RED ZONE

MANAGEMENT

Changing the Rules for Pivotal Times

Dutch Holland, Ph.D.

Dearborn™
Trade Publishing
A **Kaplan Professional** Company

This publication is designed to provide accurate and authoritative information in regard to the subject matter covered. It is sold with the understanding that the publisher is not engaged in rendering legal, accounting, or other professional service. If legal advice or other expert assistance is required, the services of a competent professional should be sought.

Vice President and Publisher: Cynthia A. Zigmund
Editorial Director: Donald J. Hull
Senior Acquisitions Editor: Jean Iversen
Senior Project Editor: Trey Thoelcke
Interior Design: Lucy Jenkins
Cover Design: design literate, inc.
Typesetting: the dotted i

© 2001 by Winford E. Holland

Published by Dearborn Trade, a Kaplan Professional Company

Printed in the United States of America

01   02   03   10   9   8   7   6   5   4   3   2   1

Library of Congress Cataloging-in-Publication Data

Holland, Winford E.
    Red zone management : changing the rules for pivotal times / Dutch Holland.
        p.   cm.
    Includes bibliographical references and index.
    ISBN 0-7931-4246-6 (hdbk)
    1. Organizational change. 2. Business planning. 3. Management games.
I. Title.
HD58.8 .H654 2001
658.4'056—dc21

2001003144

Dearborn Trade books are available at special quantity discounts to use for sales promotions, employee premiums, or educational purposes. Please call our special sales department, to order or for more information, at 800-621-9621, ext. 4410, or write to Dearborn Financial Publishing, 155 North Wacker Drive, Chicago, IL 60606-1719.

Dedication

To the kids in my life: the little kids, Hope and Win, and the big kids, Eric and Wendy.

To my wife, Jan, a lady of infinite patience who works beautifully in the Red Zone.

Thanks to my book team: my right arm, Linda Wilson, Jean Iversen, Bridgett Reed, Doris Michaels, Gerald Sindell, and Trey Thoelcke.

Special Dedication to Peter Drucker

How does a math/physics major get to be a management consultant? My key professor in graduate school, Dr. David Cleland, introduced me to the writings of Peter Drucker . . . and as they say, the rest is history. Dr. Drucker's books and articles opened a new world for me and have been an inspiration to me for 30 years. Many thanks, Dr. Cleland, and, Dr. Drucker, don't stop now!

CONTENTS

INTRODUCTION

"... and he's down on the 16-yard line, deep in Raider's Territory! How's this for drama, Howard? Key game of the season, four points behind, and the Giants have a real chance to score and win this game!"

"You're right about the drama, Dan. Now let's see if they can quickly mobilize their Red Zone offense to take advantage of this excellent opportunity. They know that if they fail to score a touchdown here, the Raiders will regain the momentum!"

"And, Howard, look how they are getting into their Red Zone offense. The offensive coordinator has just handed his headset to the head coach ... looks like he will be calling the plays. And did you see that assistant hand the coach the Red Zone play book?"

"Yes, I did ... and do you see who's going in? Campbell and Powers may be hurt, but they're going in. The Giants are putting in their star players who have been their mainstays for the entire season. This is no time for unproven rookies."

"... the snap, the play, it's Powers on a sharp slant over right tackle for four big yards! A few more key plays like that, and they'll score! What's next, Howard? What else is in that Red Zone playbook?"

"I'll tell you what's in there, Dapper Dan. It's not the regular, run-of-the-mill plays that the team uses for most of the game. It's that special set of plays that history has shown have the statistically highest chance of success in do-or-die situations like this one. All season long, the coaches have been identifying those highly productive plays with the corresponding set of best players who can produce for the team at this critical time. The Red Zone is too hot and hectic for real-time planning. They must depend on that playbook with its distillation of the year's experience. Now, in answer to your original question, expect to see the next play also going to the right, that's where the All Pros are in this Giant's offensive line. ..."

BUSINESS RED ZONES

In football, the Red Zone is the last 20 yards on the way to a touchdown. Once inside the opponent's 20-yard line, a team either scores a touchdown, the gain, or fails to score and loses enthusiasm and momentum. A team leaves the Red Zone either with six points on the scoreboard or a moral defeat at the hands of the opponent. Businesses also have Red Zones: special times when they must shift to a new way of managing to continue toward a successful future. Red Zones call for managers not only to build on but also to step beyond their usual ways of managing. Managers encounter Red Zones during critical times in the life of a company, characterized by the simultaneous presence of:

- The opportunity for great gain
- The real likelihood of great loss

In the Red Zone, failure to achieve great gain will most likely result in great loss. Figure I.1 shows the performance path of the company as it struggles through a Red Zone and emerges on the other side. Either the company makes a leap forward or takes a step backward. There is no in-between.

Unfortunately in business, however, managers don't have 20-yard markers to tell them they have entered a Red Zone. In business, managers have to recognize Red Zones by looking at the critical initiatives of their company and applying what they have learned from their own

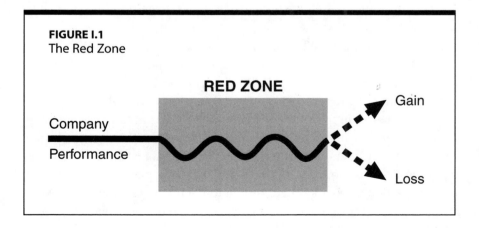

FIGURE I.1
The Red Zone

past or the history of other companies. Business history has shown that any one of the following intense conditions is a Red Zone.

- *A major shift in the company's competitive strategy.* The company either quickly moves forward in market share or burns a lot of money without producing a single percentage point of gain.
- *A merger with another significant-sized company.* The merger either propels both companies ahead in the market place or bombs, leaving both companies wishing they could rewrite history.
- *A significant internal change in the way the company does business (such as radically overhauling its organizational structure, reengineering core work processes, or changing culture).* Such change results either in important new capabilities for the company or confusion, disgust, and loss of confidence.
- *Implementation of major computer systems, like an Enterprise Resource Planning system (ERP).* An ERP either moves the organization toward greater connectivity and integration or toward major employee confusion, estrangement, and frustration.
- *Implementation of important e-business solutions, like an e-supply chain application or a major customer relationship management system.* E-business either moves the organization toward major efficiencies and cost reduction or toward supplier and/or customer revolt and dissatisfaction.

Each of these conditions brings either big gains or big losses in company momentum, market position, morale, or resources.

WHY THIS BOOK IS IMPORTANT

When more than 70 percent of reengineering projects are off target, when at least half of ERP implementations suffer outright failure, when much-touted mergers run up the tab rather than the stock price, something is wrong. I see managers undertaking Red Zone maneuvers armed more with hope and overconfidence than expertise and creativity, while they navigate intense, critical periods. When top managers consciously elect to stay above it all and leave the Red Zone management to those less key and less experienced, something needs to be done.

I believe that managers can apply the ideas in this book practically to significantly better their companies's track records of success. I believe that most management disasters associated with the major organizational shifts required for Red Zone navigation can be eliminated, putting real dollars on the bottom line while saving worker energy and preserving lifestyles.

On a grand scale, we all know that the economy needs mergers, reengineering, and implementation of value-added technology and tools to go forward. An economy needs companies to successfully navigate Red Zones. Think about the overall savings to an entire economy if companies's Red Zone navigations were more successful with less wasted time, capital, energy, and human talent. Mastering Red Zone management is surely a requirement if the economy is to become more aggressive, healthy, and vibrant. Putting it another way, a growing economy does not need the drag produced by many companies muddling through Red Zones with an unsuccessful mindset.

This book will show the critical need to shift to a different kind of management and to a significantly higher commitment level to take advantage of today's great opportunities—and avoid the multitude of failures we read about every day. I want this book to contribute to the body of business knowledge as the toolset needed to master the Red Zone.

OUR EXPERIENCE IN THE RED ZONE

After 30-plus years of consulting to organizations in the process of change, my firm and I can now look back on dozens of engagements that involved Red Zone situations for our clients. Each time our firm worked with clients in the Red Zone, our job was to help them focus on the big win/big lose situation at hand rather than on business as usual.

My firm and I worked with two large but second-tier downstream oil and gas companies as they bet the farm on a Red Zone merger to become a major first-tier player in the Midwest. We learned that strong leadership must be physically present and visible to guide the organization creatively into and through the many details that could be left to staff during normal times. We watched this company and its thousands of employees work unbelievably long hours with commitment above and beyond the call of duty for almost a year to pull off a business success that has made them the envy of the marketplace. We learned about the compelling authority of strong, innovative leadership that focused on the right things for merger success.

We worked with a major public utility in a Red Zone as it struggled to implement a major ERP system after consistently failing to implement big information technology systems. We once again saw the value of strong, innovative leadership that insisted on detailed gameplans to complete the implementation on target, on time, and on budget. We experienced the difficulties of keeping the attention of top leadership when they were considering other major changes to the strategy and configuration of the corporation. We saw the implementation completed beyond expectations using management practices very different from business as usual.

We worked side by side with one of the largest private companies in the nation as it struggled through a Red Zone to reengineer itself, meeting the formidable challenge of an invading competitor's low costs and prices. Some would say that looking Wal-Mart in the eye is the ultimate definition of business trouble. That company needed great creativity and courage to envision a potential gain and turn the situation into a win.

We worked for more than four years with one of America's premier aerospace firms as it changed its competitive strategy to meet the challenge of a foreign competitor with government subsidy connections. We saw real leadership from a CEO who made the danger of the Red Zone clear to a workforce too far from the sales process to see the danger from the rival or the real need to overhaul the company's competitive strategy. We watched as the best talent in the company was given full-time responsibility to innovate and implement a new strategy, which moved the company back to market leadership.

Are you ready for a trip through the Red Zone? Ready to learn how to maneuver your organization during those tough times that promise big wins while threatening big losses? Hang on—the journey is just beginning.

THE CURRICULUM FOR RED ZONE MANAGEMENT

Chapter 1, The State of Red Zone Management, describes the big problems that today's companies are having in the Red Zone. You will learn just how difficult these Red Zones can be.

Chapter 2, Red Zone Conditions and Maneuvers, describes in detail the different kinds of Red Zones and the maneuvers companies use to get through them successfully. You will learn the signals that determine whether Red Zone conditions are at hand.

Chapter 3, Red Zone Pathologies, identifies the key reasons why companies wind up with a loss instead of a gain. This chapter focuses on the specific actions or factors guaranteed to cause a loss across a variety of Red Zone situations.

Chapter 4, Red Zone Principles, focuses on basic underlying principles that need to be applied in a Red Zone regardless of the company or the Red Zone condition. These principles are stated in simple terms, which show that Red Zone management clearly is beyond management as usual.

Chapters 5 through 10, the Red Zone gameplans, focus on specific gameplans for six Red Zones common in business today. Companies enter them on purpose to achieve a great gain. These Red Zone gameplans include:

- Changing competitive strategy
- Mergers/acquisitions
- Reengineering work processes
- Implementing enterprise systems
- Implementing e-business solutions
- Culture change

Chapter 11, Mastering Red Zone Management, focuses on the specific actions that a company must take to build its capability to manage the inevitable stream of Red Zones it will encounter in its business lifetime.

NOTE TO THE READER

Because not all of us read alike or for the same purpose, I have constructed this book so that you have a number of options for its use.

Option 1: You Want All the Details on Red Zone Management

If that is your goal, just keep reading straight through and take in all the logical steps for what to do, what not to do, and how specifically to approach each of the six Red Zone conditions that have been game-planned for you. But even if you read all the way through, plan to re-read both Chapter 4, Red Zone Principles, and the specific gameplan chapter that applies to your next Red Zone maneuver.

Option 2: Just Give Me the Meat!

If you only have time to read a couple of chapters, make those the introduction, Chapter 1, and then Chapter 4 for those all-important Red Zone principles. If you master those principles, you can do your own gameplan for the next Red Zone condition encountered by your company.

Option 3: You Are in a Red Zone Now, and You Want a Specific Gameplan

So you are in a Red Zone now, likely up to your armpits in the details. Go straight to the appropriate gameplan chapter (see Chapters 5 through 10), then read Chapter 4 to understand fully what's behind the gameplan. You might also read Chapter 3 to see if any Red Zone pathologies are already at work in your company's maneuver.

PART ONE

RED ZONE MANAGEMENT TODAY

In today's fast-paced business world, companies are using Red Zone maneuvers as never before to get an edge on the competition and, in some cases, just stay in the race. Today's Red Zone maneuvers promise big gains but also have big downsides if not managed carefully. In Part 1, my goal is to present the reality of today's Red Zone maneuvers, to identify the pathologies or reasons for failure of many such maneuvers, and to show the ten Red Zone principles that can prevent most Red Zone difficulties.

CHAPTER 1

The State of
Red Zone Management

In football, once the offense crosses the other team's twenty, it is called the red zone because every move, every penalty, every inch, every detail, is critical. In a game of violence, nowhere is the primal urge to attack and defend more clear. Here is where the lust for blood boils most clearly to the surface. Here is where the winners are separated from the losers, the weak from the strong. Mistakes in the red zone are known to cost people their jobs, their careers, and therefore their lives.

—Tim Green, *The Red Zone,* Warner Books, 1998.

MANAGEMENT IN THE RED ZONE

The state of Red Zone management today is dreadful, absolutely dreadful. I continue to see good companies go into Red Zones expecting great things, only to realize big losses. Some losses are recoverable, but others are not. To read *Fortune* or *Forbes* is to read a veritable soap opera of Red Zone maneuvers gone bad. To make matters worse, managers, writers, and consultants are not yet tying these problems together. We read about mergers and acquisitions in one set of articles with its own set of authors, researchers, and consultants, and we read about ERP implementation and reengineering in others. We need to begin immediately to look across these big macro interventions and see them as a

3

single phenomenon. Then we can see problems across the board for what they are: Red Zones.

Right beside the articles in the popular press come the research studies of how things are going in Red Zone maneuvers, whether they be mergers and acquisitions (M&As), large reengineering projects, ERP implementations, or major changes in corporate strategy. Findings like "70 to 80 percent unmet expectations" are not uncommon for a variety of maneuvers. For example, KPMG International has found that 83 percent of corporate M&As fail to enhance shareholder value. More than 70 percent of reengineering projects do not produce anywhere near the desired results. The 1998 Standish Group International survey of 8,000 software projects found that the average large project exceeds its budget by 90 percent and its schedule by 120 percent, that 31 percent will be cancelled before they ever get completed, and that only 16.2 percent of projects will be completed on time and on budget.

Most of these studies try to look behind the few wins and the many losses and draw some conclusions about why things worked or didn't work. High on the lists of missing critical success factors we find such items as lack of top management support, failure to mobilize and gain commitment from enough people in the organization, and insufficient up-front planning.

The critical point is that many companies are not viewing Red Zones as seriously as they should to ensure success. While most companies understand the potential gains, they don't seem to understand or value the potential negative consequences. They do not seem to understand the categories of risk they face or read those risks objectively. They are not learning from the obvious experiences of others, and they are terribly misreading the complexities, the required commitment levels, and the staggering amount of innovation needed to achieve the desired gain.

MANAGING IN BUSINESS ZONES

Before I launch into the details of this chapter, let's review the basic definitions for the zones that businesses encounter over time. In normal times, managers move their businesses through two business zones.

1. Managers encounter Opportunity Zones where their companies have a chance to realize a great gain if they are innovative enough.

upset to the business.

Failure to realize the gain brings disappointment but no major

2. Managers encounter Risk Zones where their companies risk a major loss. Success in mitigating the risk prevents any major upset to the business but does not move the business forward.

Then there are the unusual times during which managers encounter what we call Red Zones, those critical times and places in the life of a company that are characterized by the simultaneous presence of the opportunity for great gain and the real likelihood of great loss. In the Red Zone, failure to achieve the great gain will result in the great loss.

To successfully navigate a Red Zone, companies must put in play both the tremendous positive motivation and creativity needed to win in an Opportunity Zone and the do-or-die, make-it-or-break-it fanaticism needed to avoid the big loss of a Risk Zone. Many, if not most, companies are not doing that.

COMPANIES THAT ARE UNSUCCESSFUL IN THE RED ZONE

Why are many companies doing so poorly in the Red Zone? Let's look at the anatomy of a typical Red Zone maneuver. First, let's look at what some cynic once said about the six phases of a big project: enthusiasm, disillusionment, panic and hysteria, search for the guilty, punishment for the innocent, and praise and honor for the nonparticipants.

While these six phases were meant to be a joke, they may contain more than a grain of truth. To get a feel for a typical Red Zone maneuver gone bad, scan the profile in Figure 1.1. If you know what a Red Zone failure feels like, skip to the next section.

FIGURE 1.1
Profile of an Unsuccessful Red Zone Maneuver

1. Realization of the need, and discovery of the "grand solution"
   - Grand intentions; we want good things to happen here.
   - We want better performance for the company.

(continued)

FIGURE 1.1
continued

- Wow! Look at this great idea.

- Isn't it a compelling solution?

- Wouldn't we be remiss if we didn't take advantage?

2. Euphoria based on the promise of the solution

- This is going to be exciting!

- The stockholders will love us.

- Won't this look great on our resumes?

- We have a great team and we can make this work.

- We have crossed a major milestone with this decision and will lead the company into a bigger and better future.

3. Grand design through the planning phase

- Early delegation; after all, the heavy lifting is over. Who, me? The Project Manager?

- Don't worry; I'll be here for you.

- Can we get consulting help from inside or out?

- Pay attention to our deadlines; we don't have time for detailed up-front planning.

- No time for detailed risk analysis; we are great problem solvers; we'll handle problems when we get to them.

4. Quickly waning executive interest and enthusiasm

- Expressions of great confidence in the troops.

- Besides, I have done my share of these over the years . . .

- Of course, all projects are messy and ambiguous at the start.

- We'll be around if you need us.

- After all, we executives *are* on the Steering Committee.

5. Project startup

- Entry of the consulting hordes to "help."

- OK consultants, communicate, communicate, communicate.

- Employees remember the last such maneuver.

FIGURE 1.1
continued

- The level of cynicism rises.
- . . . despite explanations that it won't be that way this time.

6. The devil is in the details
   - Insight into all the details . . .
   - Look at all these moving parts.
   - The "Oh No!" syndrome.
   - So many stakeholders, so little time.
   - Isn't it time for a project restart?

7. Interruption of the Red Zone maneuver by day-to-day business priorities
   - The business must go on.
   - But those are critical meeting dates.
   - We would rather have you than your representative.
   - Oops, what happened to our star players? You'll be back when?
   - What happened to that "we'll always be here to help you" Steering Committee?

8. Battles in the trenches
   - I know you have a regular day job, but we need your help!
   - Of course your world will be impacted; you heard that in the initial briefing.
   - This is really hard, and it's not fun.
   - Employee fatigue, frustration, anger, followed by apathy.
   - How will we ever get there from here?

9. Declarations of failure
   - We don't have good feelings about this . . .
   - Trial close: how would you executives react if we told you the project is in trouble?
   - Pleas for help from management.
   - The Executive: Are you sure you guys can't handle it?
   - The Executive: Here's some more money . . .

(continued)

FIGURE 1.1
continued

10. Top management wades ashore . . .

   - Top management returns to the fray . . . but too late.
   - And at a high level . . .
   - How did you guys get into this mess?
   - We warned you about those consultants . . .
   - We'll just have to do the best we can with what we've got.

11. Restart

   - We need a fresh assessment of where we are.
   - What we need is a new project manager.
   - And we need a new project plan.
   - I'm too tired, frustrated, and angry to go through this again. So this project is not going anywhere. So what?

12. Aftermath: Recovery on the inside and out

   - Let us restate more clearly what our original expectations were for this project.
   - We must consolidate our gains.
   - We really are not that far off after all.
   - Our internal rationale is sounding better and better.
   - Whatever we say, the employees will call it the "ration of bs."

13. The unlearning pause before the next new launch

   - Time for a few "Let's get this behind us" speeches.
   - Well, *those* top managers are not here any more.
   - It will surely be different this time because *we* will be leading it.
   - After all, those were "old economy" issues . . . and it's now "new economy" time.
   - Here we go again!

Does this profile sound familiar? Why? Why have we all struggled with situations like this?

WHY DON'T COMPANIES DO A BETTER JOB IN THE RED ZONE?

I think there are both some obvious and not so obvious reasons why most of us don't maneuver well through Red Zones. For instance, many companies don't really appreciate how difficult Red Zone maneuvers are. We don't realize how much innovation, creativity, and just plain savvy will be required. We don't realize the less obvious factors, such as the effect of many of the normal rules we use to run our businesses— rules that are deadly if used in the Red Zone.

It Is Difficult in the Red Zone

A huge factor that gets squarely in the way of many companies's Red Zone success is a failure to understand how tough things are going to be. I realize that you just can't appreciate some things until you have experienced them. But I want you to appreciate the difficulty of a Red Zone before you start your company's maneuver. I once had an instructor pilot give me a very valuable word picture on my first day of helicopter flight instruction. He knew that I was a very experienced pilot of fixed wing aircraft, and he sensed some overconfidence on my part. He first nodded with appreciation at the amount of my fixed wing flight time, and said that my experience would come in quite handy in flying a helicopter, especially later on. He had my attention and then said, "It's really not so hard at first. Just imagine that you jump into the deep end of a swimming pool with a basketball and then stand up on it!" Wow, that did the trick. I can assure you that when I strapped into that machine, my head and feelings were in a totally different place than they had been only a few minutes before.

I try to convince my clients from the beginning that Red Zone maneuvers are a lot like standing on that basketball, or at least the business equivalent. Getting though a Red Zone is as tough as starting a brand new venture from scratch and making it work with few if any major mistakes. Getting through a Red Zone is at least as tough and time consuming, for a period of time at least, as getting through a major product failure or losing a major customer and turning things around. Red Zone projects mean 5 12-hour days a week if they are done right or 7 12-hour days with 7/24/365 accessibility if done poorly. Red Zone projects mean creative leaps, tough decisions, hard-nosed bargaining, and face-to-face confrontation. Enough said? Bottom line, launching a Red Zone maneuver with a "walk in the park" mindset is a sure way to wind up in the deep end *under* the basketball.

Red Zone Management Experience Is a Scarce Commodity

When it comes to Red Zone management, experience is important. But proper experience isn't just a matter of being there when a company goes through a Red Zone. Just as in football red zone strategy, you need to use the "stars" who have been in the Red Zone many times and have proven themselves in action. While many of us have lived through a Red Zone, most of us were not watching how the management of that maneuver was handled. And if we were watching, most of us didn't know where to look to see the critical decisions. In fact, most of us were busy with the details of our own part of the maneuver: how our department was changing, what new skills we needed to learn, who the new players were, how we would play with them, etc.

The key factor for Red Zone experience is time at the controls of the maneuver. Very few managers have had what pilots call "stick time," actually flying the airplane rather than watching or riding. Few managers today have done multiple mergers or reengineering projects; few have implemented more than a module or two of a big enterprise information system; and even fewer have had their minds and hands on the throttles during a major change in their company's competitive strategy. So the point is that Red Zone management experience in a given company is likely to be a scarce commodity.

However, all Red Zone experience counts, whether in reengineering, implementing a major new organizational structure, merging with another large company, or implementing an ERP—all Red Zone maneuvers are similar at their cores, and experience in leading one is an advantage in leading another.

The Normal Business Rules Can Hurt in the Red Zone

Why don't we perform better in the Red Zone? One reason is that companies mistakenly apply the regular rules of business that work for day-to-day management. The helicopter instruction example works here, too. My instructor's comment about the basketball not only told me that things were going to be hard, but the things I took for granted in flying fixed wing aircraft should not be counted on for flying a helicopter. The same is true for Red Zone management.

For decades, teachers and consultants have been sending managers a steady diet of ideas to try and practices to apply. Many of these ideas have proven to be very beneficial and may very well be at the heart of the success of a lot of businesses today. Many of the messages that we refer to have been integrated into basic training for managers in everything from junior colleges to universities to company in-house training programs. And unfortunately, in many cases, these messages have been emasculated, written in generalities rather than specifics, shorted of many of their critical distinctions, transmitted by people with "I studied this in graduate school" experiences rather than "I learned this over the years in the trenches." In short, some messages just aren't effective. These contemporary management practices, good and bad, are far more a part of our implicit world of management know-how than many of us think.

In all fairness, many of us have been talking about the kind of management theories and practices that work in changing a business, not in day-to-day management of ongoing operations. While these new messages are in the public domain and are overheard in most places I go, clearly they are not yet integrated into the explicit or implicit ways we manage or conduct management education.

In addition, I want to consciously examine some key management themes that are receiving a great deal of emphasis for their potential *negative* effects on Red Zone behavior. The six themes below are most critical to note; they may very well be the regular rules that don't bring value to Red Zone management. In addition to the six themes, what we call *cultural practices* influence managers.

Good Ideas That May Not Bring Value in the Red Zone

Management systems for running a business. We design management systems to tie together important interrelated parts and steps in our business so we can be effective and efficient. Management systems work in our day-to-day business; we accept them and some of their underlying principles as good ideas. For example, we are taught to manage and measure ends and not means, to assess results and not the actions taken to get to those results. But in the Red Zone, we focus on putting in place new means or actions designed to reach new results. In addition, in day-to-day work we are taught to manage by exception, assuming most stuff will go well in our management system most of the time, and that our time as a manager will only be needed on an exception basis. But in the Red Zone, we are focused on the exceptions. In fact, everything important is an exception.

In day-to-day management, we trust our existing policies and procedures to work for us, and they do in a normal, routine world. But some of the most critical work in the Red Zone is to develop new policies and procedures for the business venture we are trying to create. We are taught to trust our budgets, plans, and controls to give us the information we need. Not so in the Red Zone, where we have only the project plan to follow. In short, our years of success with management systems contribute to our feeling that we can get lots of results for the company while our brains are on auto pilot, trusting the system to take us to the desired result. There is no auto pilot in the Red Zone.

Management development philosophies and programs. We generally accept that the best way to develop managers for long-term careers is though a series of important, challenging jobs that stretch incumbents to new capacities. We know that some managers can look back on such assignments in which they learned things the hard way. We have all looked at new players in new jobs and smiled inwardly as they bumbled about and learned critical things they could not learn any other way.

But do we really want to develop managers this way during a Red Zone? Do we want to use the Red Zone as a place to train managers inexperienced at the needed level of competence? Do we want to express our confidence in them and then leave them alone to learn on the job while the company's destiny is at stake? Sure, we will be there as their mentor, but will that be enough? No. We regularly see executives experienced in the Red Zone stand back while some of their young stars are given "developmental assignments" to lead the company through a Red Zone. The Red Zone is not the time for rookies. We lead with the best that we have, regardless of organizational position. That could even mean the CEO or the COO.

Leadership/management presence and style. The messages to leaders about leadership and management style have been clear for at least the last two decades. Good leaders and managers get things done through others. Great leaders are behind the scenes providing long-term vision, excitement, and enthusiasm through great coaching. The job of the leader is to keep a watchful eye ahead, seeing obstacles before they get to the organization and removing those obstacles before the troops get to them. Great leaders are alert to the issues inside their organizations and work with lots of input from below to ensure that any action they take makes sense and will be compelling to the troops. Good managers are taught to use a leadership style that matches the development or capability level of their troops: acting as strong teachers to the rookies in their organizations, coaches to the old pros, and sideline advisors to the top performers.

Nothing is wrong with these leadership and management messages for running the ongoing operations of a company, but in the Red Zone, such messages could be deadly. The messages, especially if mixed with the usually effective message of delegate-delegate-delegate, could say to the leader in the Red Zone that she should set up her direct reports to do the real Red Zone maneuver while she coaches and encourages them from the sidelines. If we are not careful, we might not realize that just about everybody is a rookie in the Red Zone.

An underlying assumption in many leadership messages is that the leader should be free from any hands-on work, keeping him or her available and fresh to tackle the big opportunities and problems when they come along. Because a Red Zone is exactly that kind of a situation, the leader is needed out in front, not only acting as the architect of the new business venture on the other side of the Red Zone but actively involved in leading the detailed planning and approach to get there.

Teamwork. Teamwork messages have come across as critically important for running day-to-day businesses. Everybody is on some kind of business team or teams to work together to ensure that the products and services get out the door to meet customers' every need. Cross-functional and process teams have been vital in helping organizations understand how business flows in a company and have enabled many companies to take important steps forward.

Teamwork has also become a part of the way organizations deal with change. Organizational change and task forces seem to go hand in hand, allowing organization members to put their heads together to come up with the very best ideas and become fully committed to the solution. Implicit, if not explicit, in many of these team messages is the idea of reaching consensus on issues before decisions can be made and implemented. In addition, the cultural interpretation of teamwork in many companies is that nobody can do much of anything without making decisions in a series of team meetings.

The Red Zone *is* an intense team environment. Teamwork will be critical to any successful Red Zone maneuver. But Red Zones require team members to meet, get instructions, and then to go individually to do what needs to be done. They literally can't meet and decide on everything. Frequently, there is not enough time to get everybody to a consensus level on what is to be done or how to do it. The purpose of teamwork in the Red Zone is for execution, not consensus building about each step along the way. The goal of teamwork in the Red Zone is to have people acting like team members outside of team meetings, going about their assignments with knowledge and consideration of what their teammates are doing in parallel. In the Red Zone, quarterbacks don't call an extra time—out to get a consensus on each new play.

Conflict resolution. The messages to management are clear. We want harmonious operations between departments and throughout each work process. The goal is to smooth work processes, find potential conflicts, and then resolve them. We expect managers to avoid turf wars and political infighting. The greater goal is always the overall end product of the organization: the satisfaction of the ultimate customer. Managers are told to build respect for the individual into the way they operate, and these managers in turn tell their troops to be respectful of the other departments in the company.

Once again, these messages are important and positive for ongoing operations. However, we can get in trouble when we misinterpret some of these messages and then use those misinterpretations in the Red Zone. Establishing harmony and cooperation does not mean to avoid identifying, talking about, and resolving conflicts in Red Zone maneuvers. We recently worked with two large information technology departments from two companies that had just merged—merged, I might add, without any kind of a clear organizational architecture for working together. The newly appointed leader of the two shops gave great run-the-business advice right in the middle of a Red Zone. His message was clear, "I don't want you people out there stirring up any stuff, no infighting, no conflict, just get the products and services to our users." Unfortunately, any efforts made by the organization to identify conflicts in "who was to do what for whom" were met with a strong "Cut that out!" from the boss. Confusion reigned, and performance suffered.

By definition, the Red Zone will be a conflict-intense work environment. The very way that organizations work their way through a Red Zone to a healthy business venture on the other side is to look for conflicts, surface them immediately, and then work through them as fast as possible.

The healing effect of time. Many companies and managers carry a fundamental message that time cures just about anything. If we start something new and the going is rocky, we hear, "Aw, we'll work through this in time." We know about the learning curve that says the more times we do something, the better we will be at it. We learn to count on people making a few mistakes at first, taking a few missteps at the beginning, but we are confident that we will work through it in time.

Time is the enemy in the Red Zone. Every day in the Red Zone takes its toll on energy, focus, and motivation. We must not count on people "slopping" their way through something with the hope that sooner or later they will work it out. We must enter the Red Zone with enough detailed planning and preparation so that workers can expect to get through new things quickly, with help as needed to do things the new way.

Why don't we do a better job in the Red Zone? We have examined a number of potential reasons, many of which may be in play in your company's environment. Regardless of the reasons, the challenges will be:

- To obtain the intense commitment and resources needed to work through the Red Zone.
- Not to use the normal management rules (or their misinterpretations) when Red Zone principles are needed (more on this in Chapter 4).

WHAT'S AT STAKE IN THE RED ZONE?

So what is at stake here? What does it matter if we don't start doing a better job of managing in the Red Zone? By the way, if I can't paint a fairly compelling argument that a lot is at stake for you and your company, I would be foolish to expect you to read the remainder of this book.

First, many of the great gains that could be made will not happen. In fact, many of them might not even be attempted; they just might be placed carefully in the too-hard file. Chances to reshape industry landscapes, chances to make great leaps forward in technologies or integrated services, chances to reshape the value of companies from a financial point of view—all lost or in jeopardy because of our ineptness or fear of Red Zone maneuvers. In short, we could miss out on market share gains, increased customer satisfaction, ROI increases, competitive advantage, time to market, as well as a heck of a lot of fun doing great business.

Another way to look at what is at stake is to look again at the potential losses: lawsuits from customers, vendors, and stockholders; loss of customer confidence and market share; higher costs; out-of-pocket settlements; waste from project cancellations; ruined careers, discredited managers, employee frustration, anger and bitterness; union issues; and more.

If we don't learn to manage Red Zones better, big things are at stake at the individual level—at our level. Careers have been made in Red Zone gains and lost when Red Zone maneuvers did not work. Managers and employees alike have learned both positive and negative lessons that will stay with them for the rest of their working lives. Sad to say, in many cases, the innocent have been punished by being in charge of or associated with a failed Red Zone maneuver. Looking beyond the past into the future, it would be foolish to say that we could expect fewer Red Zones in our careers. A worker in business today cannot expect to maximize a working career without skills in the Red Zone arena. So in a way, your career is on the line when you try to master Red Zone management. This book may be your chance to get a jump start on your fellow workers.

MEETING THE NEEDS
OF TODAY'S MANAGERS

This book is designed to meet the needs of today's managers involved in high-stakes gain or loss situations. Virtually all managers will experience Red Zone situations. This book meets six key needs of managers in this time of global turbulence, change, and competition.

1. Managers need to know when their firms are in a Red Zone so that they can shift to appropriate actions as well as into the needed level of creativity, commitment, and leadership to see their companies through. Managers need to identify Red Zone conditions so they can declare to the company that special behavior will be required to achieve gain and not loss.

2. Managers need to be acutely aware of the order of magnitude of the losses their companies are likely to experience if they unsuccessfully navigate a Red Zone. There are real, tangible consequences of failure that will have far-reaching effects on their businesses.

3. Managers need to distinguish between Red Zone management and crisis management. Crisis management comes into play when a company cleans up after a hurricane, recovers from an unexpected loss of key personnel, or repairs a fractured relationship with a key customer. Red Zone management is used during critical times for the company, but it could not be more different than crisis management. Red Zone management calls for disciplined, controlled actions designed to lead to a specific gain, not the conservative recovery actions of crisis management. Using crisis management when a company is in a Red Zone virtually guarantees a loss.

4. Managers need to know how to navigate formally through a Red Zone condition (such as a merger, reengineering, or ERP implementation) while successfully running the regular activity of business: serving customers and getting paid. Managers need to master formal management methods that will allow them to do these two critical things at once, and do them both very well in a high-stakes environment.

5. Managers in the Red Zone need understandable rules and principles along with detailed playbooks to achieve great gains while minimizing the chances of great losses. Managers need clear gameplans written in simple and practical terms. Managers need a way of understanding the organizational initiatives they must bring about to achieve great gains and avoid great losses. Managers don't need more theory and complex reasoning. They need specific playbooks for their company's Red Zone condition.

6. Managers need to know when their companies are not in a Red Zone so that they can manage time and resources accordingly.

Not all critical situations are Red Zones. Management must be able to tell the difference (see Chapter 2). Managers need to know when to sprint and when to run normally. Managers already recognize that neither they nor their troops can sprint a marathon.

This book will provide:

- Simple perspectives for viewing organizational situations like Red Zones.
- Straightforward gameplans for recognizing Red Zones and making change happen to navigate them successfully.
- Direct reassurance to readers that they already have much of what it takes to make it through.

That's right—managers already have many of the technical competencies they need for Red Zone management. But they may not yet have mastered the translation of their skills to successful Red Zone navigation.

CHAPTER 2

Red Zone Conditions and Maneuvers

The business world is a constantly changing, turbulent place where market forces shift with changes in economies, geopolitics, and competitive business tactics. There is no real limit to the number or kinds of factors that might impact a particular company's marketplace. However, several factors are almost sure to disrupt business as usual. Such factors must be considered on a day-by-day basis as a first step in mastering Red Zone management. Managers who have early awareness of disruptive factors have a chance to steer their organizations toward an opportunity. Managers who are unaware of disruptive factors in their marketplace are almost certain to find their organizations at risk.

DISRUPTIVE FACTORS

Disruptive factors, which can put an organization into a critical zone, fall into several general categories: market upsets, competitive scrambles, technology advances, regulatory changes, and shifts in performance expectations. As each disruptive factor emerges, some companies are impacted positively and some negatively. For example, China opening as a market was good news for many of the world's companies, but bad news for some producers inside China as they experienced a flood of new competitors. The most important role of executive management should be to envision the opportunity that can be constructed from or around the disruption.

Market upsets. Markets for goods and services, as well as for capital, are frequently upset because of product revolutions, product disasters, shifts in buyer needs, and openings or closings of market territories. Over the years, we have seen capital markets change because of a new vehicle called junk bonds. We have seen the Far East open as a major commercial market and parts of other countries close. We have seen products proliferate around new needs. We have seen the Internet develop as a new vehicle to market some products while offering real-time assistance in distributing others.

Competitive scrambles. Companies are impacted when a major competitor enters an industry as well as when a major industry competitor collapses or withdraws from the market. Formation of strategic alliances or outright mergers frequently change the competitive landscape, offering advantages to some companies and disadvantages to others. Today, start ups from nowhere may pose one of the most dangerous risks to established companies.

Technology advances. Technology revolutions and evolutions frequently cause sea changes in an industry or market, raising the bar for product performance, production cost reduction, and/or distribution efficiency. The simultaneous increase in chip computing power and decrease in chip cost allows a competitive advantage for some companies while sounding the death knell for others.

Regulatory changes. New laws upset the ways companies are doing business and require major shifts in company strategies and/or production techniques. Legislated changes in the lead content of gasoline turned companies's manufacturing approaches upside down. Declaring certain geographical regions as special areas for automotive emissions regulation creates new opportunities for some companies while banning other companies from participation.

Shifts in performance expectations. The performance expected, even demanded, from companies shifts when new ownership groups take control. On a micro level, new boards or CEOs can raise the bar on performance or predictability level. Ownership groups can require companies to move toward green commerce or away from tobacco.

Combinations of factors. Probably the most disruptive situation for companies comes when two or more disruptions are in play at one time. Imagine dealing with major competitive shifts, a technology-led sea change, and new ownership performance expectations all at one time.

HOW MANAGERS DEAL WITH DISRUPTIVE FACTORS

Managers have been dealing with disruptive factors that affect their companies since we have had managers and companies. A clear duty of executive management is to keep a wary eye on the business horizon as well as on competitors and customers to spot disruptive factors as they are emerging. Some managers personally handle this, while others enlist staff and external vendors in marketplace intelligence. It turns out that writing about this duty is easier than executing it well. Some executives have lost their jobs for being caught unaware, while others have earned high marks for their ability to read the tea leaves.

Once a disruptive force is identified, management's duty is to forecast the impact on their company. Will the disruption present a new opportunity or a new risk? How big will the opportunity be? What size is the potential risk? What's at stake—a few cents of earnings per share or the company's survival?

Once the size of the impact is determined, management's duty is to innovate or to design and execute the initiative(s) to deal with it. Can the disruptive factor be managed internally, or will new resources be required to handle it? Will we need to make minor or major innovations in the way we operate, to our scale of operation, to the way we manage the company?

The Top Six Red Zone Maneuvers

While the kinds of initiatives are literally infinite at the detailed level, companies's actions in recent years have fallen into broad categories. Each of these categories, or maneuvers, has been used many times as a means to move a company forward in response to or anticipation of a disruptive factor. The most prominent maneuvers today are labeled as follows:

- Changing the company's competitive strategy
- Merging with or acquiring another company
- Reengineering a company's core processes
- Implementing an enterprise information technology system
- Implementing major e-business solutions
- Changing the culture

Top management's job is to select one of these standard maneuvers, or craft a unique one, and build the preliminary business case for pursuing it. The business case must answer the logical questions of the company's stakeholders.

- What maneuver will give us a gain?
- How will we conduct that maneuver?
- What will be the profit when we successfully complete the maneuver?
- How will we ensure success?

In theory, at least, senior management should not move forward with a Red Zone maneuver without a business case that stakeholders find convincing. Given that a Red Zone has the potential of a big loss, a Red Zone maneuver should not be initiated if it does not make good business sense. (More will be said about the business case in Chapter 4.)

The standard Red Zone solutions are not new; in fact, they are organizational maneuvers that have, for the most part, been going on for years. Fortunately for mangers, a huge body of knowledge as well as many experts today who know the nuts and bolts of each kind of maneuver are available. Unfortunately for managers, these maneuvers have not been seen for what they really are: Red Zones, with real danger lurking behind the promise of real gain.

Now let's take a brief look at each maneuver. Let's find out its purpose and the kinds of gains it might produce. Let's examine the risks associated with the maneuver itself and the kinds of losses a company might incur. In short, let's discover why each maneuver is a Red Zone that deserves special attention and management.

Changing a Company's Competitive Strategy

A company's competitive strategy is the way it positions its products and services in the marketplace to achieve an advantage with its customers while protecting its market position from competitors. For example, after some extensive conversations with its customers, a company might decide to differentiate its products and services from its competitors's by adding additional financing packages, solution services, or bells and whistles.

After a change in competitive strategy, customers would see a new version of the business enterprise offering more attractive products and services than before. The key word here is *see* because in some cases companies try to reposition just the image of their company or product in the mind of the customer but not the physical attributes of the company or product itself. After a change in competitive strategy, competitors would see a new business enterprise requiring different competitive tactics to defeat in the marketplace.

Changing a competitive strategy can result in big gains in the marketplace, if the company does in fact make its products and services more valuable to its customers. Successful strategy change increases market share, customer satisfaction, margin, and profitability. I have worked with companies that experienced doubled market share and moved from third to first quartile in customer satisfaction by changing their competitive strategy. It is unlikely, however, that big gains will come quickly. Frequently, changing a strategy is a multimonth or even a multiyear process.

Changing a competitive strategy can result in big losses in the marketplace if the company does not make its products and services more valuable to its customers. Unsuccessful strategy change decreases market share, customer satisfaction, margin, and profitability. I have watched as some companies have failed to implement new strategies and lost huge amounts of share to other, more focused competitors. In addition, companies can experience big losses internally as new means of production do not prove to be effective or even possible.

Changing strategy is a Red Zone because of the great technical and organizational difficulty of changing products and services and the processes needed to produce and market them. The biggest problems usually come after the company has decided on the new strategy, when management is making changes to put that strategy into effect. The biggest challenge seems to be decoding and explaining the organizational changes that would make the strategy change a reality. I have seen many strategy change implementations go wrong for lack of hands-on leadership, clear direction, and meticulous follow-up. The bottom line: managers frequently misjudge the degree of difficulty they are diving into when they decide to change a competitive strategy.

Merging with or Acquiring Another Company

A company merges with or acquires another company to present itself to the marketplace more positively and/or to produce its goods and services with better effectiveness and efficiency. For example, TimeWarner and AOL came together to take advantage of complementary products and services and increased efficiencies to increase market coverage greatly.

After a successful merger or acquisition, the customer literally sees a new business venture with a different footprint of products and services available in wider markets. The company might use different brand names or blended brand names to help make the connection with its identity as a new venture.

Merging or acquiring can result in big gains in the marketplace, if the company does in fact present itself to the customer as one new company. Successful mergers can increase market share, customer satisfaction, margin, and profitability.

Merging or acquiring can result in big losses if the company does not make the two companies work as one. I have personally seen merged or newly acquired companies develop so much internal competition that both companies lost ground. I have even seen the overall image of a merged company pulled down to the level of the lowest rated participant rather than pulled up to the level of the highest.

Merging or acquiring a major company is a Red Zone because of the great logistical difficulty of tying together two companies. The biggest problems usually come in implementation, as the many moving parts of the organizations have to be synchronized. Frequently, mergers are rationalized from the beginning as a way to take advantage of economies of scale or to save money by reducing duplication of assets or people. Many merging companies have found out the hard way that it is one thing to identify potential synergies during initial planning and another to capitalize on those synergies after the companies have permission from regulators to work together.

Reengineering a Company's Core Processes

A company reengineers its core processes to take advantage of new ways of working. Take this simple example. I bought a house in 1993 that was built in 1936. The wife for whom the house was originally built said that her husband had spared no expense to make sure the house had the very best of everything available at the time, including plumbing and wiring. Unfortunately for me, or maybe lucky for me, the options I had available in 1993 were substantially better, especially in plumbing and wiring. My job was to reengineer the house by installing the best available plumbing and wiring of 1993. Reengineering a company is like that. Reengineering allows a company to put into play the very best know-how available at the current time to make existing processes better and more efficient.

The usual goal of reengineering is both to reduce costs and to make the company different or better in some way for its customers. A company might reengineer a core manufacturing process to lower production costs and sell its products at lower prices. A company might reengineer its new product development process to allow faster time to market and therefore to the hands of the customer. Reengineering enhances a company's position in its industry by putting in place newer and hopefully better processes to accomplish work.

Reengineering can result in big gains in performance if done well. Companies have reported reengineering project gains of production cycle times cut by 75 percent, direct costs in some processes cut 50 percent, response time cut by 90 percent, number of steps and handoffs in a work process cut by 50 percent, and so on. One study published in *Total Quality Management* reported that almost 70 percent of the organizations they studied had seen improvements in organizational performance of more than 50 percent.

Reengineering can result in big losses in the marketplace if not done well. Companies have lost their shirts financially, lost dozens of key employees, frustrated thousands of others, and set the company back on its heels, giving up huge ground to competitors. Some companies have spent millions and lost millions more through failed reengineering projects.

Reengineering is a Red Zone because it is disruptive and can destabilize a company. Tying back to the example of my 1993 home, designing the new plumbing and wiring was not a problem, nor was it disruptive. But rewiring and replumbing the house with a family living in it was about as disruptive as living in the backyard. Discussing the use of reengineering in preparing organizations for the age of e-business, *BusinessWeek* said, "Reengineering projects can be hugely complicated, with technology, business, and organizational upheavals all rocking the corporate foundations at once. There are harrowing risks. Casualties will include some companies that were too bold – but even more that were too timid."

Summing up Agway's reengineering experiences, Bruce Ruppert, senior vice president of planning and operations, put it even more viscerally. "You can survive the old way. You can survive the new way. It's the goddamn transition that'll kill you." It doesn't get much more Red Zone than that.

Implementing Enterprise Information Systems

A company implements an enterprise information system for several reasons. A single system connects the entire organization to provide a standard way of doing transactions across the board, positioning the company for greater productivity. Enterprise systems are designed to provide an underlying set of sound, if not industry leading, business processes. In addition, because enterprise systems are off the shelf rather than custom designed, implementing organizations can expect to benefit from regular improvement of system performance by the software vendor.

An interesting fact about enterprise systems is that most of them are not enterprisewide at all. Most are aimed at specific parts of a business and are purchased and implemented in modules: accounting, procurement, human resources, and so on. Given the complexity and difficulty of implementation of each module, most companies that have completed implementations are glad they did not try to cover the entire enterprise with one big implementation.

Enterprise systems can result in big performance gains if the contents of the systems meet the needs of the organization and if the implementation is done well. Companies have reported millions of dollars in cost savings and improvement opportunities as a result of both the system's connectivity and its built-in work processes. Not all companies have experienced such big gains, however, and some are back at work with what they call the second wave of implementation, trying to find the benefits they know must be in there somewhere.

Failing at implementing an enterprise system can produce big losses. Companies have even attributed their bankruptcy to botched implementation or flawed systems (or both). Companies with screwed up implementation have had everything from no products available to sell during key sales periods, to long delays in vendor payment cycles, not to mention missed payrolls for employees. Several companies have abandoned their enterprise system implementation in midstream at the cost of tens of millions of dollars. Others are engaged in megalawsuits of vendors and systems integrators in efforts to recoup some of their alleged losses.

Implementing an enterprise system is a Red Zone because it can be a major change to the way the company works. When a company chooses to use off-the-shelf systems to replace its present systems, many of which may have been internally developed, employees can be confused by what seems to them to be a major change in organizational strategy. How can the company be abandoning its best-in-class, proprietary system for one that any competitor can buy? In addition to the confusion, if employees are not properly prepared for use of the new system and if work processes are not aligned, the business results can be catastrophic. Companies have gone live with new enterprise systems with employees who were totally lost and literally shut down operations until they could get over-the-shoulder help in using the new technology.

Implementing e-Business Solutions

An existing company implements e-business solutions to take advantage of superfast, superefficient ways of communicating and transacting with customers, suppliers, and/or employees. E-solutions do not put entirely new business processes in place but provide alternate ways of accomplishing those processes. Examples could be anything from Charles Schwab's addition of an online trading capability for its investment customers, to Florida Power & Light's online procurement of vital raw materials.

The usual goals of e-business solutions are to broaden the company's reach while making communication and transactions easier.

Additional goals that are just beginning to be realized include accessing information about customers and suppliers that can be used to service them better and/or to increase the profit margin. Witness your very own personal greeting when you return to Amazon.com, a greeting that includes special product recommendations tailored for you based on your buying preferences.

E-business solutions can result in big gains in performance if done well. Companies have reported revenue gains in the hundreds of millions of dollars by adding e-distribution channels to their existing ways of serving up products to their customers. Some companies like Schwab have leveraged their e-business solution to upset the competitive order in their marketplace, moving from being one of the pack to being tied with the market leader in asset size.

Failed e-business solutions or solution implementation can generate big losses. While not yet widely publicized, some companies have lost millions as either their new e-channel failed to create additional business or they had to cancel their implementation because they could no longer see its potential value to the company. Border's Books's abandonment of its e-business site due to excessive costs is a prime example. Failing to implement a highly touted e-business package can be very demoralizing to an organization and undercut the business credibility of its leaders, not to mention waste tens of millions of dollars.

Implementing e-business solutions is a Red Zone because they are new to business, methodologies are not yet developed, technology is untested, and the solutions are disruptive to the existing order of things. Well-intentioned but unsuccessful e-business initiatives have done everything from anger a company's own distribution channels to cannibalize its own customers. The promotional hype around e-business solutions is still high despite dot-com disillusionment. Companies must beware the euphoria that frequently accompanies a new technology that promises great results: it may fail to deliver.

Changing the Company's Culture

A company changes its culture to do things in an improved way, evenly and consistently. While there are many definitions of culture, we stick with the simple one that says, "Culture is the way we do things around here. It's our normal way of conducting the company's business." The focus in a culture change is not on a single business process or the implementation of a computer system; the focus is on the behavior of the entire workforce. The idea is to focus everyone's thinking and mindset on an important business concept or principle, like continuous process improvement or first-class customer service.

Culture change can result in big gains in performance if done well. Companies have reported that culture changes focused on customer service and cost reduction have produced impressive results in response times and customer satisfaction. Companies have greatly improved customer satisfaction, reduced the number of customer complaints, and increased market share. General Electric continues to enjoy megabillion dollar benefits from two specific culture changes: Work Out and Six Sigma.

Attempts to change a company's culture can result in big losses if not done well. Many companies have tried culture changes unsuccessfully, getting little for their time and money and even losing management credibility. Failure in a culture change is a great way to reduce the power of management to lead in any new direction; people remember the failure and cynically say, "More talk about a new direction. This too shall pass."

Changing a company's culture is a Red Zone because focusing on the behavior of everyone in the organization is such an enormous job. Adding something new to the way a company operates is a tough enough job; focusing on changing the very way the company operates is by definition a much tougher task. Culture changes are now described by some mangers as the toughest changes they have ever tried to implement during their management careers.

Other Red Zone Maneuvers?

Have I listed the only Red Zone maneuvers? Are there only six? I have listed the big six, not the only six. For example, making the leadership transition from founders to the first generation of professional managers is an obvious Red Zone and calls for the use of many of the Red Zone principles. Implementing lean manufacturing, very much the rage today in several industries, is clearly a Red Zone maneuver. Going lean calls for elements of reengineering and systems implementation as well as the different way of thinking involved in culture change. Customer relationship management implementations are similar in that systems, reengineering, and culture change are all involved. The bottom line is simple: management uses many maneuvers to move their organizations ahead. Those that are Red Zone maneuvers should be managed as such. Fortunately, however, most Red Zones are combinations of or variations on the six maneuvers covered in this book.

COMMON FACTORS IN RED ZONE MANEUVERS

So what do these Red Zone maneuvers have in common? All of these maneuvers promise big gains if properly designed and implemented, and I know from experience that's a heck of a big *if!* All of the maneuvers can be compelling and appealing when viewed from 30,000 feet. There are many examples of successes for each maneuver, more in long-term gains than in the short term.

All of the maneuvers have high potential losses associated with failure. Implementation has proven to be highly difficult, dangerous, and risky. All of the maneuvers have many moving parts that all must come together properly to ensure the desired result. The potential loss from these maneuvers includes degraded results (e.g., not reaching original expectations) and excessive costs of implementation, including high economic and people costs.

All of the maneuvers require a great deal of innovation and creativity, whether in novel design of the venture the organization wants to become or in clever execution of that design. All of the maneuvers are costly to implement whether they achieve the big gain or result in a big loss. The economic cost of all of the maneuvers is high; changing the attributes of an organization enough for it to be truly a new business venture, with a higher chance of business success, is expensive. The energy cost to the organization can be staggering as the company tries to keep a business-as-usual posture with its clients while it completes its Red Zone maneuver.

All of the maneuvers have high people costs during implementation including longer hours, increased intensity of work, and more complexity and ambiguity. Phrases like *corporate root canal* and *18 months of hell* have been used to characterize an experience that everybody involved finds intensely challenging. While some personnel later reflect on the fun they had during the Red Zone maneuver, people often say that they do not want to go through anything like that again. For them, personal impacts include lowered morale and cynicism as well as mental and physical fatigue.

IMPORTANT TRUTHS
ABOUT RED ZONE MANEUVERS

My goal in this book is to speak out about the fact that many standard solutions being used today are really Red Zone maneuvers. I want to highlight important facts about these maneuvers and propose a new set of principles that can materially raise success rates. My thinking goes like this:

- Companies pull off Red Zone maneuvers with great difficulty. In short, most companies are not good at executing these solutions.
- While managers have been good at seeing the potential gains from Red Zone maneuvers, they have *not* been good at anticipating or mitigating the huge potential losses from the maneuvers.
- Not only does the initial disruptive factor bring a risk of loss, but the very nature of the maneuver adds more risk. The very act of undertaking the Red Zone maneuver can impact internal operations negatively and result in company or employee damage that cannot easily be repaired.
- Red Zone maneuvers are not separate and distinct but versions of a single maneuver. They are all ways of creating a new version of the enterprise that will operate effectively in the presence of the disruptive factor. In each maneuver, the firm must change some elements of who it is and how it operates. In each maneuver, the firm must alter its attributes innovatively to reach the desired gain.
- Red Zone maneuvers need to be managed differently than they are today in most companies. The business-as-usual management method used by most companies will not work in the Red Zone. Underlying principles, however, can be applied across the maneuvers to increase chances of success.

WORDS OF WARNING

Not every tough and difficult time in a company's life is a Red Zone as defined in this book. Just because your organization has some of the symptoms that we have described above doesn't mean you should suddenly scream Red Zone, panic, and pull out the chapter on Red Zone principles. I frequently see companies who are not in a Red Zone, even though to them business feels dangerous and critical. For example, when Firestone and Ford were dealing with tire failures on Explorer SUVs, they were working to resolve a crisis, but neither company was in a Red Zone as defined in this book. Both companies had much to lose, and they were working to minimize that loss, not score a big gain.

I frequently find organizations with the following situations *that I do not identify* as Red Zones:

- Individuals or departments are very busy, even too busy
- Resources are scarce, including personnel, dollars, and tools
- Employees bog down in ambiguity and lack direction
- Feelings, and facts, of being disorganized or totally unorganized run rampant
- Work processes and technology don't work right or at all
- Employees sense the organization is out of control
- Employees believe, with absolute conviction, that management is asking them to sprint a marathon

If your organization has these symptoms without being on the road to a great gain, use normal good management practices to relieve the situation.

ON TO ACTION IN THE RED ZONE

This chapter has explained the business forces that can bring about different zones or times in the life of an organization and the maneuvers that are frequently taken to navigate through them. Hopefully, I have made the case that these standard and popular business maneuvers of our time are in fact Red Zones. I also hope I have made the case that these Red Zone maneuvers are both difficult and fraught with danger and mistakes. So what is a body to do? We must beware what I call the *Red Zone pathologies* described in Chapter 3, the most frequent causes of losses in the Red Zone.

CHAPTER 3

Red Zone Pathologies

DEFINITION OF A RED ZONE PATHOLOGY

Most of the losses in the Red Zone come from the actions, or lack of actions, of the leaders and managers involved. We can't blame failure or loss on the nature of the maneuver, on business conditions, on the state of the world economy, or even on the weather. The hard fact of the matter is that managers are their own worst enemies while in the Red Zone. Whether I look across companies who have had Red Zone losses or across the different kinds of Red Zone maneuvers, I see the same general pattern of behaviors in loss situations. The patterns are so strong and the potential results so bad that I decided to label them *pathologies* to highlight their criticality.

A Red Zone pathology is a single behavior or set of behaviors that will lead to losses if used by a company in a Red Zone. Some of the pathologies are just plain bad news in any business situation but are fatal if used while in a Red Zone. Other pathologies may be laudable management practices when used in a normal business situation. But in a Red Zone, they too can be fatal.

THE RED ZONE PATHOLOGIES

The most common pathologies are:

- Lack of high quality executive support

- Lack of comprehensive and detailed up-front planning
- The organization too narrowly involved
- Inappropriate delegation for critical leadership responsibilities
- Undisciplined and incomplete project management

In each of the following sections of this chapter, my goal will be to describe a pathology and show why it can be fatal in the Red Zone.

Lack of High Quality Executive Support

The number one Red Zone pathology is lack of executive support. This pathology is far and away the most troublesome one for executives and Red Zone team members alike. Team members are frustrated when they do not see or feel executive support for the maneuver, and executives are frustrated when they think they are giving it and hear that the troops do not see it.

I visited with one steamed CEO just after his Red Zone steering committee had delicately and carefully informed him that the organization did not perceive executive support for the current reengineering maneuver. "[Expletive deleted], I am supportive of this reengineering project, and I have been there to demonstrate that support!" In this case, both views were accurate. The CEO had in fact been there; he showed up at the Red Zone team's initial organization meeting and said, "I'm for this." He also appeared a couple of months later, at the request of the Steering Committee, and made some closing remarks—that were read off pocket notes that someone else obviously had prepared. Yes, the CEO was supportive, but, no, you couldn't tell it by looking. Executive support for a Red Zone maneuver means "talking the talk" about the maneuver and being there to "walk the walk" as the organization goes through the maneuver.

The following examples illustrate the real world pathologies of inadequate executive support.

Executive neglect. The CEO of a medium-sized engineering firm endorsed the idea of making significant changes to key processes. His endorsement in words was followed by a two-day session attended by his executive team to target those processes most in need of change. After a targeting session that only located broad targets with fuzzy outcomes, the CEO was noticeably absent in the subsequent meetings of the group. He was absent for what he said were "real business reasons that dealt with real jobs for real customers."

A short time after the change initiatives were launched, the firm's market began a steep nose dive. This alarmed everybody and took more of the executive's attention away from the change. Some members of the executive team argued for aggressive pursuit of the change initiative as the best hope the organization had to change its position as a competitor in a sagging market. Despite their arguments, the CEO poured more and more attention into the day-to-day business in a vain attempt to halt the slide. Day-to-day pressures and layoffs to "size the business to the market" soon led to a true bunker mentality.

Executive pressure. The CEO of a $100 million electrical manufacturer sensed an upcoming shift in the economics of his industry, and his company had to get on board in a big way or suffer huge market share consequences. While the shift was still building momentum, he gathered his management team and told them of his concerns. The meeting ended with his exhortation to reexamine key business practices with the idea to radically change anything that needed to be changed. In further meetings with the team, the CEO repeated his wish for immediate action to reduce costs.

After more confrontations with the CEO, several members of the team launched initiatives in their parts of the organization. Though the stated purpose of these initiatives was radical surgery, the units were not able to mount a serious effort to reexamine processes or reduce costs. After some months of frustration, the CEO signed himself and his team up for a crash course in reengineering. During the course, the management team members displayed confusion about the need for change as well as a need for direction. The output from several small group exercises focused on the team's need for some picture of the future. Each time the request was made, the CEO responded with a single theme: "I don't know what we need to look like in the future. All I know is that we've got to get our costs down now!" This company failed to shift and ultimately did suffer the huge loss in market share everyone had feared.

Executive words. The CEO of a large, integrated energy company saw his firm's competitive position and stock price slipping behind major rivals. His reaction was to announce his vision for his company's future:

"to become the premier energy company." He then called for the sweeping changes needed to attain such a vision. His message was carried in written form as well as in speeches to employees. The company even produced a video of the CEO's premier speech. Employees heard the message and asked themselves what *premier* and *sweeping changes* meant. Unfortunately, no one was willing to ask the CEO for the needed clarification.

This CEO's support started as only words but moved rapidly to leadership after the CEO finally heard and appreciated his employees's need for direction and energy. Two years after announcing the original vision, he called for the firm's annual management conference to focus on the changes he had been seeking. In two days of interactive sessions at the conference, the firm's 80 top managers conveyed their need for vision clarification and for action to support change. After hearing this request, the CEO chaired a Vision Task Force that developed a detailed vision to guide change. The CEO also chartered a major change of the firm's operational planning processes, authorizing the CFO to form a team of top-notch employees working full-time on the project. This chartering of a fix for one of the firm's "sacred cows" signaled the CEO's attention, energy, and commitment.

Lack of Comprehensive and Detailed Up-Front Planning

Perhaps the second most mentioned cause of failure of a Red Zone maneuver is the lack of up-front planning about just how the maneuver will work. Lack of planning means that the firm goes into the Red Zone maneuver without simple, coordinated road maps for employees to follow. But why a lack of planning? Isn't planning a strong suit of business today? How would investors and board members allow a firm to go forward without adequate plans?

The answer is that firms do planning prior to Red Zone maneuvers, but in most cases, it is the wrong kind of planning. The planning I see has a number of shortcomings that can be fatal in the Red Zone. My observation is that most Red Zone planning is short of facts, long on assumptions, and general rather than detailed. In addition, most Red Zone planning that I see focuses on the numbers or goals that are to be met after the Red Zone maneuver is complete and not on the development of a high quality, winning business design.

For example, my firm recently reviewed a merger planning package for a major food company that focused almost entirely on explaining how great the market share of the new company would be after the merger was complete. Totally missing from the package were:

- A description of how this merger would win in the marketplace
- The key steps needed to pull off the merger in the targeted time frame
- The risks that would need to be mitigated for effective combination of the two firms

Fortunately, an alert senior executive in the acquiring company heeded good advice to look in detail at the goals, steps, and risks only to conclude that the cultures of the two companies were so radically different that a merger was probably a very bad idea. As this book goes to press, the company behind the acquisition is still looking for a more suitable target.

The following examples illustrate the real world of planning pathologies for the Red Zone.

Planning veneer. An industry-leading insurance company with a critical dependence on strong information technology initiated a strategy to ensure better and less expensive services. The heart of the new strategy was to create a separate information technology company that would then serve the various divisions of the insurance company at what was hoped would be a more responsive and cost effective arms-length relationship.

As the new strategy was unfolding, the new information technology company did extensive planning based to a large degree on the facts of the internal marketplace as they knew them from previous working relationships. But planning was kept at a very high level and focused on goals for the organization rather than on identifying the specific means needed to get the new organization into full production. As the new organization was chartered and turned loose to operate on its own, managers quickly encountered many unanticipated problems, problems that required much more time and energy than they'd envisioned in their wildest dreams. Meanwhile, the parent organization watched patiently, and then impatiently, as the new company failed miserably to meet its projections. As of this writing, the newly appointed senior manager of the information technology unit has been ordered to dissolve the separate company and reposition its capabilities back within the insurance company.

Planning sham. A well-established publishing company bought a new database of well locations that they thought would be highly useful and valuable to the oil and gas producers who used their publications. Planning to get this new database on board and to get a data production company up and running was done on the fly to support unrealistic targets for the new business. The planning was based on erroneous assumptions about the marketplace as well as about the difficulty of the information technology aspects of the new venture. To make matters worse, planning was done only at a high level. Top management of the new venture was saddled with a plan that they could not support, complete, or even rationalize to a demanding board of directors. In short order, the entire top management team was let go.

The next president got control of the venture only by doing hands-on due diligence on both the market and the information technology requirements and needed capabilities. His biggest problem at first was building credibility with both his board and his employees, who had seen a useless and misleading plan up close and personal. Credibility was finally restored after almost a year of floundering and turnover by hard-nosed, detailed planning followed by real results.

Planning fiction. One of the handful of major players in the oil field service business conceived a vision of a new competitive strategy that would integrate a number of services that major energy company customers then purchased separately. The firm hired a consulting company to go into the marketplace to validate the need, desirability, and attractiveness of such integrated services. The company reasoned that third-party consultants would be seen as more credible and less self-serving than the service firm's own employees. An extensive plan was constructed around the survey data, a plan designed to guide the new division's startup in great detail.

The company went into a full court press to organize a number of its divisions into an integrated division to fulfill the new strategy, a strategy built on and confirmed by unvalidated market data. Customer reaction was negative from the start. The service company's employees were stunned to learn from their customers that the consultant survey exercise had not correctly understood or interpreted what the customers were saying about their needs and wants. But the plan was in effect and seemed to have a life of its own. The service company struggled for almost two years, giving up market share, before learning a valuable lesson about the need to validate with the facts rather than follow a planning fiction.

Narrow Organizational Involvement

The short definition of this pathology is a failure to get all the people who will be impacted by the Red Zone maneuver involved, signed up, and prepared in time for Red Zone success. For the most part, Red Zone maneuvers are started with very narrow involvement of personnel. Obviously, when two companies enter a merger Red Zone, narrow involvement is critical, even required, until many of the legal and competitive issues are ironed out. But I still see the same level of secrecy for Red Zone maneuvers like ERP implementations, major enterprise re-engineering projects, and even cultural changes. How is it possible that major software packages are chosen with little or no user involvement (or requirements, for that matter)? How is it possible that a company shifts a competitive strategy but offers the entire employee base no explanation, wondering why they are being instructed to change every price in every store?

One might think that all the management hype and lessons learned about involvement and commitment would encourage executives to be more open and forthcoming. But such is not the case, and most maneuvers are carried out without many employees getting into the game until the last minute. But why this lack of involvement?

First, I still see executives who underestimate their managers's and employees's ability to understand basic business maneuvers. Recently, I worked with a top executive of a firm with more than 50,000 employees who stated that he didn't really need to tell workers about their upcoming Red Zone maneuver (a strategy change), because they just wouldn't "get it." This otherwise well-connected executive was unaware that a focus group of first-line supervisors had vented their frustrations with the current strategy the week before and called out for change.

The second reason for low involvement might be that executives doubt the value of information about an impending Red Zone. I heard another executive say recently, "So we tell them; what are they going to do with the information?" Sometimes I worry that we sell short our managers and employees who honestly and conscientiously try to prepare themselves and their colleagues for upcoming change.

The third and probably most likely reason for a lack of organizational involvement is simply that we forget to do it widely enough and soon enough. Planning for a Red Zone maneuver is a tough, detailed job that diverts our attention from big picture questions like, "How do we best prepare the organization for the upcoming maneuver?" Many of us are reluctant to share information about an upcoming maneuver until we have thought it through and worked out all the details.

The following examples illustrate the real world of organizational involvement pathologies.

A few good men and women. A global, high-tech producer of software and supporting services for the extraction industry launched a planning process to identify a new strategy that would make them more competitive in a fragmented market. The planning process, as requested by the CEO, involved 15 key managers and technical professionals who had been key to company successes. The group was freewheeling, innovative, challenging of the facts, and determined to come up with a winning strategy. The team met three days a month for six months to identify a new competitive strategy and to conduct detailed planning for implementation. During the strategy development and planning process, the CEO requested that the group keep their lips sealed about the direction of the strategy until ready for rollout.

Trouble joined the party when the CEO finally gave the go ahead to get the rest of the 3,000-person organization involved in what was seen as a very fast implementation. Managers and technical professionals who had not been involved in the strategy team were initially jolted by the new strategy, because it included both a change in company direction and a huge increase in the amount of crossorganization cooperation. The CEO read initial concerns from the troops as resistance to his ideas and unwillingness to embrace change. Members of the top management team who had been key members of the strategy project counseled the CEO to slow down and rethink the implementation schedule and process. At first, the CEO was unwilling to slow down, but after more than three months of frustration, he relented. His management team was allowed to conduct forums in each major global location to talk through the strategy, identify questions and issues, accept the criticism of the troops, and allow the troops to "chew" on the new strategy. While these forums were later judged as very successful and necessary, they did not do much to repair the ill will generated by the initial hard push for implementation.

Mushroom involvement. The natural gas production division of one of the largest public utilities went into an ERP implementation with full knowledge that hard-nosed project management would be needed to bring the project in on time. The internal project manager, backed by top management, stepped up to the line and ran a tight ship on the company's technical resources, the software vendor, and the third-party systems integrator. The software application went live as planned to the delight of the technical team and the almost total surprise of the user community. The technical organization knew the users were out there somewhere and the user community knew that the ERP was back there somewhere; the fun began when the computer screens changed on the morning the system went live.

Workers were not prepared for the way their computer screens now called on them to work, so they didn't work at all while they tried to figure out what to do. The scramble was on to get frustrated workers and panic-ridden managers together to plot a recovery, and recover they did—after months of work production well below their previous level. In the dark, employees were plainly not ready to get the show back on the road without getting their payback in the form of gripes, complaints, and whinings about the way this organization operated.

Pressure cooker. The very large information technology shop of a major energy company was considering the implementation of a new technical approach to data management. After some months of evaluating major software options, the CIO made a decision to go with one of the two major vendors in that data management market space. Having made the decision, the CIO initiated several waves of communication about the decision, its rationale, and about the need to change in general. To further drive home the need for change, the CIO left a copy of a new book about change on the desk of each and every employee in the department.

As the CIO attempted to move forward with contractual negotiations with the selected vendor, he became aware of a rising level of resentment and outright resistance from several key technical professionals. It seemed that the employees did not feel that management was willing to listen to or discuss their objectives, so they decided to drag their feet. The situation was finally resolved after several wasted months when a senior manager on the line side of the organization charged the CIO to "do the selection process all over again with lots of up-front involvement and dialog."

Inappropriate Delegation for Critical Leadership Responsibilities

Believe it or not, delegation consistently turns up on the list of failure factors for Red Zone maneuvers, from reengineering to big system implementations, from mergers to culture changes. In this pathology, top management hands off Red Zone leadership to unprepared or low-credibility underlings as though it were a grenade with the pin removed. But why delegation at this critical time? What are we thinking when we hand over the "change of the decade" to someone other than the most experienced staff?

The reason for the prevalent practice of handing off Red Zone leadership must lie with underestimation. Underestimation of the importance of the maneuver or of the difficulty of the task ahead surely explains why a coach would hand the ball in the Red Zone to anyone other than the best on the team.

Another explanation for recurrent delegation in the face of the Red Zone might be one of the good management practices we discussed in an earlier chapter. Managers are encouraged to ration their own time and to delegate to others, to use *their* time better while providing a developmental experience.

My experience says that most delegation occurs because top management finds leading a Red Zone maneuver to be very uncomfortable, distressing, tiring, and difficult. Plainly said, some of us run from Red Zone responsibility. And we can always use the needs of delegation and management development as excuses to get Red Zone duties off our hands.

The following examples illustrate the real world of inappropriate delegation for the Red Zone.

Rookie leadership. A large aerospace firm, dropping in market share, recognized the need to design costs out of its products. Sales results in the marketplace convinced the CEO that lower prices were an absolute requirement, and the only way to lower prices was through a totally different approach to product cost. The cost design task was first assigned to the Executive Vice President in charge of all of the company's operations including engineering and manufacturing. Immediately upon receiving the assignment, the VP turned to a 28-year-old engineer as the project lead. The young engineer was looked on by the organization as an exceptional engineer, a great employee, and he was tall, well liked, and good looking to boot.

But the task at hand was huge and daunting, and everybody in the organization knew it. The young engineer, not short on confidence, plowed gamely ahead, working out a project approach that he thought would work. The approach, heavy on new training for the organization in quality methods and fifth discipline thinking, was never able to pick up any momentum. Key organizational players would not attend the training, nor would they allow their direct reports to attend training or give time to task force meetings. The Executive Vice President tried to intervene and throw his support behind the project through a tough letter and several "let's get on with it!" speeches to the organization. Meanwhile, the organization became a bazaar for consulting firms to come show their wares and make their promises of huge payoffs (for only a small percentage of those payoffs, of course). The patient, well-mannered CEO finally called off the charade by replacing the Executive Vice President with another manager who promised, and delivered, firsthand leadership to get costs out.

Place holder leadership. A huge retail grocery organization recognized the difficulty they faced in an increasingly competitive market across the southern and southwestern United States. It saw price challenges from discount merchants who were expanding rapidly. It also saw merchants beginning to experiment in the market with fully prepared foods and a "buy here, cook here, eat here" format. Top management talked about the need for a strategy revaluation to identify alternative strategies and even the possible need to reengineer the enterprise. The newly appointed president of the organization had his hands full consolidating his new position; the CEO was clearly interested in the exercise but wanted to be a spectator and evaluator rather than a leader in strategy examination. How would they go forward? The solution was to delegate the task to a Vice President of Information

Technology, relatively new to the organization and inexperienced in business transformations like reengineering.

The IT Vice President, now the reengineering project leader, formed a team with some of the best and brightest of the second tier of management. The team began a logical process of research, discovery, and learning, making trips to several competitive organizations to understand what they were doing. The team quickly built a reengineering library and hired a consultant to provide some high-level training in enterprise level reengineering. At this point, they quickly learned that the project would go nowhere unless they could get senior management on board and participating. Meanwhile, the organization around the project team began to label the exercise as questionable because of the absence of any of the organization's shakers and movers on the team. The project dragged on for about three months, suffering from a lack of organizational priority, executive support, and organizational credibility of the IT Vice President. Finally, the project was put out of its misery and allowed to disintegrate as top management focused on several operational issues that faced the company at the time.

Ineffectual leadership. One of the key divisions of NASA faced the dual problems of rising costs for space programs and falling popularity with the general public. The result was a real squeeze on the way the organization had done business in the past, when the nation's interest in space was at its zenith and dollars were available to tackle space programs on a first-class basis. Senior management was acutely aware of the squeeze but not in agreement on what to do about it. The Director of Administration approached the leadership of the division and offered to host an effort to tackle the problem. During this era, the total quality management movement was growing in popularity, so the Administrative Director suggested that his organization host a quality initiative as a possible solution to the squeeze. Most of the leadership of the division recoiled in shock at the idea that their division was not already world-class in quality and wanted little to do with the suggested initiative.

Undeterred, the Administrative Director appointed one of his senior managers as the project lead. This senior manager was certainly a capable fellow, with plenty of gray hair to prove that he was highly experienced in leading major initiatives, even those based on still evolving management technologies like total quality management. But while the project lead was capable, skilled, and experienced, he lacked credibility.

He was a nonengineer in an engineer's world, he was from the lowest status organization in the division, and he was one notch down in civil service ranking from the majority of middle and top managers. The project manager lacked personal and organizational influence, and to make matters worse, lacked the resource budget that would have been given to any technical project one tenth the size. Surprisingly, the project had some important successes but nothing like the successes that were needed or possible had credible leadership been at the helm.

Undisciplined and Incomplete Project Management

The short definition of this pathology is the failure to use systematic project management methods to plan, monitor, and control the steps needed for completion of a Red Zone maneuver on target, on time, and on budget. Most of today's organizations in a Red Zone maneuver attempt to use some form of project management as a tool. But the overall quality of that project management in most organizations is clearly deficient, haphazard, and ineffective at best. Even those organizations with a track record of using tough, disciplined project management to build plants or refineries effectively and efficiently frequently stumble over project management in the Red Zone. Why? What's behind the consistent finding of poor project management as one of the key reasons for failure in the Red Zone?

A CEO told me recently that project management only worked for "hard" projects like building chemical plants and not "soft" ones like changing a company's strategy or its culture. His view is not unusual, but the view itself may be the source of the problem. If we view a project as hard and assign a trained, certified project manager with clear expectations to bring the project in on target, on time, and on budget, we just might get that. But if we view a project as soft, assign someone who has never worked in disciplined project management, and create loose expectations, we are likely to set up a project to become off target, behind schedule, and over budget.

Another straightforward reason for poor project management in the Red Zone is likely to be a shortage of project management talent and experience in the organization. Most managers in today's organizations have lots of talent and experience in running an ongoing business unit and little or no experience in conceptualizing, developing, and executing a one-time event like a project. This lack of experience is especially critical in a project of real size, involving millions of dollars, and impacting hundreds or thousands of people.

Failure to put hard-nosed project management in place to guide Red Zone navigation risks some heavy duty consequences. For example, poor project management can mean critical items for success are not accomplished due to neglect, failure of funding, or lack of adequate manpower. Poor project management has resulted in technical projects coming in at two to ten times their estimated costs. Poor project management has resulted in a leadership team ready to go forward with a new way of operating, while the rest of the employees are surprised to discover there is a new game plan.

The following examples illustrate the real world of project management pathologies in the Red Zone.

Hero-dependent successes. The information technology division of a Fortune 50 energy firm committed to reengineer its user service processes. The CIO ensured that the design of the new processes was managed well and even piloted thoroughly. But when it came time for formally implementing those processes across the entire organization of several thousand professionals and a dozen major user divisions, he took an almost hands-off stance. Despite strong encouragement to appoint an experienced project manager, he decided that the information technology managers responsible for service to each division of the company should "just handle it."

The net result was mixed. A few managers made major strides in changing the way they did business with users, but several of the managers made no real progress to change the ways their departments were servicing assigned customers. When called on by the company management committee for a report, the CIO hinted that he had some good managers who could make things happen and others who were really good at day-to-day business but who did not manage change well. The committee's reaction was not kind; the CIO was told to help out those mangers who were behind in their implementations personally.

Out-of-control maneuver. A large mutual fund company was growing by leaps and bounds, outstripping its competitors, and rolling in increased bottom line. The key executives of the company had a gnawing sensation in the pits of their stomachs, however, that the party would be over whenever the stock market changed direction. The 3 founding executives of the company convened a high-level strategy summit involving their top 40 or so key managers and put their fears and the problem on the table for discussion. In the summit meeting, the participants realized that they had much to gain over the long run if they put in place important capabilities and hedges for tough times and much to lose if they went into tough times unprotected.

Spurred on by that recognition, the participants identified around 20 important steps or initiatives that needed to be completed in the next 18 months or so. The meeting closed with commitments to get back together every quarter to see how things were going. The responsibility for the overall management of the 20 initiatives was left unclear, but the CFO was assigned to ensure that the next quarter's meeting was held on time.

The quarter went by swiftly, and the same participants met again for show and tell. Only three initiatives were progressing, ten initiative teams had met but done nothing, and the remaining seven were hard to identify or remember. The founding executives and participants agreed that progress was poor, but then decided to use the same plan for managing the initiatives in the next quarter.

Mix of successes and failures. A large, integrated public utility launched a major enterprise systems implementation that would impact how the entire organization did business. A technically skilled project manager was put in place to guide the overall implementation. As the effort began to unfold, however, it seemed clear that multiple projects needed to be completed to get the entire implementation done. The mix of projects included those that were purely technical, having little direct impact on users of information systems, and those that were organizational as well as technical, having high direct impact on how the users worked in their own environments.

The project manager insisted on highly disciplined project management but did not require that projects having direct user impact be planned comprehensively. The focus on all projects was primarily technical. As the overall implementation drew to a close, the report card on all the technical projects showed a very high grade, while the projects that involved direct user impact received grades from C to B+. While this story has no outright failures, clearly not requiring comprehensive action steps in all projects cost the organization time, money, and some employee frustration.

WHAT IS WORSE THAN A RED ZONE PATHOLOGY?

Only one thing is worse than having a Red Zone pathology alive and well in an organization: having *more* than one pathology at the same time. For many companies that have not achieved the big gains in Red Zones, multiple pathologies are the rule and not the exception.

CHAPTER 4

Red Zone Principles

While I believe that each of the Red Zone principles has value if used by itself, the real value comes when all of the principles are used as a set, reinforcing and strengthening each other. There are two kinds of Red Zone principles: those that describe good management practice in design, and those that describe good management practice in execution of that design.

RED ZONE PRINCIPLES FOR DESIGN OF A WINNING BUSINESS MODEL

Figure 4.1 shows five Red Zone design principles. Note that principles three, four, and five are not lock-stepped or serial but interrelated. Together, they form what we call the design engine. A firm using these design principles might need to apply them several times until it is comfortable that it has created a winning design for the new business venture that will lead to the desired Red Zone gain.

Red Zone Principle One: Declare the Company in a Red Zone

I believe that formally telling the entire organization when a company is in a Red Zone is critical. Declare and communicate when the company is in a Red Zone so that people know that special behavior

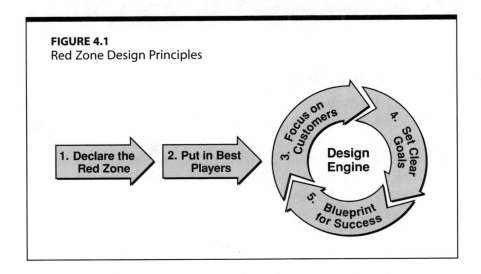

FIGURE 4.1
Red Zone Design Principles

and commitment will be required. As a part of the declaration, define that special behavior and commitment as Olympic-level motivation and creativity to achieve the gain coupled with a do-or-die resolve to avoid the loss. What better picture of needed motivation than Olympic athletes as they strive to win the highest prize? Interview after interview with Olympic contenders confirms their full-faith commitment to do their best to win the gold in the face of the world's toughest competition. The motivation for today's company in a Red Zone must be the same. In a true Red Zone, an important prize really is at stake, the maneuver really is that difficult, and world-class competitors really are standing in the way. While a sport only has its Olympics every four years, every year is the Olympics for business.

A CEO in a Red Zone has the undeniable, undelegatable, undiluted responsibility to take his or her team to an Olympic level of motivation right up front because that is what it will take. At the same time, the Red Zone CEO must ensure that the organization sees and fully understands the depth and consequences of failure, and the enormity of the loss that will result if the maneuver is not successful.

Companies and individuals in the Red Zone must show the same do-or-die level of resolve to avoid failure as the medical student who faces the last examination, as the mountain climber who sets the last piton, or as the Olympic heavyweight wrestler who faces a Russian giant who has not lost in 13 years. The Red Zone is the leader's highest calling. In the Red Zone, we must see real leadership up close and personal, strong and unbowed, like Patton before the flag. In the Red Zone, rise to that level, or prepare for the worst.

Red Zone Principle Two: Put the Best Players in the Game

Given what is at stake for a company in the Red Zone, given everything we know about the difficulty of pulling off a successful Red Zone maneuver, putting anyone into the game other than the organization's best is pure folly. Putting anyone into a key Red Zone role who does not have the right stuff should be grounds for dismissal.

"Come on! We wouldn't staff any kind of important organizational maneuver with people we didn't think were competent and could do it." I hear you say you wouldn't. But that thinking would not give you the right list of folks. You need to get your list the way Bill Gates would get his.

Imagine that an upcoming legal decision about Microsoft goes very badly for that company. Imagine that the court says that Mr. Gates must shut down his company in the United States. Imagine further that Bill says *goodbye* to Uncle Sam and *hello* to Canada. Canada says welcome, Mr. Gates, but only plan to bring a dozen people with you. Do you think Bill Gates could come up with a dozen folks to help him bring Microsoft back from ashes? You bet he could, and you bet those 12 would be hard chargers. They would be high-talent players who could create a new business venture from scratch. That's the kind of personnel you need to put in play in your company during a Red Zone.

So how do you decide who your best players are? Your gut tells you whom you should use. You have seen them at their best; you know what they've got from seeing them bring in successes and deal with failures. In addition, the organization tells you whom they want in those key roles. They tell you immediately with their hopeful attitudes or their dismal demeanor as you name potential players.

If you want to go beyond trusting your gut, consider critical attributes as you name your Red Zone team:

- *Character and personal credibility.* Red Zone is professional-level combat, and we want depth of character, integrity, grit, and resolve we can count on. Red Zones have been worked for personal advantage by unscrupulous executives to the great detriment of the organization involved. None of these people, please.

- *Leadership qualities.* The Red Zone is not consensusville; we need leaders who will take the organization where it would not have gone. We need "come on, we're going to do this" leadership.
- *Stamina and energy level.* The Red Zone may not be sprinting a marathon, but it does call for sprinting a middle distance. Leaders must have the physical resources to make the trip.
- *Commitment to the company.* The Red Zone is not a time to play politics or put personal interests first. Red Zone leaders will need to wear the company hat and fly the company flag, not the hat of their department or their own personal banner.
- *Experience and capability.* The Red Zone calls for shakers and movers who know how to get stuff done, who can innovate, improvise, and even fit an occasional square peg into a round hole. In the Red Zone we want "been there, won that" experience.
- *Knowledge of the business.* The Red Zone is about a fight for your business in an industry with world-class competitors, many of whom are experts. The Red Zone requires specific business expertise of the highest level.
- *Organizational position or company rank.* The Red Zone calls for organizationwide cooperation and coordination. It calls for leadership with the authority to make things happen. That kind of authority comes from organizational rank and title as well as from personal credibility.

That's a tough list. Yes, it is a tough list; it is your company's team for the Super Bowl. It is the kind of Red Zone leadership team you will need to field to achieve the gain and avoid the loss.

By the way, if you select your organization's best for the Red Zone and your key executives are not on that list, heaven help you. You may want to do some restaffing before you dare start your Red Zone maneuver.

Beyond identifying your best, you also must deal with the critical question of who is qualified. You may have found your best, but they might not all be at the level you need to get through your Red Zone maneuver successfully. Unlike a pro football team in the Red Zone, you can draft and field players from other teams if you need to, and sometimes you do. The CEO's job is to ensure that the team taking the field in the Red Zone has the right stuff, and that CEO must go to whatever lengths are necessary to get them from inside or outside the organization.

I cannot stress enough the need to give Red Zone assignments to those managers in key organizational roles, placing direct responsibility and accountability on them for achieving the desired gain. Our firm usually audits an organization's readiness for Red Zone success by going through all the key jobs on the organization chart and asking the CEO exactly what the Red Zone role is for each of his key reports. Organizations without specific Red Zone assignments for their CEO, COO, CFO, CIO, and CHRO clearly are not ready to begin any kind of Red Zone maneuver.

Red Zone Principle Three: Focus on the Customer

Use your customer's perspective to see clearly through the Red Zone. The key to successful navigation of any Red Zone is to look beyond the zone to the ultimate destination. For a business organization that destination is the marketplace, the world of the customer. The bottom line is simply this: if the Red Zone maneuver does not have a positive impact on the customer and the marketplace, think more than twice about doing it.

I believe that the ultimate value of an organization is determined by the impact it has on the customers and the marketplace. While an organization must satisfy other stakeholders, like its investors and its employees, making customers the maneuver's reference point is critical for design purposes. Organizations with a firm fix on what they can do for the marketplace through their new venture are more likely to complete a Red Zone maneuver successfully.

Isn't focusing on the customer during a Red Zone maneuver obvious? Isn't that the reason we go to all the trouble to merge, reengineer, change our culture, and so on? No. Many organizations enter the Red Zone with motives other than customer value improvement. I have seen organizations undertake Red Zone maneuvers for what can be called financial engineering reasons. That is, some companies want to change the way the company looks to investors and Wall Street without changing the way the company does business in the customer marketplace. Most of us have seen Red Zone maneuvers driven primarily by key executives who desire personal wealth. While most organizations profit when executives are financially motivated to grow the business, many organizations suffer when executives pursue financial wealth at the expense of the company. Focus on finding the customer value improvement to smoke out healthy or unhealthy reasons to conduct a Red Zone maneuver.

How do you keep your eye on the customer when your organization is working through a Red Zone? The approach that seems to work best explicitly incorporates the attributes of the organization's products and services, the organization's current position on those attributes, and the competitors's likely position on those attributes. Figure 4.2 shows an example of a Red Zone customer scorecard that was used to identify the value that one organization wanted to bring to the marketplace through its Red Zone maneuver. The data in our sample figure shows how a huge retailer saw its position (plus = better, minus = worse, 0 = same as) relative to its three top competitors (C1, C2, and C3) on two key customer values: shopping convenience and fulfillment of needs in the shopping experience. The needed action column on the far right sug-

FIGURE 4.2
Red Zone Customer Scorecard

Customer		Present Position				Desired Position				Needed Action	
Value	Attributes	Our	C1	C2	C3	Our	C1	C2	C3	Advance	Hold
Shopping Convenience	Location	+	0	+	−	+	0	+	0		✓
	Access	+	+	0	0	+	+	0	0		✓
Fulfillment of Needs	Price	0	+	−	−	+	+	0	0	✓	
	Quality	+	−	0	−	+	+	+	0	✓	
	Service	−	0	+	0	+	+	+	+	✓	

gests that any Red Zone maneuver attempted by the company would need to help the company advance dramatically on the value dimensions of price (requiring the lowering of costs) and customer service, while holding its position on quality of goods sold.

The completed scorecard allows the organization to see the basis of its relationship with its customers, where it might gain value by improving its position, and where it would need to hold its value position with respect to its competitors. The use of such a scorecard during Red Zone design clearly focuses management attention on the ultimate challenge and sets the stage for concrete Red Zone goals, including explicit customer relationship management goals. The bottom line is this: companies should plan to better their relationship with customers in every Red Zone maneuver. Red Zones are tough enough without this customer relationship improvement constraint, but failing to take the customer into explicit account is likely to be a tragic flaw.

Red Zone Principle Four:
Set Clear Red Zone Goals

Organizations need a handful of crisp, clear goals to follow in the Red Zone. A firm enters the Red Zone when it decides to pursue a significant gain using one of the Red Zone maneuvers discussed earlier. By their very nature, these maneuvers can lead to great gain for the firm or result in significant loss. The challenge is to complete the maneuver successfully. I have found that the first step toward the desired gain is to set clear goals for the maneuver. Without those clear goals, mounting the kind of organizational effort necessary for success will be practically impossible.

One of the fundamental reasons for setting clear goals is to drive innovation and creativity. Red Zone goals should be set after what amounts to a feasibility study that pays explicit attention to the customer scorecard discussed earlier. Red Zone goals should identify desired organization outcomes that can be produced by increasing customer value. For example, a strategy change Red Zone might have as its goal increased market share. But that market share goal needs to be anchored in a value improvement for the customer. Setting an increased market share goal without planning to add customer value will put a Red Zone maneuver in jeopardy right from the beginning.

Unlike the outrageous goals recommended by many writers for a reengineering project, Red Zone goals should be management's best effort to describe what it wants to make happen with some degree of certainty. While outrageous goals are used to jar folks into thinking outside the box, Red Zone goals should be set to guide what management believes should be obtainable. If the organization approaching the Red Zone is a public company, the same guidelines should be used for goal setting as are normally used to let shareholders know what the company expects to do over a designated time period.

Red Zone Principle Five: Blueprint for Success

It is important to have a new perspective or a new way of thinking about a Red Zone maneuver. One should think about how the organization will look and operate after the maneuver is completed. After the maneuver, if the job has been done right, the organization will be a new business venture that will be more successful than before. That is, the new business venture will allow the organization to meet its Red Zone goals by adding value to customers and the marketplace.

Another way to think about a Red Zone maneuver is to visualize the organization, or venture, after the maneuver as we would visualize a remodeled house. We can envision a remodeled house by using a set of blueprints. We choose the word blueprint rather than the word vision because blueprint normally implies precision and detail while vision may imply something more fuzzy and ephemeral.

Remember why we are doing a Red Zone maneuver: to allow our organization to achieve some future gain while preventing some future loss. For our organization to succeed, it must have different attributes or qualities than it currently has. The purpose of the blueprint is to depict the organization as it needs to look to achieve the desired gain, with those new attributes in play alongside the organization's other attributes. For a home remodeling, we understand what is about to happen to our home by comparing our house today with the blueprint for tomorrow.

While most of us would not even entertain the idea of launching the construction phase of a major home remodel without a blueprint, I see senior managers do just that for the Red Zone all the time. Why?

Because most of us managers think in terms of checking tasks off our priority lists as we run our day-to-day businesses. We don't often have the need for blueprint thinking that will lead to a new venture.

There are two obvious reasons for building a blueprint for a Red Zone maneuver. First, the completed blueprint of the organization as it will look after the maneuver allows organization members to picture the desired destination. Their mental picture provides the context for the actions needed to reach the desired gain on the other side of the Red Zone. Second, the presence of a completed Red Zone blueprint allows organization members to generate lists of tasks to reach the desired gain. I believe that it is critical to derive task lists from the overall blueprint and not to make lists by concentrating on what we know will be pieces of the maneuver. For example, making task lists for an entire organization by focusing only on a particular systems implementation will produce a much less comprehensive list than focusing on the overall organizational blueprint.

What is in a Red Zone blueprint for a maneuver like a merger, reengineering, or an e-business implementation? We can take guidance for our blueprint from the remodeled home example introduced earlier. Included in those home blueprints will be the elevations that show how the house will look from the outside; the floor plans that show how it will look from above; and the inside views of each room, including traffic patterns, appliances, and sometimes furniture. While I will show more specific blueprint contents in the gameplan chapters to follow, the organizational blueprint generally should include pictures, diagrams, and narratives for the following:

- The organization chart that will be in play after the maneuver is completed, with as many members' names as are known at the time of blueprinting.
- Organization goals and measures that will be used to run the business after the maneuver is complete.
- High-level process diagrams that show how the work of building the organization's products and services will be done as well as how customers will be served.
- High-level systems diagrams that show what and where new systems will be deployed including, if needed, how new screens will look to workers.

- Narratives or vignettes that describe how employees will be working after the maneuver; i.e., with the new processes, with new systems, toward new goals.

The last step in the blueprinting process is to validate the business case for conducting the Red Zone maneuver. Now is the time to take a hard look at the business situation and to decide if the initiative really makes sense. While top management may already have a high-level business case, this is the time to plug in the blueprint-based revenue and cost projections, which should tell you whether to continue, modify the plan, or cancel.

Isn't this blueprinting pretty elaborate? Won't blueprinting be a lot of work? Well, sure it is elaborate, and it will take a lot of research and due diligence, not to mention brain-stretching creativity. But after all, we only have the success of the company at stake. After all, we only have a few hundreds of millions of dollars in play. After all, we will only impact most of our customers and employees. Still don't think it's worth the time and energy? Give me a break; go do it.

Don't Move! Don't go to Red Zone execution principles until a clear picture of the improved business design has been drawn.

- How the Red Zone maneuver will positively impact the customer is clear.
- The maneuver has clear goals.
- A completed blueprint for the organization after the maneuver, as it achieves those goals to satisfy customers, is in place.

This is the last chance to stop the Red Zone maneuver before execution begins. Do not go past this point without a sensible business case and a blueprint on which you are willing to bet the firm. Because you are.

RED ZONE EXECUTION PRINCIPLES

There are also five Red Zone execution principles as shown in Figure 4.3. Note that principles six, seven, and eight are interrelated, forming the engine that drives a successful execution of a Red Zone design.

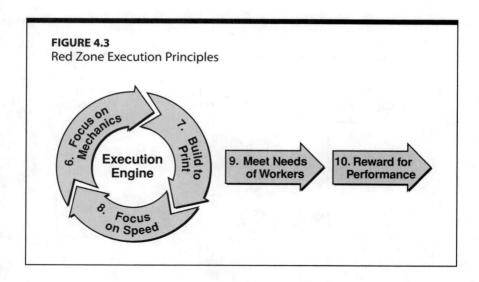

FIGURE 4.3
Red Zone Execution Principles

A firm using these execution principles might need to apply them repetitively during the execution phase to ensure success in the Red Zone.

Red Zone Principle Six: Focus on the Mechanics for Operations Integration

Regardless of the kind of Red Zone, much of the work to complete the Red Zone maneuver will be the same. We look at organizations as having a finite number of moving, mechanical parts that must be altered to move an organization from where it is to what it will need to be after the Red Zone. Figure 4.4 makes the point that all Red Zone maneuvers have the same mechanical parts that must be altered to move toward the new business design, integrating the design into the company's operations. This operations integration step is clearly the most important element of the execution of the Red Zone design. Nothing good happens for the company until the Red Zone design is fully integrated into the day-to-day operation of the company.

The organization's mechanical parts for alteration are as follows:

- *Work processes.* The detailed steps the organization takes to do business, the steps that employees take to produce and deliver products and services.

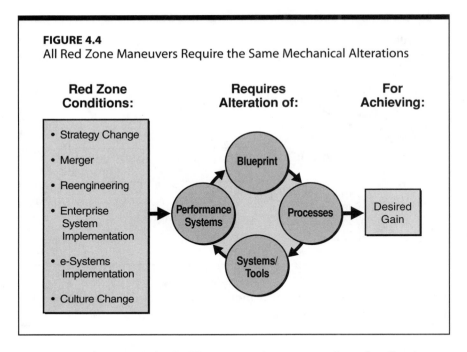

FIGURE 4.4
All Red Zone Maneuvers Require the Same Mechanical Alterations

- *Plant/equipment/tools.* Those concrete assets that the firm's employees use in the firm's work processes to produce and deliver products and services.
- *Performance systems.* The organization's collection of roles, role (or job) descriptions, goals, training programs, and incentive structures that enable workers to do the work of the firm; i.e., to use the firm's plant/equipment/tools in work processes to produce goods and services for clients.

These mechanical parts obviously will need to be changed differently based on the type of Red Zone maneuver and the nature of the Red Zone blueprint and goals, but the underlying point is still simple. If you want an organization to behave differently, these mechanical parts are the valves you adjust to make something different happen. In our view, each Red Zone maneuver can be looked at as an engineering problem. Until all the alterations required by the Red Zone blueprint are made, the change will not be integrated into operations, and the organization will not reach its desired goal.

For example, if a firm enters a reengineering Red Zone, by definition it will be changing work processes. But those work process changes must be coupled with changes in plant/equipment/tools to fit the changed processes, and the performance system that guides worker behavior must be changed to fit process and tool changes. For a firm entering an e-business Red Zone, alterations will need to begin with information systems (e.g., plant/equipment/tools), extend to work processes, and then on to performance systems.

Figure 4.5 makes the point that a change in any one mechanical part of the organization will require a change or alteration in the other parts to get them back in sync. The springs shown in the diagram attempt to illustrate the interdependence between the mechanical parts. More information about the changes a particular Red Zone maneuver needs will be provided in the gameplan chapters to follow.

Now, let's summarize this Red Zone principle. Once goals have been set for a Red Zone maneuver and the blueprint for operation after the maneuver has been sketched, Red Zone managers can make a list

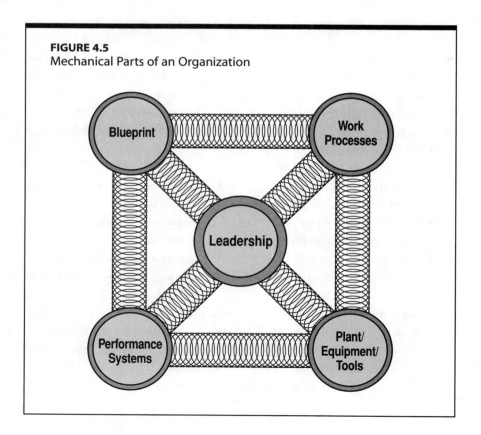

FIGURE 4.5
Mechanical Parts of an Organization

of things that need to get done by looking at required alterations of work processes, plant/equipment/tools, and performance systems. For many managers working through their first Red Zone, the number of items on the action lists is staggering, running into the hundreds or even thousands. But keep in mind, a lot of arms and legs are available to help once the people in the organization understand the blueprint. I have found that Red Zone managers who focus on precisely identifying and then executing all of the required alterations in the mechanical parts of their organization are far more likely to produce the new business venture that gives the desired gain. Fortunately, our next Red Zone principle describes program and project management tools.

Red Zone Principle Seven: Use Program and Project Management to Build to Print

Once the new organization or venture is blueprinted, building it requires intense management. That needed management can be supported by two mature management disciplines that are not often used in a normal, run-the-business environment: program and project management.

Project management is used to bundle small sets of the alterations just discussed in principle six. Program management is used to oversee the sets of projects. Program management focuses on several important issues as it achieves the organization's long-term interest, or vision, represented by the Red Zone blueprint.

- Identifying of all the steps needed to build out the Red Zone blueprint and then organizing those steps into manageable projects.
- Ensuring that all projects have the resources to complete important steps on target, on time, and on budget.
- Ensuring that projects have necessary coordination and cooperation to keep them from colliding, conflicting, and taking resources from each other.
- Including formal risk management, systematically identifying and mitigating the most likely risks to the Red Zone maneuver.
- Flexing projects around the highs and lows, ebbs and flows of the business to keep the right overall amount of organizational energy focused on achieving the blueprint.

In short, program management works with the senior executives to ensure that needed changes are fully integrated into the operations of the company (Figure 4.6).

Project management focuses finite resources on the completion of unique assigned work—on target, on time, and on budget. Project management brings concrete results to a given Red Zone initiative in a defined time period. For example, we might use project management to plan and control the alteration of the employee performance system in a merger to ensure that employees of both companies are paid from the same compensation structure.

Project management needs to be done in a similar fashion across projects to enable program management to understand overall status or progress toward building out the organization to the Red Zone blueprint. Failure to adopt a uniform project management method ensures a poor job of managing change and that change initiatives that run simultaneously will not be comparable, making overall program management practically impossible to do well.

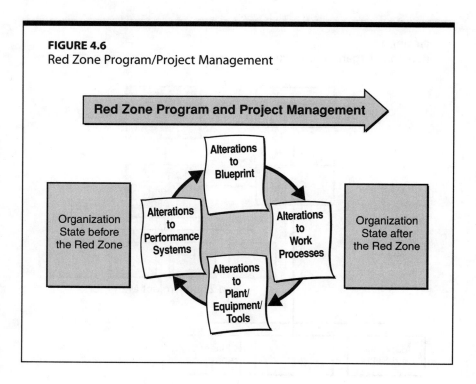

FIGURE 4.6
Red Zone Program/Project Management

Red Zone Program and Project Management

Alterations to Blueprint

Organization State before the Red Zone

Alterations to Performance Systems

Alterations to Work Processes

Organization State after the Red Zone

Alterations to Plant/ Equipment/ Tools

The use of program and project management allows the organization in the Red Zone to assign clear responsibilities and accountabilities for the various parts of the Red Zone maneuver. Of course, the ultimate responsibility and accountability for any maneuver rests with the CEO. The CEO can delegate the day-to-day work of program management to another Red Zone team member with the needed experience, capability, and organizational rank and credibility. Red Zone projects can then be assigned to other Red Zone team members with the right stuff for project success.

For Red Zone program and project management to be effective, I believe that both the program and project managers should be formally appointed and should show up on the firm's organization chart. Figure 4.7 shows the basic organization chart format that I think best communicates the Red Zone maneuver's importance and priority. Note the direct attachment of Red Zone program management to the CEO. Note also the steering committee structure above program management. Generally, the members of the steering committee are the CEO and the

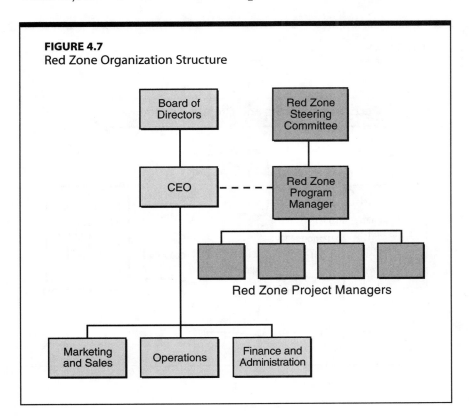

FIGURE 4.7
Red Zone Organization Structure

Board of Directors

Red Zone Steering Committee

CEO

Red Zone Program Manager

Red Zone Project Managers

Marketing and Sales

Operations

Finance and Administration

CEO's direct reports, although on some occasions, other members might be added depending on the nature of the Red Zone maneuver.

Red Zone Principle Eight: Focus on Speed

Speed is important in the Red Zone for a number of reasons. Time is money and when you are going after a big organizational gain, the faster you can get to it, the better things are economically. In other words, the faster we move, the sooner we can reap the benefits of the Red Zone maneuver.

Speed is also important for strategic focus. It is very difficult for a top management team to keep its eye on the strategy ball while they are engaged in a day-to-day battle to get through a Red Zone maneuver. The sooner the company puts the Red Zone behind them, the sooner top management will be able to look out to far horizons to plot the next maneuver.

Moving briskly through a Red Zone may also be a competitive advantage in the short term as the company moves to a new configuration, which competitors then want or need to match. The result of any Red Zone maneuver should be a new way of working, or competing, that gives advantage. As a company demonstrates that it can move quickly through a Red Zone, investors discover that they have shares in a more valuable venture. The market seems to place a premium on those companies that demonstrate speed and agility.

The last reason to value speed in the Red Zone has to do with decreasing critical risks. In the hot and heavy work of the Red Zone, the risk of doing something that will negatively impact customers is always present. In addition, the organization runs the very real risk of workers running out of gas, time, and energy.

It is possible to move too fast, however. Just as keeping employees in the Red Zone too long is a risk, so is working them too hard and too fast. Moving too fast can produce burnout, frustration, and the loss of valuable personnel. In addition, moving too fast may encourage sloppy implementation, inadequate planning, and otherwise doing things so poorly that they have to be redone later. Moving too fast can mean slamming in systems with the hope that the organization will find time to fine-tune them later. Unfortunately, many organizations wind up with systems or work processes that lack the integrity to deliver good products or services to customers.

Optimal speed through the Red Zone can be achieved by using disciplined program and project management with a critical path approach to building out the Red Zone blueprint. Focusing on a good master schedule with interim milestones also will reduce Red Zone cycle time. Adding quality checks and face-to-face audits increases the chance that the organization will understand where it stands and at what pace it can move. Last but not least, sensitivity to people and their workloads will allow top management to make the Red Zone journey at best speed.

Red Zone Principle Nine: Meet Special Needs of Workers

Workers will lose heart and energy before the desired gain is realized if they don't receive intense attention and support while in the Red Zone. The Red Zone is a tough time for employees and families as we expect much more of them than during normal business times. We can organize our thinking about special attention for workers as follows:

- *Workload management.* While everyone in an organization in a Red Zone is impacted and should be considered, particular attention must go to managing the workload of the Red Zone team members. Special concerns for program and project management include:
  - Leveling workloads between people
  - Making arrangements to cover regular workloads for team members
  - Being flexible enough to allow the changing of team members before burnout or around personal situations
  - Arranging for job protection for workers on teams
- *Hygiene factors.* Working conditions are especially critical during a Red Zone maneuver. Care should be taken to ensure that workplaces are comfortable and convenient (or even special), and that basic needs are cared for, ranging from meals brought in, to special transportation, to expense account relief, to special hats and T-shirts.
- *Recognition and appreciation.* We want to show special appreciation to all employees during and after a Red Zone maneuver. We recommend special incentives or bonuses to show appreciation for

those folks who are keys to the success of the Red Zone maneuver. First and foremost, we want to ensure that personnel who have performed especially well in the Red Zone get performance appraisal credit; the last thing we want is for employees to feel, or be, penalized for their special work in the Red Zone. Beyond personal recognition, consider organizational celebrations both to mark progress and show appreciation.

- *Budgeting for special needs.* Hard costs are associated with making people special during any Red Zone. We recommend that organizations budget for those costs as a part of the overall investment to achieve the desired gain in the Red Zone. We have seen many projects get in trouble because Red Zone managers did not have the dollar resources for the care and feeding of the firm's Super Bowl athletes.

- *Leadership example.* Last but not least is leadership example. Nothing seems to beat the impact of the organization's executives mixing it up with the troops and working the long, hard hours with them during a Red Zone. One of the single biggest mistakes an executive can make at this critical time in the life of an organization is to be either unavailable or aloof. A leader needs to be in the thick of things, showing employees what's in it for them and getting their opinions and feedback.

Red Zone Principle Ten: Reward Management for Red Zone Performance

Beyond strict responsibility and accountability, managers designated for key Red Zone roles must be rewarded heavily for success. Failure to provide direct, valuable monetary incentives for Red Zone results will seriously jeopardize the maneuver.

This principle sounds like a slam dunk, but it isn't. Why are so many companies not doing it or doing it dead wrong? Figure 4.8 shows the very simple combinations of possible incentives for management working in and around the Red Zone. Most companies regularly use incentives every year to reward senior executives who have reached the company's annual business plan goals. During the time of this writing, our firm has 25 clients in some form of Red Zone, and every one of those clients is planning to give incentives to senior management for meeting or exceeding normal business goals.

FIGURE 4.8
Motivation for Maximum Performance in the Red Zone

Types of Motivation	Incentives for Meeting Normal Business Goals	Incentives for Meeting Red Zone Goals
No Motivation	NO	NO
Motivation for Disruption	NO	YES
Motivation for Inertia	YES	NO
Motivation for Maximum Performance	YES	YES

"Incentives for achieving Red Zone Goals" literally means additional incentives given for meeting Red Zone milestones and/or for achieving the Red Zone goals described in Principle Four. Such incentives are frequently a problem for companies entering the Red Zone. Failure to pay for Red Zone goal accomplishment while paying incentives for normal goal accomplishment produces a kind of organizational inertia, making the changes needed for the Red Zone even more difficult to accomplish.

A handful of the companies we are working with today are having great difficulty rationalizing the payment of extra incentives to management to lead through the Red Zone. Their difficulties stem from a variety of sources: compensation managers who are concerned about upsetting balances and equities; staffers who maintain that the company has never done it that way; senior executives who don't want to spend the money or who worry that someone will make too much money; and concerns about how such incentives would appear to the organization's workers. For a variety of reasons, strong incentives are frequently not given to executives in the Red Zone. This omission is clearly linked to the number one Red Zone pathology: lack of sustained management support.

I sometimes see companies paying incentives for Red Zone goal accomplishment seemingly without concern for the day-to-day performance of the company. This approach is almost guaranteed to produce disruptive results as the Red Zone changes are implemented without proper consideration of the normal business of the company. I have seen a number of examples of disruption when senior managers responsible for a comprehensive ERP implementation were rewarded solely for implementation of the technical systems without any incentive impact for normal work goals. The net result of this kind of situation was frequently systems that worked from a technical point of view but that disrupted users's work environment and productivity.

I believe that the best motivation for the Red Zone is to provide dual incentives for meeting Red Zone goals as well as for meeting normal business goals. The simple truth of the matter is that companies must continue doing their normal business while they work their way through a Red Zone like a merger, reengineering, or system implementation. I have seen the best motivational successes when both sets of goals were in play simultaneously and when the biggest management payoffs were linked to organizational performance in the first two to three years after the Red Zone maneuver was complete. Such long-term linking of incentives clearly says to senior management that not only getting through the maneuver counts, but reaching that new, more successful, business venture *really* counts.

I want to close this discussion of the ten Red Zone principles with a bit of context. In the introduction to this chapter, I said that each one of the principles would help out in a Red Zone situation. Let me say now that one of these principles is probably more powerful than the others. Archimedes said that he could move the world with a long enough lever and a place to stand. With Principle Ten, I will make more progress in managing a Red Zone maneuver than with any other.

GETTING RED ZONE PRINCIPLES INTO PLAY

Let's just make sure we are clear on whose job it is to get and keep Red Zone principles in play. Ultimately it is the CEO's job. The CEO will be held accountable for either the success or the failure of the Red Zone maneuver. As I said in an earlier chapter, the CEO's job is to read the tea leaves of the business environment and to anticipate those business disrupters that might make opportunities possible. Then the CEO must lead the organization into the kind of Red Zone maneuver that will allow the company to operate more successfully in the future. Finally, the CEO's job is to shift the organization into Red Zone operation to ensure that future success.

While shifting the organization into Red Zone operation is challenging, keeping it there is even more challenging. The biggest challenge will be the press of day-to-day business: meeting customer needs, dealing with the inevitable interruptions and upsets of business life, solving manpower problems, and dealing with every organization's tendency to revert to business as usual.

One of the best ways to get the Red Zone principles into play and to keep them there is to produce a specific management gameplan for an organization's Red Zone. This management gameplan is very much like the special Red Zone playbook used by football teams inside the 20-yard line, customized for the specific team they are about to play. The gameplan should be like a primer for the organization about to launch a Red Zone maneuver, providing context for the maneuver as well as basic guidelines for managing it. By Red Zone gameplan, I do *not* mean the specific technical methodology for the maneuver. For example, the Red Zone gameplan for reengineering that follows in Chapter 7 will not provide the how-to-do-it reengineering detail that can be found in a number of books or consulting methodologies. My goal in writing this book is to cover the essential *management principles* that must be put in place at the highest level to achieve overall success in the Red Zone. Once a company elects to reengineer major processes, for example, senior management should complete their company's reengineering gameplan and select specific technical text(s) or methodologies to guide the detailed reengineering work.

A key point made earlier is that all Red Zone maneuvers can be treated as basically the same. That is why the ten principles just covered can be applied so broadly. But there *are* some nuances, some aspects of each of the six Red Zone maneuvers covered in this book, that are unique to the maneuver. The next part of the book focuses on specific gameplans that concentrate on the details and nuances of each maneuver.

PART TWO

THE RED ZONE MANAGEMENT GAMEPLANS

In Part Two, my goal is to detail a specific gameplan for each of the six most common Red Zone maneuvers. Each gameplan chapter is constructed around a primer of basic information about the maneuver followed by the ten Red Zone principles focused specifically on that maneuver. While Red Zone maneuvers are very similar in structure, unique aspects of each maneuver need more detailed explanation.

CHAPTER 5

Red Zone Gameplan for Changing Competitive Strategy

In this first of the Red Zone gameplan chapters, we will discuss the toughest of the Red Zone maneuvers. Changing a company's competitive strategy is toughest because it has the most moving parts, involves more of the total organization, and has a more immediate impact on the company's customers than any other Red Zone maneuver. This chapter will begin with a high-level primer on the subject of competitive strategy and will end with a discussion of the Red Zone principles as they apply to changing a company's competitive strategy.

THE PRIMER ON CHANGING COMPETITIVE STRATEGY

A Definition of Competitive Strategy

What do we mean when we talk about an organization's competitive strategy? Strategy is the approach the company uses to present itself to the marketplace, the rules it uses to win in the marketplace, and the actions it takes to protect itself from competitors.

Succeeding at business might be a bit easier if it were more like the game of Monopoly. Players lucky enough to land first on the hot properties could just buy them with funds from that wonderful endowment each receives by agreeing to follow the rules. Building infrastructure on the newly acquired properties would yield higher rents, and this income could be used to buy more properties and improve infrastructure.

About the only strategies required would be rampant acquisition and accumulation of all the properties in various color-coordinated categories, plus occasional diversions like accidentally knocking the dice off the table if a roll landed an ultracompetitive player on someone else's greatly improved Park Place. The game even gives us $200 in subsidies when we pass each "business cycle."

Looking back on those childhood Monopoly games, the same few kids usually seemed to win. It's not that they were luckier with dice. It's not that they got more from the Community Chest. Well, maybe they did play banker more often. But what they did do unfailingly was to develop an approach to each game, based on where they landed and where others landed, and nurture a ceaseless desire to win. They knew when to trade for a property or buy it on the side before anyone else could see a pattern. They knew just how many jelly beans, or similar tokens of appreciation, would negotiate down a price. We could say they had aggressive and successful competitive strategies.

Strategy 101

In any industry, some companies, like those high-performing Monopoly players, will always outperform their competitors. They have been able to establish and sustain a competitive advantage over others. To survive, every company has to have some degree of competitive advantage. Even in cases where advantage is minimal—where products or services are virtually identical—companies can remain profitable. For a Dunkin' Donuts franchisee, competitive advantage might be a better location than the Krispy Kreme. In most industries, competitive advantage is a more complex issue, arising from a combination of product appeal, production capacity, pricing structure, marketing programs, distribution channels, leadership quality, and a culturally inherent desire to win. Competitive advantage is sustainable when the strategy that produces it cannot be easily copied by competitors.

More than ever, leaders and managers must view the development and execution of competitive strategy as an ongoing activity that defines the company's direction and steps, inspires the quality of people and performance, and builds in the capacity and competence for change as conditions alter to reach success.

A Strategy Is a Strategy Is a Strategy

When does a company have a true competitive strategy? According to the all-time strategy guru, Michael E. Porter, you will know a true strategy when you see the following five characteristics:

1. A company with a true strategy can demonstrate that it delivers distinctive values that are different from its competitors.
2. A company with a true strategy carries out a set of activities to deliver the product in a different way from its competitors.
3. A company with a true strategy will have come by it through debate, struggle, and tradeoffs, sacrificing some of its subsidiaries or opportunities to focus on the strategy.
4. A company with a true strategy ensures that all its activities align with its goals and strategies.
5. A company with a true strategy demonstrates continuity in execution, not developing one strategy for 2001 only to trash it for a completely different one in 2002.

In a September 2000 interview titled "Soothsayer of Strategy," for London's *Sunday Telegraph,* Porter said, "the best CEOs are able to give a clear purpose to their organizations. You find they endlessly repeat their strategy to their employees." The interviewer asked Porter why successful corporations can be doomed to eventual failure, even if they have magnificent strategies. His reply: ". . . many companies undermine their own strategies—a lot of the problem is internal. Once you are successful you want to grow. It's natural. But the very act of growing can undermine a successful strategy. Then, of course, there can be structural changes in the environment that undermine a strategy."

Approaches to Competitive Strategy

Porter published his seminal work *Competitive Strategy* (his latest version was published by the Free Press, 1998) some 20 years ago. The book continues to be a best-seller today and is considered one of the important works by most of today's big decision makers. MBA students and management consultants worldwide study his idea that five basic factors drive competition within industries.

1. Threat of new entrants
2. Threat of substitute products or services
3. Bargaining power of suppliers
4. Bargaining power of buyers
5. Rivalry among existing firms

In response to these five factors, Porter identifies three sources of competitive advantage, which he refers to as *generic strategies*. In his February 2000 *CMA Management* article, "The Quest for Competitive Advantage," Raymond Suutari summarizes the sources of competitive advantage along these lines:

1. *Cost leadership—having the lowest costs in the industry.* Cost advantage varies between industries. It is generally based on economies of scale, preferential access to natural resources/raw materials, and superior, proprietary technology. Cost leadership is effective only if a company can command prices close to the industry average and avoid discounting practices.
2. *Differentiation—making a product or service so unique that people will pay higher prices and/or many people will buy it and continue to buy it over time.* Differentiation can be tangible, based on superior quality of performance, or intangible, based on image or brand. Differentiation can be derived from product/service characteristics or distribution channels. This strategy may impose a higher cost structure on a company, which is acceptable as long as the price premium covers these costs.
3. *Focus—adopting a narrow competitive scope in an industry.* Opportunities for advantage may arise from buyer characteristics, product specification, or geography/location. Focus can be based on targeting a segment with unique needs not served by others (differentiation) or having specialized equipment that can handle target market needs more efficiently (cost).

The Red Zone Alert: The Changing Competitive Landscape

Competitive strategies may well have to change unexpectedly, or at least be designed to allow for significant adjustment, because the environment in which companies operate changes. The economy of a region might collapse or boom, new technology could easily end a product's life cycle, or new regulations or legislation can dramatically alter the competitive landscape. When a new CEO arrives, that event itself is often a signal for strategic change because the board likely charged this officer with doing so. Whatever its basis, the ultimate success of a competitive strategy depends in equal parts on the soundness of the decision and actions identified, and on the effectiveness and aggressiveness of its implementation.

As long as the pace of change was relatively predictable, companies in well-defined industries could compete successfully using long-favored competitive strategies based on quality and productivity, giving customers the best value for their money. As the pace of change accelerates, preoccupation with existing competitive strategies is likely to erode a company's market share and profitability. Success can be a company's undoing. Failing to act on the undercurrents that change the conditions of competition, IBM and GM missed major shifts in the marketplace and struggled for years to adjust and recapture customers.

The average life span for most organizations is estimated to be 40 years. Well, age is relative, but the desire to dodge the old corporate age bullet drives a growing business to seek corporate renewal consultants. Companies's, and leaders's, demises are too often the result of failure to understand and address emerging needs for new markets, for new products, and for new means to distribute them—the future competitive "space."

The Red Zone Problem: Changing the Competitive Strategy

Divining competitive strategies used to be an exercise to develop great answers to the fundamental question, "How do we position our company to gain or increase advantage in a known environment?" The more relevant question today is, "How do we position our company to keep the horizon of an ever-evolving environment in view and figure out what's to our advantage and what's not? Can't we just stop time until we get this figured out?" Sorry folks, it doesn't work that way.

Recent literature advises leaders to rethink the basis for planning strategy in today's very fluid environment. Rather than positioning a company in a given industry space and focusing the company's collective energies on the position relative to competitors, leaders should consider how they can influence their competitive environment—create it or shape it.

- In a collaborative arrangement with Philips, the European electronics manufacturer, Sony reshaped a market environment and quickly moved to capture it before Philips or other firms had grasped its potential. Philips saw the tape recorder as an expensive office product; Sony envisioned a commercial product—the Walkman—that could reach millions of customers. Philips saw the CD player as a luxury product; Sony envisioned a middle-of the-road product and quickly scaled up capacity to preempt the market.
- Amazon, eBay, E*Trade, and Priceline have helped create the dynamics of a new competitive space as well as influence that of many traditional industries.

To shape an environment, leaders start the planning process first by imagining the environment and then charting the direction and formatting the elements (major milestones) along the way. Speed of reaction is a critical element of competitive strategy, and it is not tied to a time clock or corporate planning calendar. Rules of engagement are created in real time as leaders refocus and readjust their approaches to competition and redefine the environment. Competitive strategies will change.

No primer on strategy would be finished without some real examples of companies that succeeded and failed in the Red Zone of strategy change. These examples are designed to give life, color, and great complexity to the simple theories discussed thus far. The examples are designed as much to get the juices flowing as they are to make specific points about Red´Zone principles. Hopefully, the examples make the point that fooling around with an organization's competitive strategy, its way of approaching its marketplace, is serious business.

Toys R Us: A Failure in the Red Zone of Changing Competitive Strategy

Our story is focused around one company's attempts to harness the power of the Internet as it approached the all important holiday seasons of 1999 and 2000. We'll cover more of the impact of the Internet in the chapter on e-business implementations. In the case of toysrus.com, let's examine how this company went about changing its competitive strategy. We'll find some very important lessons for playing in the Red Zone.

As with most traditional retailers, opening an online channel allowed Toys R Us to extend its brand to a new market space, acquire new customers, and increase share-of-customer. The strategy was also supposed to protect market share from virtual upstarts like eToys, as well as category killer Wal-Mart. In April 1999, Toys R Us announced three key initiatives to support their e-commerce strategy, the goal of which was to be the leader in the online retail market for toys and children's products by fourth quarter 1999. (Some Web-savvy readers might observe that at this point, Toys R Us was already late to the e-party.) The key initiatives were:

1. The establishment of toysrus.com as a separate subsidiary, encompassing all Toys R Us businesses including Toys R Us, Babies R Us, and Kids R Us. The existing Web site would be completely rebuilt and launched in the second quarter 1999, offering many customer-focused enhancements over the old site.
2. A strategic partnership with Benchmark Capital, a leading Silicon Valley venture capital firm (VC), which would invest $10 million in toysrus.com. Best known for its investments in eBay, E-Loan, Ariba, and other Internet startups, the toysrus.com venture represented their initial foray into bringing clicks to bricks.
3. Acquisition of a 500,000 square foot, state-of-the-art, fully automated distribution center strategically located in Memphis, complete with an experienced fulfillment team, purchased from a direct catalog company.

Robert Nakasone, Toys R Us's CEO at the time, commented in an April 1999 company press release, "This is an exciting time for Toy R Us, and we're confident that these elements will help toysrus.com deliver exceptional value to our customer and shareholders." A noble promise at a challenging time. Duff & Phelps Credit Rating Co. had lowered its ratings of the company, citing an increasingly competitive environment that had produced a steady deterioration in market share and profitability. The aggressive new Internet strategy promised to provide the basis for longer-term improvement and restore investor confidence. In tandem with the new online strategy, Nakasone had also launched the *C-3 initiative,* a strategy to improve customer service, price/value perceptions, and supply chain improvements, in addition to improving store layout.

In August 1999, a mere four months after the toysrus.com press conference, Nakasone resigned abruptly. Chairman Michael Goldstein was named acting CEO, effective immediately. In an August 1999 AP Newswire story covering the leadership change, Goldstein said, "We've had a lot of stumbles, there's no question about it. But our business is good, and soon we will start to show some results." Headlines describing those recent stumbles could read: (1) Dot-Com CEO Resigns Shortly after Launching New Venture; (2) Dot-Com's VC Partners Pull Plug on Bankroll; and (3) Earnings Fall Short of Expectations. A November 1999 *Fortune* article, "Can These Marriages Be Saved?" detailed the stories behind the headlines.

Resignation. In July, toysrus.com's new CEO, Robert Moog, backed out of the job, saying that the relationship quickly got hung up on a variety of operations and control issues. Essentially, Moog's vision was a major strategy change for the company.

- Toysrus.com should carry a broader selection than the retail locations, not just a subset.
- Stores would have online kiosks so customers could order out-of-stock items.
- The cost of transferring goods would be carried on the books of Toys R Us, not on the dot-com (a frequent practice for bricks with clicks).
- When necessary, Moog would have the freedom to underprice the stores.
- In the event of a sudden shortage of hot items, he didn't want the parent company hoarding inventory.

In short, Moog says, in an August 1999 AP report, "I thought we should have all the benefits that Toys R Us could offer us and at the same time have the flexibility to do things independently." He wanted to operate more like an Internet pure play.

Moog said the definition of the "free hand" Nakasone offered him was different than his experience. While Nakasone didn't outright refuse Moog's demands, he didn't sign off on them either—sort of decision by nondecision, a dangerous practice in a speed-of-light world. Chris Vroom, an e-commerce analyst at Thomas Weisel Partners, commented, "They [Toys R Us] just couldn't let go; they were seized by this cannibalization inertia." Moog summed it up well, "Toys R Us misjudged how much of a free-spirited entrepreneur they wanted."

Irreconcilable differences. Also, shortly before Nakasone's departure, Benchmark Capital announced that it was pulling out of the struggling toysrus.com. Officially, the companies said they could not come to terms on the structure of the deal. In a not-so-indirect reference to the experience, Bill Gurley, a Benchmark partner and *Fortune* columnist, talked about PowerPoint inertia. "They say, 'Great, let me put together a PowerPoint presentation and get back to you.' So they go three managers deep, and all of a sudden you've got 15 PowerPoint presentations at an hour apiece about how the dot-com will interface with the company. That is the exact bureaucracy that keeps big companies from moving on the Internet alone. I tell them, 'This is why you're not doing this internally.'"

Earnings shortfall. Nakasone's resignation came eight days after the company reported disappointing second quarter earnings—an 11 percent drop in quarterly net income, including a $4 million charge for establishing toysrus.com.

Examining the reasons behind Nakasone's "resignation," analysts commented that the store remodeling had not gotten off the ground as quickly as it needed to. Sean McGowan, a toy analyst at Gerard Klauer & Mattison, said Nakasone's departure was probably most related to the company's failure to develop a competitive strategy for toysrus.com. He added, "If I'm a board member, maybe I grew increasingly concerned about when I was going to start to get some signs of progress."

All this happened right before the most important buying season of the year. Christmas wasn't going to be very merry for toysrus.com; media actually called it an online retailing bloodbath. The company's main e-tail competitor, eToys, had sales of $107 million compared to $39 million for toysrus. Beyond the orders, fulfillment was more of a nightmare. While the exact details are not known, we do know the result: in early December, the company e-mailed some of its customers saying it would not be able to fill their online orders by Christmas, and it offered them $100 gift certificates for use in its stores. Not very helpful, especially for customers without a nearby retail location. As a matter of fact, the Federal Trade Commission fined the company for failing to notify customers of the delayed shipments.

On December 31, 1999, the *San Francisco Business Times* ran a short epitaph on the deal, "Benchmark Capital," which pretty well summed up a dismal year. "The corporate divorce, coupled with internal management shake-ups at Toys R Us, cemented the company's reputation as an Internet also-ran, especially when faced with competition from aggressive e-tailers like Amazon.com and eToys."

RED ZONE MORAL TO THE STORY

Getting clear on a strategy is tough. Getting clear on how to execute it is much tougher. Getting all the top executives on the same page is critical. Strong leadership is needed to get key stakeholders on board and then to cut through organizational inertia and make the right things happen.

Telus: A Company that Succeeded in the Red Zone of Changing Competitive Strategy

In July 1998, *Telephony* magazine published an inspirational story of a telecommunications company that changed its competitive strategy to operate and prosper in a changing environment. Telus was formed as a holding company when the province of Alberta, Canada, privatized Alberta Government Telephone (AGT) in 1989. The Telus name was derived from a combination of *telecommunications* and *universality*, to convey the notion that the company that was both friendly and forward thinking.

In 1995, the company acquired Edmonton Telephone, a former competitor. Initially both companies continued to operate under their own names, marketing a variety of branded products and services under the AGT and Ed Tel names. As such, these subbranded products and services projected an old-fashioned, slow-moving, government-owned image and did not do well in the market. At this point, fewer than 10 percent of Alberta residents even recognized the Telus name. As its share of the long-distance market began to erode, Telus executives knew they needed a change in competitive strategy.

George Petty, the company's maverick CEO, recognized the competitive advantage of projecting a unified, customer-focused image. Known for his inscrutable manner and deal-making audacity, Petty, a former senior executive with AT&T global business services, was rumored to be working toward a merger with BC Tel, a move that could topple the Bell Canada-dominated alliance of 11 provincial phone companies to which Telus belongs. Petty had even courted Bell Canada's archrival AT&T when Telus attempted to buy a portion of AT&T Canada's long distance operation.

Under Petty's direction, Telus initiated a major evaluation of their brand identity structure, hiring a consulting team to help the company develop and implement a master brand strategy. The resulting approach called for a single name for most operating units and a goal to be seen as open, accessible, responsive, dynamic, trusted, and uniquely Albertan, yet world class. The Telus brand identity included dynamic visuals for all print materials, promotional programs, and signage on company facilities, vehicles, and uniforms. Communications were planned and executed with extraordinary attention to detail.

- A detailed plan established guidelines for communicating a unified message about the strengths, culture, style, and future direction to each key audience: end users, employees, agents/partners, potential employees, and the financial community.
- A teaser campaign helped generate awareness that *something* was about to happen. Several publicity coups helped to launch the brand. Across the province, Telus held ceremonies to "retire" existing brands with dignity and respect. Also, just before the public brand launch, a repairperson and truck, both displaying the new Telus logo, appeared prominently in an episode of the highly popular TV show, *The X-Files* (which was filmed in Canada at that time).
- Employee involvement was essential to produce maximum impact. A massive implementation effort, facilitated by employee volunteers, incorporated the new Telus identity virtually overnight on more than 16,000 pay phones and 2,000 vehicles.

Beyond the visual elements, the business operations also needed to portray a newly energized, customer-centered enterprise. To improve customer service and support the change initiative, the whole company was involved in a series of service-driven initiatives. Each initiative was timed to support the launch of the Telus master brand.

- Employees were trained to help customers in a more friendly and responsive way.
- A new 24-hour repair service was introduced.
- The pricing strategy became more competitive.
- A separate "new promise" campaign introduced Telus's new brand attributes.

Results from the change in strategy were dramatic. AGT had a top-of-mind awareness among 52 percent of Albertans. Within just 6 weeks of the Telus master brand strategy launch, Telus achieved a 60 percent top-of-mind awareness (surpassing management's 40 percent goal). Within this same 6-week period, ratings for the company's image attributes also outdistanced AGT's. Longer-term results were equally favorable. Telus has retained a 70 percent market share in long distance, while other provincial operators lost 8 to 10 percent in market share. With these success rates, changing competitive strategies almost sounds like fun—a fun and creative marketing campaign, well executed, supporting and supported by internal operational improvements. That fun was underscored with lots of hard work behind the scenes and fueled by an unwavering commitment to win from a remarkable, visionary CEO.

THE RED ZONE MORAL TO THE STORY:

Strong executive leadership to develop a good design is the right place to start.

Involving employees and getting the needed outside expertise into play is

critical. Top it off with an implementation that has passion and panache!

PRINCIPLES

Now for the Red Zone principles that apply to changing competitive strategy. The goal in this chapter is not to duplicate the principles of

Chapter 4; instead we want to show variations and distinctions of those principles for the Red Zone maneuver of changing competitive strategy.

Red Zone Principle One: Declare the Company in a Red Zone

When changing the company's competitive strategy, special commitment is needed. That needed level of commitment really is Olympic-level motivation and creativity to achieve the gain coupled with do-or-die resolve to avoid the loss. Even though changing the competitive strategy is the most difficult Red Zone maneuver, convincing the organization that special commitment is needed may, in fact, be easier for this maneuver than others because strategy is directly connected to customers and competitors.

Our experience suggests that the most effective way to get the organization into the spirit and importance of this Red Zone maneuver is to compare clearly and boldly the organization's intention and performance to that of major competitors. In this Red Zone, management should be able to show direct competitive impact, such as decreasing market share, decreasing customer orders and interest in products and services, customers changing from the Red Zone company to the competitor, and so on. Following are successful tactics to communicate the Red Zone condition to employees in the organization:

- Setting up a scorecard that shows the company's market share and/ or financial performance compared to the leading competitor.
- Buying the competitor's product and making it available for the organization's employees to use, measure, compare, evaluate— and, therefore, worry about.
- Conducting and publishing customer satisfaction surveys that directly compare the company's products with those of competitors.
- Cleverly using graphics to show the competitive challenge. Bell Helicopter distributed 3×5 cards with the Bell logo sprinkled with two or three small red laser spots. The CEO was able to say convincingly that "competitors had Bell in their laser sights."

Management should not assume that everyone understands the company is in a Red Zone; the Red Zone message must be stated clearly and explicitly to all. Have the leadership team all acknowledge publicly and privately that the company is in the Red Zone and, ideally, give a clear signal to their troops. Consider using a code word to indicate Red Zone management, an obvious one such as "Red Zone," so you can communicate and mobilize the organization more quickly. Tell the organization *why* you are in a Red Zone, and the trigger that put the company there. Organizational leaders are sometimes reluctant to admit they are in a Red Zone, especially if it is viewed as failure, but it should be viewed as a strong leadership move to "take the hill."

Red Zone Principle Two: Put the Best Players in the Game

Changing competitive strategy is really top management's game. In fact, it is the CEO's game. Organizations just don't change strategy without the CEO being in the thick of things. Changing strategy will not be a consensus move without his leadership. This maneuver calls for bold leadership. The CEO must see the new strategy in his sleep and feel it in his bones as well as talk it and walk it around the company.

Changing strategy is the place for integrity, grit, and resolve, and for tough leaders who will take the organization where it would not have gone. The CEO must know the team, including everyone's strengths and weaknesses, and play to the strengths. This is not a time for training and development.

Changing competitive strategy begins with the design of the new strategy and ends with that new strategy's execution throughout the organization. This execution step must be taken in an organized and comprehensive way. Changing strategy takes quick, bold movement, not incrementalism, so leaders with authority are needed to get things done.

Every top executive should have a Red Zone role. That is, they should each have an important and visible piece of the Red Zone action in addition to their day job, or their usual duties in day-to-day operations.

Red Zone Duties of the Chief Executive Officer (CEO):

- *Chief customer advocate.* The CEO must stay tuned to the marketplace during the strategy change maneuver, ensuring that the strategy change is hooked to adding value in the marketplace.

- *Chief strategy advocate to the board and to investors.* The CEO should keep the Board of Directors informed, involved, and supportive. Keep the investor community informed—they can be your ally or your downfall; manage that relationship proactively.
- *Chief communications officer to the firm.* Only the CEO can be credible in explaining, pushing, and insisting on the strategy change, making the case for both the change and its specifics.
- *Master designer.* The CEO must use a leadership style that includes top-down direction while hearing and incorporating bottom-up feedback, ensuring during the design phase that the specifics of the new strategy meet marketplace objectives.
- *Master program manager.* The CEO insists that building is to spec and is the major provider of resources and internal obstacle remover. In addition, the CEO must keep the ultimate time clock on the maneuver, insisting during the execution phase that mechanical changes get made on time.

Red Zone Duties of the Chief Operating Officer (COO):

- *Intimately involved in the design of the strategy.*
- *Chief executor of the new strategy.* The COO and direct reports will be the folks on the spot for implementing the strategy change.
- *Day-to-day owner of the customer scorecard.* The COO owns those parts of the organization that must be altered to produce the desired customer scorecard.
- *Day-to-day change leader.* Works with the CEO and the program manager to understand what changes in work processes and plant/equipment and tools will be necessary.
- *Leader in day-to-day executive teamwork.* Provides leadership to the executive team as it focuses on internal issues. (The CEO works external as well as internal issues.)

Red Zone Duties of the Chief Sales Officer (CSO):

- *Customer advocate.* The CSO is responsible for key customer interaction and market impact, focusing on customer relationships during the shift to a new strategy. The CSO also keeps the organization informed, communicating the strategy shift's potential impact on customers.

- *Marketplace information resources.* The CSO keeps the CEO and the executive team in sync with the marketplace. Communicating trends and changes during and after the strategy shift.
- *Chief marketing officer.* The CSO rationalizes product and market strategies to support the overall change in competitive strategy.
- *Chief communicator to customers.* The CSO explains how the strategy change will produce value. The company's advertising and public relations should be aligned to the new strategy, fit with the customers' needs, and signal a strategy change to the marketplace.
- *Chief pricing officer.* Works directly with the CEO, COO, and CFO to pick price points that complement the changed strategy.

Red Zone Duties of the Chief Financial Officer (CFO):

- *Leader in metrics.* The CFO measures the results of strategy change, making adjustments to the company's balanced scorecard.
- *Assistant to the CEO.* Helps apply needed resources to change the strategy.
- *Challenger of assumptions.* In discussions about investing in the strategy, plays devil's advocate.
- *Compensation and incentive designer.* The CFO works with the CEO and the human resources officer to ensure that monetary incentives are in place to motivate key organization members to make the strategy change.

Red Zone Duties of the Chief Information Officer (CIO):

- *Chief customer information officer.* The CIO works with the CEO and the CSO to identify the information the firm must manage to ensure success.
- *Chief information technology strategist.* The CIO ensures that the company's technology strategy accommodates the change in competitive strategy.
- *Leader in metrics.* The CIO works directly with the CEO and CFO to put in place the metrics and scorecards for measuring strategy results. Works with top management to ensure that IT resources support scorecard changes and provide real-time information for progress reporting.
- *Information technology resource provider.* The CIO works directly with program management and the COO to ensure that IT

resources/systems support both work and management process changes.

Red Zone Duties of the Chief Human Resources Officer (CHRO):

- *Staffing leader.* The CHRO helps to identify and recruit the personnel needed to run the business while the company's best players work on Red Zone.
- *Training and development leader.* The CHRO leads the charge in identifying new skill sets to be recruited and hired and/or trained as changes in competitive strategy call for them.
- *Chief people advocate.* The CHRO monitors stress and strain on the organization and recommends support for people as needed.
- *Performance management leader.* The CHRO leads the employee performance management systems to focus on the new strategy. Also works directly with CFO to design alignment of changes in incentive compensation criteria.
- *Line management support provider.* The CHRO provides trained human resources generalists to assist line management in making important changes during strategy change execution.
- *Executive team development leader.* The CHRO plays a key role in ensuring that the executive team is working well together.

Not only is changing competitive strategy the place for strong individual leaders with authority, it is the place for top-notch executive teamwork. The executive team must be absolutely together on this one. Top management may require several team building sessions until they are all in sync on the need for changing the strategy, the direction of the new strategy, and the execution plan. The team must work seamlessly without even needing lengthy communications. Because strategy change is likely to impact most of the organization in thinking or doing things differently, the top management message must have no chinks in its armor.

This Red Zone maneuver is the place for the very best technical expertise available anywhere. In no other Red Zone does the organization need as much business expertise in the form of expert knowledge of the industry, of customers and what they want, and of competitors and where they are going. While most companies have industry expertise and market knowledge, this is not the time to trust that internal knowledge exclusively. The source of expertise is not critical; management just must have the courage to go get it—from consultants, contractors, study institutes, panels of customers, and/or competitor refugees.

Red Zone Principle Three: Focus on the Customer

While every Red Zone maneuver should explicitly consider the customer as the ultimate reference, the strategy change maneuver lives or dies by what happens to the customer. The goal of a strategy change is to show the customer a different face, with new or altered products or services and new attributes or performance of those products/services. Constant use of the customer scorecard, like the one shown in Chapter 4, is required for strategy work. The understanding and measurement of progress on the customer scorecard is at the heart of the entire strategy exercise. Use the scorecard to think through the impact that you want to have on the marketplace, and use actual measures to know where you want to come out of this strategy change maneuver with respect to your customers and competitors.

The scorecard can be used to identify alternative ways of winning with the customers and defeating competitors. For example, a company using the scorecard might conceive of different combinations of values and attributes in terms of Michael Porter's tools covered in this chapter's primer.

- Further differentiation of the company's products and services
- The move to a low price/high value approach to the customer
- The move to a niche strategy

Identification and then evaluation of these various alternatives become the heart of what we described earlier as the Red Zone design engine, the recycling of scorecard, goals, and blueprint until the company has a design direction that will work in the marketplace.

The customer scorecard exercise seems to work best if real live customers are involved. How is that for novel and creative thinking in the Red Zone? We have had clients successfully use panels of customers to help lay out the scorecard as a part of designing the strategy change. Those panels have then been used to keep track of the progress of the strategy implementation in terms of customer impacts.

A variety of actions can be taken to ensure the strategy change is going right for desired customer impact.

- Categorize your customers based on their response to change—progressive early adopters, middle-of-the-roaders, and late bloomers. Test your proposed strategy moves with the progressive early adopters rather than the late bloomers for a true read.
- Get early adopter customers to help you differentiate your products/services in the marketplace based on benefits and successes they realize using your product/service.
- Help your early adopter customers translate the strategy shift into a *win* for them. By going through that translation exercise, you may identify hidden benefits as well as traps.
- Validate proposed changes of products and/or services with other customers.
- Project competitors's position down the road; don't use their current position.
- Quickly and visibly respond to customer feedback. Let customers know you hear them and appreciate their input.

Red Zone Principle Four:
Set Clear Red Zone Goals

The primary reason for changing competitive strategy is to increase the company's appeal to customers at the expense of competitors. Either we want to take market share from competitors, or we want to create products and services that will make market—that is, cause buyers to enter our marketplace. Market share and margin are the key here.

After fully understanding the customer scorecard, top management's job is to set goals for the strategy change that the organization can understand and follow. The best goals for this kind of Red Zone maneuver are as follows:

- Market share (units and dollars)
- Competitive ratings (i.e., relative moves in rankings of products and services compared to competitors)
- Profitability (by unit and totals for market segments)

Goals should be derived from estimates of marketplace reaction to the changes the company proposes on the customer scorecard. That is, we are doing the maneuver to impact the market by changing our product and service attributes so that they will be more valuable to customers. That increased value should translate into market share and profitability. If the translation is no increased market share or profitability, then the scorecard thinking must be redone until we are able to anticipate improvement in share and profitability.

The review of market data is critical in this step. While speed is of the essence in the Red Zone, obtaining a high-quality reaction from the marketplace about the proposed scorecard changes before making a call on goals is usually worth the time it takes. Many Red Zone goals are pure guesses. We want to go for market-educated guesses.

What about other goals areas? What about the balanced scorecard idea of serving up several goals to ensure that the organization keeps a balanced focus? It is a good idea to have balanced measures during normal times, but a Red Zone change of competitive strategy demands goals biased toward the ultimate desired impact—market share.

To corroborate these set goals, top management can ask employees whether or not the set goals communicate the fact that the company is in a war, a business battle with the bad guys for the hearts of customers. If the battle is not clear, it will be difficult to get the organization mobilized for success in the Red Zone.

Red Zone Principle Five: Blueprint for Success

The goal of the blueprint step in Red Zone strategy change is to build a picture of the organization serving up its products and services to customers in a new way, a way that will provide better overall value to the customer. To say it another way, the blueprint is how the organization will describe its new business design or model to its employees in a way that they can understand, evaluate, and then use as an end target during Red Zone execution.

The heart of the blueprint should be a compelling picture of how customers will use the products and services that will follow the revised customers scorecard. The heart of any strategy change should focus on customers relating differently and better to the organization's product and service offerings. In the blueprint step, management must picture that way of working with the customers so that it seems feasible and logical.

In addition to describing how the organization will work with customers, Red Zone managers must picture the company's manufacturing and customer service processes as they will need to operate to deliver the products and services on the scorecard. The final piece of the blueprint for Red Zone strategy change should be a description of how employees will need to work differently around changed processes.

Completion of the blueprint is the final step in the Red Zone design engine that links the customer scorecard and Red Zone goals with how the organization will need to look and operate after implementation. In a way, the blueprint step is one more test of the organization's ability to change its way of operating to achieve the desired strategy change. We have had clients at this step literally say, "We just can't ever see our organization operating the way it will need to operate for that strategy change." Such a statement should immediately be followed by another cycle of the Red Zone design engine, starting with a reexamination of other scorecard options that might be both winners with the customer and deemed possible by the organization.

Don't Move! Don't go to Red Zone execution principles until a clear picture of the improved business design is in place, including:

- A clear understanding of how the Red Zone strategy change will positively impact customers and negatively impact competitors.
- Clear goals for the maneuver in market share, market dollars, margin, and competitive ranking.
- A completed blueprint for the organization after the maneuver, as it achieves its goals to satisfy customers.

RED ZONE PRINCIPLES FOR EXECUTION OF A NEW STRATEGY

The Red Zone execution principles for strategy change are especially critical, because the Red Zone goals and blueprint are likely to represent a comprehensive and challenging change to the organization. A lot of leadership horsepower will be needed in this execution phase.

Red Zone Principle Six: Focus on Mechanics

The goal of this step is to identify those mechanical parts of the organization that must be altered for the blueprint to come to life. Once again, those mechanicals are:

- Work processes
- The plant, equipment, and tools needed to support those work processes
- The performance systems that help focus employee behavior on those processes and tools

For a change in competitive strategy, identifying and altering the mechanicals can be a major and difficult operation. The difficulty of the needed alterations will be dependent to a large degree on the amount of desired strategy change. For minor changes in strategy, the required alterations might be minimal, but for a major strategy change, the needed alterations will likely be significant.

- *Work processes.* The detailed steps the organization takes to do what it is designed to do. For a strategy change, the critical processes to be altered are as follows:
  - The manufacturing, production, and operational processes that will produce the company's products and deliver its services.
  - The marketing processes that will position the firm in the marketplace, and the sales processes that will be used to obtain orders from specific customers.
  - The research and development (R&D) processes that support the technologies behind the work processes mentioned above.
- *Plant/equipment/tools.* Those tangible items that are used by the firm's employees to support its work processes. A strategy change requires alteration of the company's plant, equipment, and tools to support changes in work processes. While we can't say which tools will need to be altered, we can say that such alterations will be required and are likely to be extensive.
- *Performance systems.* The organization's collection of roles, goals, training programs, and incentive structures. These systems will need to change to reflect the new strategy. The changes should tie back directly to the process alteration identified above.

Red Zone Principle Seven: Use Program and Project Management to Build to Print

The job of program management should focus on getting the new strategy implemented by tackling the needed changes in the mechanical parts of the organization. Program management for strategy change will likely need to be formal and disciplined to ensure that the many changes required for strategy change are brought under management. Program management will need to identify and form multiple projects to achieve concrete results per the blueprint. Our experience suggests that a formal program management structure, run by an experienced manager reporting directly to the CEO, will make strategy change much easier to control.

The projects that make up the strategy change program are best organized around changes in work processes, plant/equipment and tools, and then performance systems. My experience strongly suggests that each of these projects or sets of projects should be crossfunctional in membership and orientation to have the broad view needed for comprehensive strategy change. Placing change projects inside functional organizations (such as marketing, sales, or manufacturing) should be avoided at all costs because of the bias normally found in such organizations. Functional organizations will find either that they are already doing a version of what the blueprint requires or that the blueprint cannot be executed at all at their level.

Consider formal risk management including contingency plans with predetermined trigger points. Program management of strategy change should look just like an engineering/construction project or a big systems project. It should have a work plan including activities in a predetermined sequence, deliverables, responsibilities, and target dates. Other impacts, as well as those of the specific strategy change, should be managed. Plan for interim milestones to celebrate progress along the way to end results.

Red Zone Principle Eight: Focus on Speed

Because the goal of a strategy change is to have a positive impact on the marketplace, speed is critical. The idea is to come to market with a new strategy that gives the company an advantage, even if it is short term. The CEO, as the timekeeper during the Red Zone, must drive the strategy change as fast as possible to gain the market advantage, while not going so fast that the organization cannot make the needed internal changes effectively and efficiently. A strategy change's time frame can range from a few months in a fast-cycling industry that makes PCs, to two years or more for a basic industry like aerospace or energy. The best way to set a timetable seems to be to factor in the times it has taken other similar firms to make such changes and the CEO's estimate of the organization's change capacity.

Red Zone Principle Nine: Meet Special Needs of Workers

Workers who are a part of a Red Zone strategy change often have special needs if they are sprinting a marathon. Implementing a strategy takes intensive efforts for a long time, and workers wear out. Important considerations for workers during this Red Zone include:

- Making sure that workers on the Red Zone project team have someone covering for them in their regular jobs.
- Ensuring that project personnel have job protection (i.e., their jobs will not go away as a result of the shift in strategy).
- Ensuring that interim, public recognition is given for progress through the Red Zone, both in the form of individual recognition and team celebrations for hitting important milestones.
- Ensuring that recognition includes all those contributing to the Red Zone strategy success, not just the select few.
- Making recognition visible and keeping it tied to progress metrics.

Last, but not least, highly visible leadership is needed from the CEO and other executives to show their continuing commitment and excitement about the strategy change. Leaders who lose interest, lose the strategy game.

Red Zone Principle Ten:
Reward for Red Zone Performance

The incentives that we have seen work best have been based on the strategy change goals and include:

- Market share (units and dollars)
- Competitive ratings (i.e., relative moves in rankings of products and services compared to competitors)
- Profitability (by unit and totals for market segments)

Explicit recognition must be given to the strategy change goals along with the accomplishment of normal year-to-year goals. Incentive compensation amounts should be commensurate with the success of the strategy change maneuver and should be over and above normal incentive compensation. Ending this section on a negative note, I have not been a part of a strategy change that did not have a few managers and employees who, for whatever reason, could or would not support the change. Those unsupportive workers should lose all incentives and risk demotion or even termination.

APPLYING THE GAMEPLAN

There is a lot to know about the Red Zone maneuver for changing competitive strategy. But this gameplan chapter will be your jumpstart as you get ready for this most difficult maneuver.

CHAPTER 6

Red Zone Gameplan for Mergers and Acquisitions

Merging two companies or making an acquisition is a thorny problem because of the sheer complexity of mechanical issues in making all the tangible pieces fit together and because of the need to come out of the merger with a single workable culture or way of doing business. This chapter will begin with a high-level primer on the subject of mergers and acquisitions and will end with a discussion of the Red Zone principles as they apply to this difficult situation.

THE PRIMER ON MERGERS AND ACQUISITIONS

A Definition of Merger/Acquisition

Writing (and reading) financial news does not often become a humorous exercise. However, the topic of mergers and acquisitions seems to inspire a certain creativity among journalists covering the topic. Some pertinent headlines from *The Economist:*

- *"Stop Me before I Merge Again."* Discusses the disastrous results that led to a little-protested Congressional moratorium on rail company mergers in the United States.
- *"Road Rage."* Speculates on merger mixes and matches among the world's leading auto makers.

- *"Oil Mergers: Rigged."* Describes recent coups of British Petroleum's CEO in taking over Amoco and (impending at the time) ARCO.

Global merger and acquisition activity has reached unprecedented heights across almost every industry. Sounds like hog heaven for investment bankers, attorneys, and CPAs, but what about shareholders and other corporate stakeholders? To continue quoting *The Economist,* a July 2000 article, "How Mergers Go Wrong," noted that many of these mergers are "like second marriages, a triumph of hope over experience" and have "even higher failure rates than the liaisons of Hollywood stars."

KPMG research has found that as many as 80 percent of the deals struck over the past 10 years never created the value that management or shareholders expected. A McKinsey & Co. study found that nearly 80 percent of all mergers failed to recover the costs incurred in the deal. Nevertheless, CEOs and boards seem as undaunted by statistics as those sweethearts on the silver screen. According to Thomson Financial Securities Data, the value of corporate mergers and acquisitions worldwide rose to a record $3.5 trillion in 2000, up from $3.3 trillion in 1999.

But before we launch into our Red Zone discussion, let's get a working definition in play. *Merger* is the generic term for a full and final coming together of two previously separate corporations or commercial interests. An *acquisition* is an addition to an established entity or group. To the participants, especially in situations where one entity is considerably larger than the other, many mergers feel like acquisitions. Whether the union is a joining of equals or of different sized organizations, the legal partnership preserves only one corporation. We use the accepted term *M&A* to refer to the Red Zone condition under discussion in this chapter.

The Urges behind the Merges

It's important to understand that M&A is not an end in itself but a means, a strategy, to achieve corporate goals. Let's take a brief look at some of the reasons corporate leaders get the urge to merge.

- Some M&As are defensive, initiated in part because the companies involved are under threat, perhaps from contracting markets, falling commodity prices, excess capacity, rapid technological change, or soaring R&D costs. McDonnell Douglas merged with Boeing in part because its biggest customer, the Pentagon, was cutting spending in half.

- Some boards operate under the maxim that the best defense is a good offense, setting out with determination to buy first rather than be bought. Look at the dizzying dance among car makers in the wake of the once admired DaimlerChrysler merger: would VW buy BMW, would VW buy Rover, would GM buy a piece of BMW, would GM buy Daewoo, or would DaimlerChrysler pair up with Peugeot Citroen?

- CEOs face constant pressure to do deals that drive growth and improve their company's competitive position. Waiting for organic growth, especially in a mature market, is a slow and nonenergizing process. M&A activity, on the other hand, is more exhilarating and gains CEOs the attention of bankers, brokers, and financial media. When the former Chemical Bank and Manufacturers Hanover merged with Chase Manhattan, the result was a remarkable megamultinational institution with leading product lines in retail banking, wholesale lending, underwriting and loan syndications, trading, and advisory and venture capital services.

Growth through M&As has moved from a trend to common practice in America's fast-growth firms. A 1997 study by then Coopers & Lybrand found that acquisitions have become a cornerstone of the expansion plans in the fastest growing companies. Typical firms with a growth-through-acquisition strategy have already acquired an average of five smaller businesses over their first 10 to 12 years of corporate life. The acquiring firms grew significantly faster than their peers that relied exclusively on internally generated growth.

The Usual Suspects: Motive, Means, and Opportunity

Given the last decade's robust economic conditions in the United States, corporations have had both the means (financial liquidity) and the opportunity (excess capacity) to pursue new targets—to motivate CEOs and directors to continue making M&As a central business strategy.

The market's retrenchment in 2000 and complex regulatory hurdles in many merger-happy industries (e.g., oil, telecommunications) may signal fewer headline-grabbing megamergers on the $182 billion AOL/Time Warner scale; nevertheless, M&As are business as usual here and abroad.

Enough smaller scale deals, in the $16 billion and less category, took place to set yet another record for 2000 M&A activity in the United States. According to Thomson Financial Securities data cited in a March 2001 article, "A Slower Beat for the Mating Dance," in *Institutional Investor*, U.S. corporations engaged in $1.8 trillion of M&As in 2000, significantly ahead of the $1.56 trillion of M&A deals in 1999 as well as the record $1.61 trillion in 1998.

Some Approaches to M&As Work Better than Others

Statistics vary depending on the source, but one does not have to be a statistician to conclude from the available evidence that the majority of M&As fail to meet objectives on one or more levels.

- In a March 1999 article, "Best Practices in Acquisitions," for *The New Straits Times,* Andersen Consulting cites a 1999 survey that nearly 50 percent of U.S. companies involved in M&As indicate that they did not gain access to new markets, grow market share, or add products three years after the close of the transaction. In addition, more than half of these same companies underperform relative to their peers.
- In a January 1998 article, "Why a Large Number of Mergers Fail," in *The New Straits Times,* a PricewaterhouseCoopers executive director related that up to 77 percent of recent merger deals did not recover costs; 50 percent of these destroyed shareholder value, while 50 percent recorded the same or lower productivity or profits.
- J.P. Morgan examined 116 major acquisitions (each involving more than $1 billion) made over the last 15 years and found no added value three years after the deals were made. The research, highlighted in a January 1999 article, "Signs of Caution Lie Ahead for Merging Companies," in *The Kansas City Star,* suggests that just 56 percent of mergers create value for the acquirers.

In their 1997 report, "Speed Makes a Difference: A Survey of Mergers & Acquisitions," then Coopers & Lybrand researchers concluded that a rapid transition can lessen the adverse effects on key measures of business performance, including profits, employee morale, and productivity. "The distinguishing characteristic of fast-transition companies is that they ruthlessly prioritize and focus on the 20 percent of postdeal actions that drive 80 percent of the value with the highest probability of success," comments Mark Feldman, partner and managing director for Coopers's M&A consulting. "Above all, that means doing what's needed to boost revenue."

Companies that operate in fast-transition mode, adds Feldman, facilitate the merger or acquisition at a pace faster than that at which the firm normally operates. The reverse holds true for slow-transition companies. Feldman remarks, "Unfortunately, companies that transition slowly have their priorities confused subsequent to the deal. They're too focused on cost cutting. The result is these companies lose market share to competitors. Productivity and employee morale decline, while labor costs, the duplication of work, and employee turnover go up." One memorable example: Compaq's efforts to digest Digital Equipment Corporation (DEC). While Compaq and DEC were involved in postmerger turmoil, Dell Computer geared up a slick ad campaign to take market advantage. After the merger, Compaq's 1998 second quarter domestic growth rate was 11 percent, while Dell's was 72 percent.

Measuring Success for M&As

Expressed as an equation, the general idea behind a merger is that $1 + 1 = 3$ or more. As such, stakeholders inside and outside organizations involved in such transactions should be able to see clear readings on their M&A score, and grasp at a basic level why the deal makes sense. In a 1999 study of worldwide M&A activity, KPMG researchers found that M&As generally were undertaken to improve the company's visibility in its markets: 41 percent of respondents cited increasing or protecting market share as the purpose behind their M&A activity; 28 percent wanted to obtain new or increased presence in other geographic markets; and 11 percent were after economies of scale.

Yet when it came to scoring, results were not always so clear. While the companies surveyed tended to view their M&A transaction as successful, over half did not have a formal posttransaction review policy.

Some companies may not have adequate measures to use in budgeting restructuring costs and assessing whether those budgets were met. Some companies may lack objective benchmarks where more precise success measures can be used, or do not know what measures to use.

Overall, respondents thought that their strategies for different facets of the transaction (such as HR, IT, or culture) were not well planned at the outset or planned too late. They recognized they were weak during the postmerger stage but were unclear how to go about improving their performance.

Why M&As Are a Red Zone Condition

What happens between and inside each company involved in a merger is clearly not business as usual. Leaders must continue running their current operations to the satisfaction of multiple stakeholders while designing, under prescribed parameters and tight scrutiny, different and better ways to operate at some future point to the satisfaction of even more stakeholders of a yet-to-be completed organization. Whew!

The value and consequences of M&As mean different things to different people. Each corporate constituency—directors, shareholders, regulators, analysts, lenders, management, employees, unions, alliance partners, suppliers, and customers—defines such value in different and often conflicting ways. It's the job of the CEO and executive team to identify and examine the opportunities that best fit the company's goals and to reconcile these competing positions. This means lots of customized communication about the strategy to each group, under prescribed disclosure conditions, and then the crucial, step-by-step engineering of a vast variety of transactions to meet the needs, enact the strategy, accomplish the mission, and achieve the desired results.

With billions of dollars at stake in a single deal and an unforgiving marketplace all too ready to pounce on the weak and punish the failed, there are few opportunities for do-overs. Company leaders have one chance to get it right.

Why M&As Fail

While many reasons contribute to mergers achieving less than desired results, a February 1998 article, "Right Measures to Reap Benefits of Successful Mergers, Acquisitions," in *The New Straits Times* cites three important reasons: "unclear case for union, inexperience, and integration issues."

Unclear case for the union. Reengineering guru and author James Champy wrote in a November 1997 article, "What Ned Johnson Can Teach Sandy Weill," for *Forbes*, "Synergy, an investment banker told me, is the excuse given for a merger than can't otherwise be justified." Strategic due diligence before and throughout the preunion period simply has no substitute. Beneath the surface, not every deal looks as good as it did at the outset. CEOs who walk away from flawed deals should be hailed as heroes. When a deal keeps going south, it's better just to say "no" rather than push ahead, only to end up facing years of factional scheming, damaged reputations, alienated customers, and declining share value.

Inexperience. While a lot of current M&A activity is happening, a large number of rookie stakeholders are still involved in negotiations and postmerger integration. These stakeholders have never been involved in an M&A and may not go through another in their careers. Common practice is to hire accountants and attorneys with M&A expertise on the front end of the deal, and hiring end-to-end merger management experts to support leaders during the transaction and throughout integration is becoming increasingly prevalent. Just like some leaders find it hard to say "no," however, others find it hard to say "help!"

Integration issues. By their very nature, M&As represent no small degree of risk to at least two companies. Typically, the stabilization and integration phases of the M&A life cycle takes between 15 to 30 months before the targeted benefits are delivered. Proceed too fast and risk damage to employees and customers, business processes, and technology performance. Proceed too slowly and the next two or three big company initiatives could easily distract key management attention and derail the whole transition process. Leaders's jobs don't end when the ink dries but rather when the company is well on the way to achieving the results it projected at the outset of the deal.

No primer on M&A would be finished without some real-life examples of companies that succeeded and failed in the Red Zone. These brief examples were selected to show some of the adventure and complexity of the real world of M&A.

Getting It Wrong:
Boeing and McDonnell Douglas

After a courtship that began in 1994, Boeing, the world's largest jet maker at the time, acquired longtime rival McDonnell Douglas—and its outspoken leader—in the Summer of 1997. Boeing CEO Philip Condit would remain CEO, with McDonnell retaining Harry Stonecipher as president and COO of the new Boeing. At the time of the announcement, the move was hailed as a strategic and financial coup. McDonnell's military business would boost Boeing's revenue from defense-related projects to 40 percent of the new entity's combined total revenue and help smooth the financial impact of cyclical demand for commercial jetliners. Investors looked for quick improvement in profitability with the elimination of duplicate facilities and jobs. The Pentagon expected to be a primary beneficiary of cost savings gained by combining forces and trimming down.

Over a year after the acquisition was first announced, Boeing was still plagued by a series of setbacks. The process of merging the cultures of intense rivals with a workforce of some 235,000 employees was difficult by itself. Added to that challenge, McDonnell's commercial product line experienced larger losses and write-offs than projected. Its defense and space operations posted slimmer profit margins as the Asian economy stumbled and countries cancelled or postponed contracts for fighter jets. Boeing took a larger than expected $1.4 billion pretax charge to phase out a pair of slow-selling McDonnell jetliner models, closing at a loss of $498 million for the fourth quarter of 1997. This effectively meant that Boeing was really paying more than $15.5 billion for 85 percent of McDonnell's revenues.

Then the unthinkable, or surely the unmentionable, happened. According to an April 1998 article, "The Titanic Effect," in *Interavia Business & Technology,* at a March 1998 address to the Seattle Rotary Club, Stonecipher told business leaders that Boeing's financial results were dismal. He said that he was less threatened by Airbus Industrie (the company's chief European rival) or Lockheed Martin than by Boeing's own "failure to execute inside." He added that Boeing was "arrogant" and had yet to earn its self-proclaimed global status. A follow-up article, "Stonecipher's Boeing Shakeup," in the September 1998 issue of *Interavia Business & Technology* noted that "Stonecipher's comments had less impact than, say, Kruschev's denunciation of Stalin, but not by much." The comments came a week after Boeing had frozen management salaries and bonuses for 1998 and a day before the report in the *Seattle Times* about a meeting with leaders of northern European airlines in which they expressed increasing frustration about delivery delays and Boeing's unwillingness to share bad news. Boeing simply did not air its dirty linen in public nor, evidently, with customers.

Meanwhile, Boeing was struggling to recover from the effects of severe bottlenecks, parts shortages, and inexperienced workers. Company officials said it would take $2.6 billion in charges and unforeseen expenses to bring its factories in sync with the current order boom for its commercial aircraft. They continued to postpone significant reductions in personnel and gave no information about any plans to close or refurbish McDonnell's outdated commercial jet facilities, either of which could have eased the bleeding.

As the Dow Industrials soared, Boeing wrote off $4 billion and for fiscal year 1998 reported its first annual loss in 50 years. The stock tumbled. Boeing leaders were blamed for their failure to acknowledge the extent of the problems and for delays in designing and implementing a comprehensive plan to manage them. Critics said that the focus on correcting production snafus was diverting the attention of top executives from pressing issues involving the McDonnell acquisition, as well as their 1996 acquisition of Rockwell International's aerospace assets.

Here was a group of dedicated, talented people who had designed some of the most sophisticated products in the defense and aerospace industries, with a century's worth of combined program and project management experience, and they still couldn't get an effective plan going. What had looked like a showcase corporate marriage had some pretty dismal looking, and feeling, partners.

Outside pressures increased. The Pentagon was threatening to withhold billions of dollars earmarked for McDonnell's latest Super Hornet models unless performance improved. Inside the company, morale among former McDonnell employees continued to sag as they waited for information on plant closures and layoffs. Many McDonnell employees were still describing themselves as *McDonnell* defense workers or *Douglas* workers. Industry analysts observed that the Boeing-McDonnell

Douglas merger actually involved three separate cultures: Boeing and McDonnell employees—and Douglas employees who, they believe, were never fully integrated with McDonnell.

Decision making was lengthy and laborious, even over minor decisions. It took more than a year for the company to decide on a standardized in-house mail envelope. Getting to that decision involved convening a mail council from 20 geographic areas to evaluate the 13 different kinds of envelopes used between the companies.

The integration was in trouble at the top of the organization as well. High-ranking executives made little effort to get to know one another. At a meeting of the 200 top executives a year after the acquisition announcement, Stonecipher asked, "How many of you know 50 percent of the people in attendance?" A small number of hands went up. At 60 percent, only a few hands were raised. At 70 percent, the number was almost zero. Little wonder that actions and results at the line level of the company were so hard to come by.

Here's an interesting piece of luck to bring a happier ending to this tale. Boeing's Phantom Works, an in-house think tank that was a serendipitous creation during these tumultuous times, ended up being a key force in speeding the integration process by developing new products and refocusing the company on its diverse customers.

THE RED ZONE MORAL TO THE STORY:

Responsibility for the setbacks in this M&A started at the top of both organizations. The difficulty in senior executive integration was mirrored at the line level. When operating in a Red Zone, leadership must be united and switched over to a do-or-die level of commitment, or risk certain loss—in time, profit, market share, market value, and credibility.

Getting It Right: Time Warner and Turner Broadcasting

Time Warner CEO Gerald Levin had a vision, shared by his media peers, of the modern media conglomerate. In the coming deregulated era, production (content) linked with distribution would allow one company to seamlessly create and deliver new information and entertainment products for the digital age through multiple channels. Time Warner's acquisition of Turner Broadcasting was based on this clear, compelling vision, executed in a relatively straightforward fashion as megamergers go, and most likely saved Levin's job.

Time Warner itself had been created by a merger of Time, Inc. and Warner Communications in one of the biggest deals of the 1980s. By the mid–1990s, Levin's situation was not enviable. At the time, Time Warner was plagued by debt, years of underperforming stock prices, and involvement in poorly conceived deals that tied up its best assets as well as management energy. Meanwhile, rivals were doing the kind of deals that got them closer to the big seamless vision: Disney had bought Capital Cities/ABC, and Viacom had bought Paramount and launched UPN. Levin asked shareholders and the board to hang on while he got things straightened out.

The situation, for both Time Warner and Levin, didn't get better anytime soon. One of the deals, a strategic partnership with U.S. West (among others) and TW's Entertainment Division, landed Levin in court over potential competition between the partnership and Levin's new deal to merge Turner Broadcasting into the parent company—a violation of the partnership agreement.

Dealing with the mercurial Ted Turner in the merger process wasn't punishment enough. Adding to Levin's woes, to win the approval of a big Turner shareholder, TCI's John Malone, Levin structured a side deal giving Malone a 20-year, 15-percent discount on TBS services such as CNN, TNT, and the Cartoon Channel. The arrangement prompted an investigation by the Federal Trade Commission (FTC). Analysts predicted the imminent breakup of Time Warner and a major management shakeout.

Long story short and from pillory to praise—Levin finally pulled off his dream deal. In July 1996, the FTC finally blessed a slightly altered version of Time Warner's acquisition of Turner Broadcasting, restoring Time Warner's position as the world's largest media company.

Along the way, Levin had dumped executives and directors who did not share his vision. He proved himself capable of giving up a sacred cow, cable operations. In a marked departure from the strategy that drove him to make nearly $5 billion in cable system acquisitions in

1995, Levin told analysts he was working on a deal to restructure the U.S. West partnership, conceding both majority ownership and management control of the company's cable system to them. Levin was now, finally, delivering on a plan to restore the company's financial health by eliminating $8 billion of debt by selling off significant stakes in its cable systems, aggressively cutting operating costs and generating new revenue through the TBS acquisition.

As the months passed, the question remained: would Levin's dream end up becoming his nightmare? The rumormill cranked out stories about behind-the-scenes management power struggles, many of which were based on the sheer size and consequent unmanageability of the vast enterprise. In addition, critics predicted that it was only a matter of time before Turner, made Vice Chairman in the deal and openly critical of the high costs and inefficiencies in Time Warner operations, took over completely.

Instead, Levin listened to Turner (though anecdotes suggest that it's hard *not* to) and delivered the cost cuts and synergies in record speed. Ten executives were hired to act as bridges between the different divisions to facilitate comarketing arrangements, and operating protocols were established. The two leaders, Turner the showman and Levin the staid executive, complemented, and complimented, one another. "I love working with Ted," Levin told *Fortune* in a March 1998 article, "Suddenly, Jerry Levin's Stock Is Hot." "He's one of the most interesting people on the planet." For his part, Turner says, "We just have a ball together, but I try not to waste his time."

A year after the acquisition, the reinvigorated company's stock rose 34 percent, and market value nearly tripled, from $35 billion to $100 billion. Shareholders and Wall Street cheered both Turner and Levin. The man whom analysts had given only months in his job stuck to his vision and ended up a hero.

Just look at what happened a few years later. As a result of the successful Turner integration, Levin acquired a reputation for understanding how to make mergers work. One day he got a call from Steve Case, chairman of AOL, asking him to start off the year 2000 with the biggest merger in U.S. history and become CEO of a combined AOL-Time Warner. This time around, a four-person committee of top AOL and Time Warner executives are focusing on how to merge AOL's resources with Time Warner's and divide responsibilities within the combined company.

THE RED ZONE MORAL TO THE STORY:

Gerald Levin demonstrated a do-or-die commitment to this merger. By bringing

in experienced players to oversee the TBS transition and integration, he was

putting the strongest managers and employees into the thick of Red Zone

management. Using the four-person committee of senior executives for the

AOL-Time Warner integration demonstrates that both Levin and Steve Case

recognize that they are in a Red Zone, which requires special behavior and

commitment from everybody, especially key managers.

RED ZONE PRINCIPLES

Now for the Red Zone principles that should apply to the merger and acquisition maneuver. The goal in this chapter is not to duplicate the principles of Chapter 4; instead we want to show variations and distinctions on those principles for the Red Zone maneuver of mergers and acquisitions.

Red Zone Principle One:
Declare the Company in a Red Zone

When merging or acquiring another company of equal size, an amazing amount of detail must be managed and managed well. And managing detail well takes time, lots of time, and energy. M&A brings together two companies with different cultures with different ways of doing business, communicating, and viewing the business world. The large number of details and the differences in the companies require a high level of enthusiasm, motivation, and commitment to make a successful merger happen. That needed level of commitment really is Olympic-level motivation and creativity to achieve the gain coupled with do-or-die resolve to avoid the loss.

Capturing the attention of employees in either company is not a problem. People are aware that M&A makes change happen and that jobs are immediately at stake. People have been through enough mergers or heard enough about them to know that the situation is going to be tense. The problem for management is to turn employee attention toward the hard work of the merger and away from the woe-is-me victim mentality into which employees can easily fall.

The two leaders involved in the M&A must quickly reconcile their positions, agree to the roles they will play in the new company, and take their strong leadership on the road to the employees. Both leaders must be credible in telling the employees about the stronger future they intend to create for the combined organization. They must also articulate the business reasons for the combination, giving employees time to make sense of the M&A maneuver. Last but not least, those leaders must make sure workers understand that they are all in a Red Zone together until the final step of integration is complete.

Red Zone Principle Two:
Put the Best Players in the Game

M&A is a two-executive team game. Both executive teams must play actively and aggressively: playing as visible winners, standing tall and straight, and avoiding the frequently seen winners and losers syndrome. Playing as winners starts with both teams respecting each other and honoring the business deal that put the two companies together. Going beyond that, both teams must continue their moral leadership responsibilities to their troops as the details of the merger become clear.

Rarely are the two teams equal in power in the M&A game. The more powerful team will be known early on and will have a very special responsibility to set the tone for the entire merger. Putting egos aside is a leadership requirement as the more powerful team works with the other team to put the official slate of executives into place for the new company. Executive team members who do not wind up with a leading slot on the new team must continue to play and set a leadership example for both organizations. Leaders who get caught up in what they see as personal loss must either hide their disappointment and play well or take their leave early on.

The new executive team must get to know each other quickly and begin to play very well as a team, because they have a lot to do in identifying and making the hundreds of changes needed to get the two companies together. Teamwork is the responsibility of the CEO of the new company. The quality of the teamwork that will emerge, however, is frequently determined by the example set by the other, former CEO and immediate reports. The new CEO should ask for and get complete cooperation from the former CEO or immediately arrange for that person's departure. While almost half of the CEOs who are merged into a more powerful organization wind up leaving, the goal is to have them play as strong, effective business leaders, fully supportive of the new organization until their departure time.

Every top executive should have a Red Zone role in addition to their usual duties in the day-to-day running of the company.

Red Zone Duties of the Chief Executive Officer (CEO):

- *Chief merger advocate to the organizations.* The CEO's primary responsibility is to ensure that proper strategic due diligence is done and that clear goals are set for the merger. The CEO, above all people, must understand each company's distinctive market franchise and what specific advantages are to be gained by the merger.
- *Chief merger advocate to the board and to investors.* The CEO's goal should be to keep the Board of Directors informed, involved, and supportive of the merger, particularly when the inevitable surprises happen.
- *Chief customer advocate.* The CEO ensures that the merger really does meet marketplace goals and brings additional value to customers.
- *Chief communications officer.* Communicates the business reasons for the merger, the specific merger goals, and the continuing status of the merger to the firm. The former CEO needs to be a co-communicator of the CEO's message.
- *Master architect.* During the premerger phase, the CEO ensures that the blueprint of the new organization will allow merger goals to be met.
- *Effective leader.* The CEO must use a gracious, compassionate, but forceful leadership style that understands workers's sensitivities while ensuring that work is effectively handled. Once again, the former CEO, if still in play in the combined firm, must show high-quality leadership right beside the CEO.
- *Master program manager.* The CEO is the major provider of resources, internal obstacle remover, and ultimate time clock keeper.

Red Zone Duties of the Chief Operating Officer (COO):

- *Designer.* Intimately involved in the design of the merger blueprint, owning many of the operating details.
- *Chief executor of the merger blueprint.* The COO and direct reports will be on the spot for implementing the blueprint, including the removal, if needed, of redundant organization units and personnel.
- *Day-to-day owner of the customer scorecard.* Because the COO owns those parts of the new organization that touch the customer, he or she handles one of the biggest potential problems in any merger, the loss of customers from the merged-in organization.
- *Day-to-day change leader.* The COO works with the CEO and the program manager to understand, identify, and schedule all the integration activities to combine the new company in such a way that merger goals can be set.
- *Leader of day-to-day executive teamwork.* Provides leadership as the new executive team focuses on internal issues (the CEO works external as well as internal issues).

Red Zone Duties of the Chief Sales Officer (CSO):

- *Customer advocate.* The CSO is responsible for key customer interaction, the impact of the merger on the now larger market, and prevention of customer loss.
- *Chief marketing strategist.* The CSO is responsible for rationalizing the branding, product, and market strategies of the two organizations into one.
- *Chief communicator to customers.* The CSO explains how the merger will serve the customer better. The merged company's advertising and public relations strategies should be aligned to continually send a positive and engaging message to the marketplace.
- *Chief pricing officer.* Works directly with the CEO, COO, and CFO to pick price points that make sense for the merged operation.

Red Zone Duties of the Chief Financial Officer (CFO):

- *Leader in financial due diligence.* Success depends on knowing the full financial implications of merging the two companies and their assets.

- *Leader in metrics.* The CFO measures the results of the merger, including measurements that make progress visible, worrying later about reconciling the sacred cow metrics of the two companies.
- *Financial systems leader.* Ensures continuous financial and accounting operations.
- *Challenger of assumptions.* Devil's advocate for investment in the merger as well as for the overall use of capital for the now combined company.
- *Compensation and incentive designer.* Works with the CEO and human resources officer to ensure that monetary incentives are in place to motivate key organization members for merger success.

Red Zone Duties of the Chief Information Officer (CIO):

- *Chief information technology strategist.* The CIO ensures that the merged company's technology strategy starts with the merger and quickly aligns with long-term goals, working directly with program management and the COO to align information technology resources/systems to ensure continuous operations in the new company.
- *Leader in metrics.* The CIO works directly with the CEO and CFO to put in place the metrics and scorecards for measuring merger results.

Red Zone Duties of the Chief Human Resources Officer (CHRO):

- *Staffing leader.* The CHRO works directly with the CEO and COO to ensure that employees are named in all key executive and operating roles as soon as possible.
- *Legal impact manager.* The CHRO works directly with the COO to ensure that all impacts of the merger on people are executed in a fair and legal way that protects the long-term franchise of the organization.
- *Compensation and benefits leader.* The CHRO aligns the human resources systems for compensation and benefits as soon as possible to promote workforce continuity, confidence, and security.
- *Performance management leader.* Aligns employee performance management systems to focus the new organization on the short-term and long-term objectives of the merger.

- *Line management support provider.* Provides trained human resources generalists to assist line management in carrying out the required operations of the blueprint.
- *Chief people advocate.* Monitors stress and strain on the merged organization and recommends support to people as needed.
- *Executive team development leader.* The CHRO plays a key role in ensuring that the new executive team is jelling and pulling together well.

The new executive team must be absolutely together for merger success. If the new executive team is blended, they must play as one team without the two-subteam mindset with its destructive sneak circuits of unauthorized communication to other employees of the two companies. The executive team must provide moral leadership and set the standard for getting on with business. They must look ahead and not back; they must get over hard feelings between the two companies and release any baggage that would keep the merged organization from moving forward to success.

Red Zone Principle Three: Focus on the Customer

While the vast majority of mergers are publicly rationalized by increased marketplace impact, the party most likely to be lost in the shuffle is often the customer. The difficulties encountered in a merger frequently seem so daunting and time consuming that the customer is the last to be served. Ironically, the customer's vote is likely to be the only one that counts in the final measurement of success.

Red Zone principle three recommends that a customer scorecard for the products and services of both organizations, like the example shown in Chapter 4, become an explicit driver for the planning and execution of any merger. The idea in a merger is not immediately to change the way the customer sees the offerings of the new firm but to protect the way the customer sees the offerings. As managers and employees alike face customers from the organization with which they merged, they must keep intact the attributes those customers valued.

Red Zone Principle Four:
Set Clear Red Zone Goals

Crisp goals are important for any Red Zone maneuver, and M&A is no exception. Three kinds of goals are particularly important: rationale goals, synergy goals, and operational goals. The primary rationale for merging varies: examples include acquiring new markets or distribution channels, acquiring complementary products to broaden lines, acquiring mass or size for economies of scale, diversifying, and so on. Whatever the specific rationale, it should be turned into explicit, and where possible, quantified goals.

Specific goals should be set for any synergies that were a part of the reason for merging. These synergies are typically stated in terms of costs to be saved and/or additional sales (which could be made, for example, by making more product lines available through the sales outlets of the combined companies).

The final category of goals has to do with the business operations of the combined organization immediately following the merger. The best goals to use for this kind of Red Zone maneuver are as follows: market share, competitive rankings, profitability, and return on investment.

Clear merger goals are essential, allowing employees to understand where they need to go as well as to measure progress. Clear goals also become the targets for incentive compensation to motivate merger success.

Red Zone Principle Five: Blueprint for Success

The goal of the blueprint step in Red Zone M&A is to build a clear, concrete picture of the organization as it will look one to two years past the transition period, when goals have been met and synergies realized. Critical dimensions for the blueprint are as follows:

Vision, strategy, and values. The blueprint should begin with a description of the organization as it should look in the future, including its marketplace position, its desired competitive ranking, and its goals.

The blueprint should also state the single, unifying competitive strategy that the merged organization will use to win with customers and compete against rivals. For merging organizations whose operational units will be kept separate, the intention to keep independent competitive strategies in play must be stated explicitly. The blueprint should also include the values and operating principles that will provide guidance and boundaries for operation of the merged firm.

Organizational structure and leadership. Top management must state in the merger blueprint, with as much precision and certainty as possible, how they intend to structure and manage the organization. Failure to state clearly the structure and provide leadership positions with names will encourage continuing rounds of positioning and lobbying for opportunity as the merger unfolds.

Markets and geographic coverage. Painting a picture of the extent of the merged company, including both the markets (customers) that will be served as well as the geographic regions that will be pursued, should be a key goal of the blueprint.

Product and service lines. The merger blueprint should show how the company's products and services will exist together; i.e., which will be primary products and which will be complements. The picture of products and services must match the customer scorecards completed earlier.

Operating processes. The blueprint should contain a description of how the merged organization's business processes will work together to produce products and services across its geographic and customer markets. While all the details of operating processes may not be known for some time, exactly how the organization will operate after the merger should be outlined in as much detail as possible.

Don't Move! Don't stop the Red Zone design engine and go to execution principles until a clear picture of the merged organization exists, including:

- How customer value will be protected in the short run and strengthened in the long run.
- How the organization will be structured and where it will operate.
- What the company will stand for in the marketplace.

RED ZONE PRINCIPLES FOR EXECUTION OF A MERGER

The Red Zone execution principles for M&A are especially critical because so many moving parts and details must be reconciled in a short period of time for the organization to reach its goals successfully. Strong leadership is required to focus on those parts of the merger that are critical and to direct energy away from those parts that may seem important but that in the long run will not impact success.

Red Zone Principle Six: Focus on Mechanics

Successful execution of the Red Zone merger properly begins with the identification of the mechanical moves that must be made for success. The first challenge is to reconcile the differences between the two companies to get the organization operating as a single entity. Such reconciliation ranges from changing signs to reflect the name of the merged company to changing customer numbers to fit them into a single accounting system. Additional mechanical changes will include employee numbers, files, records. . . . The list seems endless.

The second challenge is to identify the mechanical changes needed for the newly merged company to meet its purposes. If, for example, a primary purpose of the merger is to share distribution channels, mechanical changes must allow new product to flow and be promoted in existing channels. While some mechanical changes will be relatively simple, others may not. For example, if a primary reason for companies to merge is to blend the two companies's technologies to develop and market products that are new to both, the needed mechanical changes will be neither simple nor obvious.

To make the identification of mechanical changes even more onerous, each change requires support by second-order mechanical changes. In other words, any one change needed for the merger, like distributing one company's product lines in another's distribution system, will require changes in work processes, equipment, and in the roles and performance of workers. While these changes are simple and logical, they become complex because of their sheer number. That complexity can be managed in the disciplined program and project management environment suggested in the next Red Zone principle.

Many of the needed mechanical changes can be worked out by managers and employees in near real time as they understand and settle into their roles in the merged organization, provided that they know those roles and that they have access to the Red Zone blueprint. That is a big proviso for many organizations. I have found that clarifying the merged organization's structure and performance management system is critical during the very early stages of the merger.

Top management must rapidly agree on an organization structure and name key managers to populate that structure. Once named, those key players should be encouraged to name the players that will be on their teams, and so on. I have found great value in rapidly naming players by organizational level and then conducting teambuilding sessions as they take over their responsibility. The teambuilding sessions should cascade down from the top management team until every organizational unit has been covered. Critical in those teambuilding sessions are the merger blueprint, the development of that organization's version of its own blueprint, the clarification of roles and responsibilities for each member of each team, and then the charge to work through the details that fall under each manager's purview.

Red Zone Principle Seven: Use Program and Project Management to Build to Print

The CEO has his or her hands full during a merger. The first concern is to keep the organization moving forward, serving the customers, and getting revenues. Meanwhile the CEO is also ultimately responsible for ensuring that all required merger actions are taken in a rapid and systematic way. I have found that a program manager reporting directly to the CEO can be an alter ego and lead the mechanical transition steps.

The job of program management should focus on getting the merger completed in the shortest possible time by systematically tackling the needed mechanical changes. The role of the program manager is to act for the CEO to ensure that the right merger actions are taken at the right time, while keeping the CEO informed of and lined up for those critical merger actions that only he or she can handle up close and personal.

Program management must adopt a slam dunk attitude, that doesn't settle for less than 100 percent success, for the Red Zone. While the overall goal of the program manager is to make sure that the organization accomplishes all of the mechanical changes identified in any earlier step, some mechanical actions will count more than others. Program management must use the 80/20 rule to find that 20 percent of actions that will result in 80 percent of the results. Once those 20 percent are identified, program management must work directly with the CEO and the executive team to ensure that those actions are slam dunked.

Beyond slam dunking the critical 20 percent, program management must work with amazing detail. Program management for a Red Zone merger needs to be formal and disciplined to ensure that the thousands of changes required for the merger are brought under management. Program management needs to identify and form multiple projects to achieve concrete results and take the company to the blueprint.

The projects that make up the merger program are best organized around merger goals. Experience indicates that each of these projects should be both crossfunctional and biorganizational in membership and orientation to have a broad view. Having project team members from both of the merging organizations will allow the team to use the best of both organizations's thinking and practices. For example, if a merger goal is to reap $50 million in cost savings, a project team might be appointed to help an assigned executive find those dollars.

Red Zone Principle Eight: Focus on Speed

Speed may be more critical in M&A than in any of the other Red Zone maneuvers. Nowhere are the risks as high for moving too slowly. Customers and employees suffer when the merger does not rapidly remove uncertainty about how the organization will operate. If the merger is really about increasing market presence and opportunity, moving fast gives advantage, while moving slowly allows competitors time to reap benefits during periods of lingering uncertainty. The faster the organization moves, the less adverse the effects on key measures of business performance: profits, employee morale, and productivity.

The timeline for an effective merger varies directly with the type of merger. Mergers that form portfolio companies whose assets and operations are merged only on financial statements can move to complete the mechanical parts of the merger in less than six months. Mergers that combine operating units may take many more months. The CEO, as the timekeeper during the Red Zone merger, must drive the merger as fast as possible to gain the desired merger goals, while not so fast that the rest of the organization can't still effectively and efficiently make the needed combinations and deletions.

Red Zone Principle Nine: Meet Special Needs of Workers

The most important need of managers and employees alike in the merger Red Zone is certainty of having a job, the nature of the position, its location, reporting relationships, and compensation. Workers going through a merger will work effectively only so long without certainty. Top managers must focus on bringing clarity to all employees about their status in the organization.

Be fair with those workers who might be leaving the company. While the merger maneuver does not automatically mean reductions in head-count between the two organizations, such reductions are common. All workers are impacted by the way the top management team handles those reductions. Obviously, the employees whose positions have been eliminated will be impacted by the quality of outplacement packages and services. The remaining workers in the merged company will be acutely aware of what is happening to their former coworkers. What is happening will be either encouraging, that the new executive team is fair and humane, or discouraging, that they might not really want to work for the new team in the long run.

Provide extra support to those workers who are on special teams to work out the details of the merger. Some of the two organizations's best and brightest will likely be called on to reconcile the many differences. These team members should not be forgotten as they return to regular work after serving on teams or task forces.

Provide strong leadership to settle merger conflicts. Merger teams can sometimes be bogged down by attempts to reach a consensus on every issue. Strong leadership keeps workers focused on high-priority matters and quickly resolves issues not critical for long-term success.

Red Zone Principle Ten: Reward for Red Zone Performance

Provide real, substantial incentives to top management for bottom line results over the first three years of the merger. The idea of a merger is to create a new organization with more value then the two starting organizations. If the merger is successful, that increased value should show in two to three years, and should be the driver of the primary top management incentives. Putting the big bucks several years into the future focuses top management attention where it should be, on increased future value.

Additional incentives should match the different classes of merger goals. The key to proper incentives is to tie them to the accomplishment of multiple goals, not just to one key goal. For example, tying primary incentive compensation for the chief executive solely to the accomplishment of a synergy goal, like a savings target, will likely cause intense interest on meeting that goal to the exclusion of other purposes of the merger, like building long-term franchise value.

Explicit recognition must be given to the accomplishment of merger goals along with the accomplishment of normal year-to-year goals. Incentive compensation amounts should be commensurate with the success of the merger and should be over and above normal incentive compensation. Ending this section on a negative note, I have not been a part of a merger yet that did not have a few managers and employees who, for whatever reason, could or would not support the merger. Those uncooperative workers should lose all incentives and risk demotion or even termination.

APPLYING THE GAMEPLAN

Wait. Don't begin applying the merger gameplan yet. Go straight to Chapter 10 and read the Red Zone Gameplan for culture change as well. One of the biggest obstacles to a successful merger maneuver is the cultural differences between the two organizations. To better understand how to tackle the culture issues with a merger, try Chapter 10 on for size.

There is a lot to know about the Red Zone maneuver for M&A. Fortunately, many M&A experts have been there and done that and can help with the technical details. But the consistent application of the Red Zone principles is up to the top management team. Only they can give this maneuver the importance and priority it deserves.

CHAPTER 7

Red Zone Gameplan for Reengineering Work Processes

In this Red Zone gameplan chapter we will discuss one of the most important and most heavily criticized of the Red Zone maneuvers. From the moment that the word *reengineering* burst on the business scene more than a decade ago, business folks and writers alike have praised it highly yet doubted its claims. As participants in the reengineering movement, our firm has been a firsthand witness to both its value and its abuse as a business tool. In my work, I have found the process of managing a large reengineering effort to be widely misunderstood and poorly done.

THE PRIMER ON REENGINEERING

A Definition of Reengineering

Over the past 15 years, reengineering has become the stuff of management legend, moving through the same stages as many Hollywood careers—from young, enthusiastic starlet to too much, too soon disillusionment, and finally into battered but mature appreciation. Hundreds of books, thousands of projects, and billions of dollars later, we can finally talk about reengineering without defining it, damning it, or defending it—mostly. But beyond all the hoopla, just what is it?

Michael Hammer and James Champy, in their best-selling work *Reengineering the Corporation: A Manifesto for Business Revolution,* define reengineering as "the fundamental rethinking and radical redesign of business processes to achieve dramatic improvements in critical, contemporary measures of performance, such as cost, quality, service, and speed." The term reengineering has been used somewhat indiscriminately to describe different kinds of reorganizations, most often those associated with reducing costs and downsizing. Reengineering is a balanced, nonetheless intense, approach to performance improvement that pursues multiple improvement goals concurrently—quality, cost, flexibility, speed, accuracy, customer satisfaction—to deliver dramatic returns in productivity, capacity, and profitability. Other programs focus on fewer goals or trade off among them.

Clelland Johnson, a Computer Sciences Corporation partner, puts it all together nicely: "Reengineering is the fundamental analysis and radical redesign of business processes to achieve dramatic improvements in performance. It is developing creative and innovative ways of doing business, managing the organization's human resources through these changes, and implementing the appropriate information technology to support the new environment."

Motivations for Reengineering

The concept gained popularity as the right cure-all that appeared at the right time and got an extraordinary amount of promotion. In "It's Totally Radical," an article published in the *Journal of Business Strategy*, Ray Manganelli, president and CEO of Gateway Management Consulting, explained that in the late '80s and early '90s, "Business executives have had to adapt to a new economic world order. Consumer demand has plummeted, competition has increased, and the ability to raise capital by diluting equity has slowed markedly."

Difficult and dangerous as reengineering may have seemed, given the tenor of the times, leaders were willing to try this innovative concept that promised a fresh start. Major corporations made intensive efforts toward reengineering, hoping that it would be the route to future success in a highly competitive marketplace where product costs could mean the difference between success and failure.

Research has shown that 88 percent of the large corporations in North America were already implementing business process reengineering (BPR) in 1993, at an average rate of 4 projects per firm. As some of the most competitive companies in the country began launching reengineering projects, many others, rightly or wrongly, jumped on the bandwagon. The notion of tapping the combined talents of corporate strategists, technologists, and human relations experts to bring hard and soft skills to bear on complex issues made great sense. But too many "me-too" projects were launched without leaders doing the proper homework or preparation.

Depending on the source and the point in the decade, somewhere between 50 and 85 percent of reengineering initiatives launched by the mid-90s were deemed unsuccessful. Yet some 70 percent of the companies who said they had reengineered were planning to invest more in their reengineering efforts. A survey by Deloitte & Touche, cited in the March 1998 issues of *National Real Estate Investor,* found that nearly 75 percent of 400 large North American firms were planning to increase the number of BPR projects in 1995 and 1996. According to an April 1997 article in *Computerworld,* "Reengineering Needs to Get Quicker and Leaner, but in Today's Rapid-Fire Business World, It's More Vital Than Ever," the Gartner Group projected the reengineering market to grow by 20 percent per year through 1999, with businesses investing some $8.7 billion in professional reengineering services by 1999.

Success can be slippery to define and fleeting in hindsight. In an August 1993 *Datamation* interview, "Does Reengineering Really Work," Michael Hammer said that although 70 percent of firms did not achieve all their BPR objectives, most achieved a large part of what they wanted to do. Other studies at the time supported his assessment. Yet, over the next few years, the literature and spokespersons who had once praised reengineering's payoffs were now describing it in decidedly less favorable terms. When *The Reengineering Revolution* appeared in 1995, authors Hammer and Steven Stanton admitted that, "Reengineering has not been an unqualified success. Many companies have undertaken reengineering efforts only to abandon them with little or no success."

The Enduring Legacy of Reengineering

As a discipline that now has an extensive body of knowledge based on implementation, reengineering has become an accepted tool for focusing intense effort on fundamental performance improvement. Reengineering efforts can raise performance to new heights or help rescue a business from stagnation. Throughout the last century, we've taken the best techniques from each fad and integrated them into the general body of management knowledge and practice. The practical application of reengineering ideas continues to have a significant influence on how we approach any business improvement project. In addition, a disciplined format for continuous reexamination and rethinking of how work is organized and performed is essential in competitive corporations.

The fundamental reality is that reengineering, applied intelligently, can produce powerful results that make the organization work better for its customers, its shareholders, its suppliers, and its employees. As part of their management repertoire, companies can use reengineering techniques when and where the situation calls for them.

When companies embark on a complex technology implementation, shared services implementation, a major change in distribution channel, or a merger or an acquisition, they can apply reengineering tools and techniques to improve results. With the boom in electronic commerce and increase in business-to-business data sharing throughout the supply chain, the discipline and techniques of reengineering are more vital than ever.

The Red Zone Problem:
Reengineering the Right Work Processes

Too often, process costs are reduced and quality improved, yet profits decline. In an excellent overview article in the August 23, 1993 *Fortune,* "Reengineering: The Hot New Managing Tool," Tom Stewart summarizes the effects of this paradox. "A computer company reengineers its finance department, reducing process costs by 34 percent, yet operating income stalls. An insurer cuts claims process time by 44 percent, yet profits drop. Managers proclaim a 20 percent cost reduction, a 25 percent quality improvement, yet in the same period, business-unit costs increase and profits decline." Reengineering is all about operations. Only strategy can show which operations matter, and matters of strategy are the province of the CEO and executive team. Reengineering without strategy leads to market-blind cost cutting. Robert Tomasko, author of *Rethinking the Corporation,* advises leaders to get the strategy straight first. "Don't fix stuff you shouldn't be doing in the first place."

In our *Business Horizons* article in July 1995, "Getting Past the Obstacles to Successful Reengineering," Sanjiv Kumar and I argue that selection of processes to reengineer should be based on added value to customers and on gaining a concrete competitive advantage. Some processes differentiate the company in the marketplace or form the basis of the company's identity. Others determine how well the company performs relative to its competitors, where a 10 percent improvement could translate into success or a loss of 5 percent into failure. Such key processes are critical to the firm's strategic intent.

The selection of processes to engineer, therefore, must be guided by those two criteria. In my experience, companies that picked process targets that were neither valuable for the customer nor focused on gaining the competitive edge were worse off for the time and energy spent in reengineering.

Some companies target well. Agway, the large farm supply co-op that sold cattle feed to farmers and gardening tools to grandmas, served two very distinct sets of customers with different needs. The order and billing system had considerable redundancy because customers ordered directly at the stores but received their goods from Agway mills and warehouses. After a strategy review, the executive team decided to split its commercial farming and retail businesses, then proceeded to reengineer the selling processes in the new businesses. As a result, service to both farmers and grandmas improved, and a complex layer of costs was eliminated.

Mutual Benefit Life (MBL), one of America's oldest and largest carriers, went from being reengineering's first poster child to whipping boy in fairly short order. During a five-year period, MBL spent millions revamping every major information system, including automating its policy issuance process. At the time, not much thought had gone into questioning the efficiency of the work rules and premises behind how policies were issued. In the late '80s, MBL's president launched a project to reengineer its life insurance policy issuance process. After reengineering, 30 jobs were compressed into one; the entire process was handled by a single case manager. Turnaround went from 22 days to 3 days. Brilliant!

Meanwhile, another area of the company was making disastrous real estate and mortgage investments—about $1 billion dollars worth—eventually forcing the company to seek protection under the New Jersey State Department of Insurance in 1991. Too bad for shareholders and employees that process analysis and reengineering didn't occur in all the right places.

Companies that focus on reworking administrative processes (often because they're easier to attack) while ignoring the tougher, politically charged, customer-centric ones are expending valuable energy and resources in the wrong direction. Companies that focus on reworking the right processes for the wrong reasons also learn expensive lessons. In his *Fortune* article, Stewart tells a story that illustrates the point. Under the assumption that its customers needed more expertise from its sales force, a computer company spent tens of millions of dollars on reengineering its selling operations, training its sales force in consultative selling techniques, and providing them with expensive electronic sales tools. The only problem was that customers didn't care how much the salesperson could demonstrate on spiffy laptops or relate to their business issues. What mattered to them most was price.

How Really Matters

In line with its own public relations business process, reengineering had caused a revolution in business. The revolution was not without costs and consequences, yet the concept of BPR made too much sense to discard. In fact, with experience did come wisdom about how—and how not—to do it. Doing it is no simple matter.

Reengineering is applicable, with little variation in concept, to all types of organizations—manufacturing, service, nonprofit, private, or public. The study, "Business Process Reengineering: Learning from Organizational Experience," published in the March 1999 issue of *Total Quality Management,* shows no significant trends or differences between sectors in terms of length of projects, methods applied, or results achieved. Apart from a regional variation in Asia, the basic concepts are being applied throughout the world in all different cultures. Examples of reengineering are found at all levels: department processes, crossfunctional processes, whole organizations, and supply chains. The success factors and problems are the same; however, tactical moves and implementation details differ enormously. No two organizations reengineer in exactly the same way, but they all reengineer.

Almost all of the popular management literature assumes that the organization and implementation of change efforts makes a difference. The conceptual development and codifying of the *how* of organizational change is one of the enduring contributions of the reengineering movement. Influential books by Michael Hammer, James Champy, Tom Davenport, James Collins, Ray Manganelli, and John Kotter suggest key factors that make the difference between success and failure: leadership commitment, credibility of project managers, stakeholder buy-in, communication, customer-focused scorecards, new reward and recognition systems, crossfunctional teams, and assigning the best people to the project.

Both this book and my previous book, *Change Is The Rule,* intend to add a practical, highly structured how-to tool to the leadership arsenal for those critical times and places in the life of an organization. In fact, *Change Is the Rule* was one of the first books to show change management as more of an engineering challenge at the detailed level of leadership, vision, work processes, and performance systems.

One Story Has Many Lessons for the Red Zone

As readers will note with stories in other gameplan chapters, sometimes multiple Red Zone maneuvers are going on in an organization at the same time, some maneuvers going well and some not going so well. Companies in the Red Zone frequently face the daunting task of managing several maneuvers that are part of a bigger organizational effort. For instance, during a merger, the two companies have to deal with integrating enterprise information systems while at the same time blending cultures. Changes in competitive strategies may be achieved by reengineering several business processes. Our first story concerns a failure of strategy, with a strong reengineering flavor and a dose of botched system implementation.

A Bumpy Ride for Greyhound

In 1991, after a crippling six-month strike and subsequent Chapter 11 bankruptcy, Greyhound Lines emerged leaner and ready to get back in the transportation game. The company faced a challenge to win back ridership, already eroded by inexpensive airfares. Executives announced their plan to reengineer the company along the lines of an airline, with a hub-and-spoke system, a new computerized reservation system, and higher fares for people who waited until the last minute to purchase tickets. Effects of the aggressive cost cutting from Chapter 11 reorganization were beginning to hit the bottom line, and the company produced a narrow profit in 1992, its first since 1989. Wall Street rewarded its efforts and its promises, and the company's stock rose from about $12 to over $21 per share.

The only problem with the promises was that many of the assumptions made as a basis for the project were erroneous. Running a bus company was not like running an airline.

- Greyhound operated 2,400 buses over 2,600 terminal locations, about 10 times more craft and locations than most airlines.
- Average one-way bus fare was about $^1/_{10}$ of average airline fares.
- The average bus rider earned less than $17,000 per year and bought tickets shortly before a trip, using cash because many did not have credit cards.

Compounding the problem, the development of its new computerized reservation system, appropriately called TRIPS, was more difficult than originally anticipated. A preliminary test of the system revealed some serious flaws in the technology and the preparation of the people using it. With the new system, clerks took twice as long to issue a ticket. Remember, company executives had assured investors, lenders, and securities firms that TRIPS would be up and running for the 1993 summer vacation season. Any bad news that Greyhound's reengineering plans were off track would doom the company's critical $90 million stock offering. Eager to deliver on their promises, top Greyhound management overrode the executive in charge of developing the system and declared that TRIPS would go online at the scheduled time, software bugs or no bugs, adequate preparation or not.

So TRIPS was rolled out in July 1993. The system continued to malfunction, and terminals often froze up, frustrating both agents and customers. At that point, the database didn't include all Greyhound destinations. To do ticketing for those cities, reservation agents had to check log books and do manual tickets. Some agents went back to writing tickets by hand to avoid the five-minute wait to print a ticket using TRIPS. Customers calling in with reservations encountered problems of a different kind. The new system had been designed to work with a new toll-free reservations number connected to 400 operators. The complexity of the interface was too much for the flawed system, however, and it often crashed. On average, customers had to make a dozen calls before they could get through to reserve a seat.

Given these challenges, the organization, already short of resources, was now even less capable of serving customers than before the reengineering project. To make matters worse, over 80 percent of the people who made reservations were no-shows, so many buses sat empty or nearly empty at the terminals. Because most of Greyhound's customers did not have credit cards, the company had no practical way to force them to pay. Worse yet, agents couldn't sell tickets to people who actually went down to the terminal, cash in hand, to buy a seat on the nearly empty buses because the system wouldn't let them.

No surprises here: ridership fell and customers defected to regional competitors. Revenues were down 12.6 percent and losses totaled $72 million in the first nine months of 1994. The stock dropped to $1.75. Top executives resigned. Shareholders sued after the company lost more than $100 million in 1994.

According to a 1998 article, "Right Strategy—Wrong Problem," in *Organizational Dynamics,* during this painful period, industry veteran Craig Lentzsch took over as CEO, bringing in a new management team. They averted bankruptcy through some financial restructuring, and by the end of 1995, the company was again showing a profit. More importantly, Lentzsch de-engineered, dismantling the airline business model and scrapping TRIPS, replacing it with a basic service and sales concept: "If you want to travel by bus, you show up at the terminal and within a reasonable time you get a seat on the bus at an affordable price. If we fill up the bus that is supposed to leave at 10 AM, we will keep rolling out buses until everyone has a seat."

The Greyhound debacle has the distinction of being the poster project cited for one of *Chief Executive's* "Seven Deadly Sins of Reengineering," published in the May 1996 issue, using reengineering to avoid making hard decisions. To quote *Chief Executive,* "A few years ago, troubled Greyhound Lines decided the key to future success was to reengineer its reservation system to the point where it could analyze ridership, fares, take phone reservations, and guarantee travelers a seat. But what it really needed to do, analysts say, was largely to abandon the long-haul business and concentrate on shorter trips [which Lentzsch did]. By constantly promising that the new reservation process would dramatically alter its business, management delayed the move that ultimately proved inevitable."

> ## THE RED ZONE MORAL TO THE STORY:
>
> Getting strategy straight is critical, and picking the processes that are going to
>
> make the most difference from a customer and business point of view are key.
>
> Forcing a reengineered process with its attached computer system into play
>
> when the rest of the organization isn't properly prepared is a great way to wind
>
> up in the doghouse.

Cookin' with Gas

At press time, Brooklyn Union Gas (BUG) was the country's sixth-largest gas utility. As a result of its reengineering efforts, the company created a culture of customer friendliness and technological achievement that put it ahead of its competitors. While many organizations relied exclusively on outside consultants in the early years of reengineering, BUG also developed reengineering talent from within. Bill Feraudo, the company's self-taught specialist and coincidentally senior vice president of marketing, estimates that 80 percent of his time is spent educating and convincing people about reengineering. Feraudo's comments about the project appeared in "Gas Attack: Brooklyn Union Gas Is Posed to Profit from Energy Deregulation," published in the August 25, 1997 *Forbes ASAP Supplement.*

Back in the early '90s, Feraudo was information systems vice president with a reputation as a take-charge guy who could inspire a sense of mission. Feraudo and his reengineering team had a budget of $46 million and a deadline of $2^1/_2$ years; $48 million and $2^3/_4$ years later the system went into effect as did Feraudo's promotion to head of customer service. "My reward for building the system was having to live with it," he said.

Living with it, Feraudo soon discovered gaps in the company's work processes. Sales and marketing didn't work closely enough with the customer service representatives to identify selling opportunities quickly. Customers with problems were transferred from rep to rep and required to reexplain their problems with each transfer, and then any installation and repair work had to be scheduled far in advance, making service waits extensive.

Foreseeing intense competition for customers under deregulation, he reasoned that the only way to retain existing customers while growing new business would be to "reorganize the company from the customer's point of view." Feraudo began his educational odyssey by attending reengineering seminars and then taking his findings to his boss, CEO Robert Catell, who understood well the impact of the coming deregulation. Because gas and electricity were becoming commodities subject to competitive pricing pressures, profitability would come mostly from new services.

Senior management embraced his vision, and Feraudo was given a mandate to reengineer BUG's customer service organization from the bottom up. His first step was to establish a business transformation team of ten general managers from various functions across the company. In turn, the team sought out CSC Index to help them learn how to rebuild every customer interface process.

The team first targeted BUG's largest market, the residential sector. Based on customer feedback, they set three broad goals:

1. Create customer satisfaction
2. Enhance growth opportunity
3. Increase net profitability

Under this scenario, a customer with a gas-heated home could be sold gas lights or a gas pool heater. This meant that every employee in contact with customers, from customer service reps to meter readers to appliance installers, would need to understand and promote the benefits of gas.

Reengineering the sales process was a top priority. Starting with the weakly performing, 36-member Advanced Energy Options group, a sales unit that handled leads for the residential sector, the transformation team reengineered the unit out of existence and replaced them with a new process. Leads would now come into a presell qualification center where reps were trained to do much of the work that the sales force used to do: qualify and categorize leads as well as schedule appointments, mail product literature, and answer general questions.

The team bundled the technical and sales positions. Leads went to plumbers (or installers, as the company calls them) instead of a sales force. On a computer-run rotating system, a certified master plumber, contracted and trained by BUG, was assigned appointments set by the presell qualification center. The installer would be responsible for explaining the benefits of the particular product the customer had inquired about, closing the sale, and installing the product. Installer oversight was managed by a seven-member team called *trade ally reps*. They trained installers in sales, safety, and new installation requirements and were held accountable for installers's performance standards.

Turning a plumber into an effective salesperson wasn't easy, so the company invested heavily in training. BUG middle managers, used to a command-and-control style, had difficulty transitioning into effective coaches and facilitators. They too received customized training in what BUG called *the supervisor of the future*. Most importantly, BUG transformed the way it compensated its employees, starting with a noncash reward system for groups that improved profitability. Ultimately, a portion of all customer contact employees's salaries would be tied to customer satisfaction ratings.

Among the new benefits achieved by the reengineering were:

- Customer records were now transferred along with the call with the press of a key.
- Information about contract maintenance options and other possible cross-selling opportunities popped up automatically when reps scheduled appliance installations for customers.
- Salespeople could go to a phone and download complete, up-to-the-minute histories of industrial customers before making sales calls.

By 1996 Brooklyn Union Gas had reengineered about a third of its processes, including customer service, marketing, and sales. Feraudo had been personally involved in at least 15 of the projects. Feraudo also masterminded the development of BUG's unregulated businesses, under the umbrella name KeySpan. He says, "I've had so many different roles at this company that I'm not sure what to call myself. I guess you could say that I build things."

Something sure helped build revenues. Revenues for 1996 reached $1.43 billion, up $216 million over 1995, and earnings have risen an average of 15 percent over the past 5 years, climbing to $97 million in 1996 excluding gains and charges related to an IPO. As KeySpan, the company is now the largest distributor of natural gas in the Northeast, with 2.4 million customers. The company closed out 2000 trading at a

52-week high, and CEO Catell announced that earnings for 2000 would be $2.40 per share, significantly ahead of estimates.

THE RED ZONE MORAL TO THE STORY:

These folks did it right. They developed the detailed expertise needed for big-league reengineering, dedicated strong resources to the job, and kept top management in the lead. What a great set up for the Red Zone Principles of Reengineering.

PRINCIPLES

Now for the Red Zone Principles that should apply to the management of the reengineering maneuver. The goal in this chapter is not to duplicate the principles of Chapter 4; instead we want to show variations and distinctions on those principles for this particular Red Zone maneuver.

Red Zone Principle One: Declare the Company in a Red Zone

When employees in today's businesses hear that reengineering is afoot, alarm bells go off. Over the past ten years, many of the changes that organizations have made have been labeled as reengineering whether process redesign was the focus or not. Unfortunately, some managers and the business press have labeled restructuring, dismantling of organizations, slashing of costs, and massive layoffs as reengineering. In short, reengineering has gotten a bad name it may not deserve.

The reengineering maneuver is all about making fundamental changes in work processes for radical performance improvements to improve business results. Such business changes will be difficult to design and even more difficult to test and implement. The challenge for top management in the reengineering Red Zone is to ensure the organization fully understands the reasons for reengineering, the consequences of not reengineering, and the most likely outcomes of the reengineering exercise.

As a part of declaring a reengineering Red Zone, I recommend that top management use the mantra for that special behavior and commitment needed for this very difficult maneuver: Olympic-level motivation and creativity coupled with do-or-die resolve to avoid loss. But rather than focusing the declaration on the word *reengineering*, we recommend labeling this Red Zone maneuver with terms that describe the business reasons for the reengineering, like *service excellence* or *added value to customers*.

Red Zone Principle Two: Put the Best Players in the Game

Reengineering is the chance to start with a clean sheet and use the very best available resources to work in a new way. Not everybody in the organization will have the perspective and skills to do such an exercise. The organization must go for those managers and workers who are the best thinkers for the reengineering design phase, regardless of their current roles or importance in the organization. In addition, those managers who will be critical for the implementation phase of reengineered processes will need to be pulled into play. Surveys of failed efforts through the mid–1990s showed that many companies failed to budget adequately for the reengineering project in terms of people. Selecting the very best people to lead the project is critical. The company capitalizes on their expertise, ability, and credibility to lead the process and enlist support from other members of the organization.

As with any Red Zone maneuver, reengineering requires massive amounts of direct leadership from the executives of the organization. Each and every executive has a distinctive role they must play well for the organization to enjoy success.

Red Zone Duties of the Chief Executive Officer (CEO):

- *Chief advocate of reengineering to the organization.* The CEO knows in the gut that reengineering is needed and is willing to put the organization through the ordeal to do it.
- *Chief strategy officer.* The CEO ensures that the competitive strategy of the organization is clear from the start. Reengineering must further the long-term interests of the organization and requires a clear statement of strategy up front.

- *Chief process selector.* The CEO works with the COO to target the processes for reengineering. The CEO retains the final say on which processes are chosen.
- *Goal setting leader.* The CEO works with the COO to set business goals for the project.
- *Chief customer advocate.* The CEO ensures that reengineering really does add value from the customers's point of view.
- *Chief communications officer.* The CEO communicates the business reasons for reengineering, the specific business goals that are to be reached, and the continuing status of the change to the firm, the board, and investors.
- *Master program manager.* The CEO is the major provider of resources, internal obstacle remover, and ultimate time clock on the maneuver and the business objectives associated with it.

Red Zone Duties of the Chief Operating Officer (COO):

- *Chief targeting officer.* The COO ensures that the right and best processes are targeted for reengineering.
- *Goal owner.* The COO owns the project's specific business goals.
- *Designer.* The COO is intimately involved in the design and approval of the new processes that come out of reengineering.
- *Chief executor of the reengineering blueprint.* The COO insists that mechanical changes necessary for the reengineering get made on target, on time, and on budget.
- *Day-to-day owner of the customer scorecard.* The COO owns those parts of the new organization that touch the customer.
- *Day-to-day change leader.* The COO works with the program manager to understand, identify, and schedule all the mechanical changes needed to meet the business objectives of the reengineering project.

Red Zone Duties of the Chief Sales Officer (CSO):

- *Process selector.* The CSO works directly with the COO in targeting processes for reengineering.
- *Customer advocate.* The CSO ensures that a customer scorecard is completed during the targeting process to explicitly take into account the improvement of customer value. Responsible for key

customer interaction, market impact, and prevention of customer loss, focusing on customer relationships during reengineering.

- *Marketplace information resource.* The CSO keeps the CEO and the executive team in sync with the marketplace during and after the reengineering.
- *Chief communicator to customers.* The CSO explains how reengineering will serve the customer better.

Red Zone Duties of the Chief Financial Officer (CFO):

- *Leader in metrics.* The CFO measures the results of the reengineering initiative, making progress toward the specific business goals of reengineering visible. Also, works with the CEO to understand and document the economic need/gain for reengineering.
- *Resource manager.* The CFO assists the CEO with the resourcing needed to complete the initiative.
- *Compensation and incentive designer.* The CFO works with the CEO and human resources officer to ensure that monetary incentives are in place to motivate key organization members for reengineering success.

Red Zone Duties of the Chief Information Officer (CIO):

- *Chief systems architect.* The CIO works directly with the COO to ensure that the information systems needed to support reengineered work processes are identified and implemented.
- *Information technology resource provider.* The CIO works directly with the program manager and reengineering project managers to ensure they have the needed information technology resources to identify and redesign new work processes.
- *Leader in metrics.* The CIO works directly with the CEO and CFO to ensure that the metrics and scorecards for measuring reengineering results are in place.

Red Zone Duties of the Chief Human Resources Officer (CHRO):

- *Performance management leader.* The CHRO works with the COO in aligning employee performance management systems to focus on the new, reengineered work processes as well as changes in incentive compensation criteria.

- *Organizational development leader.* The CHRO works directly with the COO to identify and work through reengineering's impact on people.
- *Training and development leader.* The CHRO identifies the worker competencies needed for the reengineered work processes and provides training to develop those competencies.
- *Chief of outplacement.* The CHRO assists the COO in dealing with the performance issues of workers who are unwilling and/or unable to align with the reengineered processes. Unfortunately, one commonly finds individuals who, for whatever reason, absolutely refuse to change behaviors. The CHRO supports the transfer or termination of such workers.

While reengineering should have a big impact, its focus will be on specific work processes, not the entire organization. Regardless of the processes selected for reengineering, the entire executive team must be in sync and supportive of the effort.

Red Zone Principle Three: Focus on the Customer

Reengineering may or may not point directly at increasing customer value. For example, reengineering might have direct customer relationship management goals: to increase the speed of customer order processing for one market segment or to smooth the billing process for another segment.

In other cases, however, the purpose of reengineering might be only indirectly related to customers, for example, to lower manufacturing overhead costs. Hopefully, lowering costs will eventually translate into lower prices and therefore better customer value. Reengineering also poses the risk of disrupting the company's relationship with customers.

Regardless of the purpose of reengineering, a customer scorecard, like the one illustrated in Chapter 4, should be completed as a part of the Red Zone design sequence. This scorecard will be the single most important tool for keeping the reengineering project focused in the right direction and for resolving inevitable conflicts. The choices of new process designs are many, and the company needs some way to evaluate those choices. I recommend using questions based on value to the customer as the best tools for making clear choices in reengineering. Asking the following question can help clarify design choices: "Would this proposed redesign bring more or less value to the customer than other proposed designs?"

The competitor sections of the scorecard absolutely should be filled in for the reengineering Red Zone. If your company feels that reengineering of processes can be of value, odds are that your competitors have a similar feeling. Anticipating where competitors are going with the way they do business is critical, and the best way to understand their anticipated directions is to translate them into a completed customer scorecard.

Red Zone Principle Four: Set Clear Red Zone Goals

Clear goals are vital for the proper management of Red Zone reengineering. Needed goals fall into two categories: process goals and company result goals. Process goals describe desired results from redesign of work processes. For example, a process goal might be to reduce the cycle time for new product development from 18 to 12 months or to reduce the time it takes to solve a customer's problem from 4 working days to 1. At least one of the process goals should reflect the company's desired gains on the customer scorecard. Setting a specific goal that speaks to the company's relationship with the customer is critical for keeping the reengineering initiative moving in the right direction.

Result goals describe the desired business outcomes of reengineering work processes. Common result goals are stated as costs reduced, revenues gained, market share expansion, and return on investment. For example, result goals might be to increase market share by 5 percent or reduce development costs by 15 percent by fielding new products more quickly.

While both kinds of goals are critical, they are used differently in the management of a reengineering maneuver. Process goals can have a great impact on the quality or creativity of the process redesign. Setting a goal of 5 percent improvement in a process will likely encourage evolutionary thinking by the design team, while a goal of 50 percent improvement will call for revolutionary thinking. The outrageous goal of

50 percent will stimulate creative thinking and may not be a totally realistic expectation. By the way, I haven't seen a top management team yet who would be upset with only a 45 percent improvement in a business process.

Result goals, on the other hand, should be set like other business goals: at feasible but challenging levels. In a mature industry filled with established companies, major changes in business results are unlikely. We do not recommend launching a reengineering project with the business goal of cutting overall product costs by 50 percent or increasing market share by 50 percent. Such goals will be seen by managers and workers alike as impossible and will not serve as good direction or motivation for working hard.

All process goals, however, should be ultimately linked to business goals. For example, a good test of reengineering targeting is to draft process goals and calculate the business results they could bring the company. If the calculation shows that big improvements in process performance are not likely to change overall business results, then the wrong processes have been targeted for reengineering.

Red Zone Principle Five: Blueprint for Success

The goal of this blueprint step is to generate a picture of the organization as it will operate in the future with reengineered processes in place. In reengineering terminology, blueprinting is very close to what is called *process redesign*. However, blueprinting goes further to picture the whole organization, not just the redesigned processes.

The first and most important step in building the blueprint is process redesign. Reengineering or redesign methodologies are common in both the business literature and among consulting firms who do reengineering. While the words vary a great deal across methodologies, the ideas are essentially the same and include steps like these taken from our firm's *Change Management Toolkit for Reengineering:*

- Target key organizationwide processes with the potential to enhance organizational performance.
- Understand those processes in terms of customer needs, design weaknesses, or technology weaknesses.

- Identify performance targets and investigate innovations that may allow those targets to be met.
- Develop a picture or vision of a radically improved process and validate that vision with others who have a stake in the process.

Once a stable vision of redesigned process(es) is in place, an organizational blueprint can be constructed to give employees a picture of the new venture the organization will become after reengineering is complete. For the blueprint to be valuable in execution and communication, it should contain the information as listed in Chapter 4: Red Zone Principles.

I have seen much confusion in reengineering projects because of failure to provide the organization with a comprehensive blueprint. Many organizations focus on providing information only about the reengineered work process without giving the kind of detail employees need to understand the whole Red Zone maneuver. It's far better to have too much information about the desired future organization than not to have enough.

Don't Move! Don't stop the Red Zone design engine, the sequence of design steps, and go to execution principles until you have a clear picture of the organization as it will operate after the reengineering. Before execution begins, top management must be clear on:

- How the improved, reengineered processes will enhance both customer value and business results.
- How the organization's major processes will work to meet those enhancement goals.

RED ZONE PRINCIPLES FOR EXECUTION OF A REENGINEERING

The Red Zone execution principles for reengineering are especially critical because the change process will likely be very disruptive to personnel working on and around the targeted processes. In an overview article in *Fortune,* Tom Stewart warns, "All change is struggle. Dramatic, across-the-company war." Once the new design is presented, he says, "The true test of leadership begins."

Red Zone Principle Six: Focus on Mechanics

Successful execution of the Red Zone maneuver properly begins with identifying the mechanical moves needed for success. In reengineering, the focus is on targeted processes from the beginning of the maneuver, so those mechanicals should be identified before leaving the design steps. However, our firm has never been involved in a reengineering exercise without finding needed process alterations other than those targeted. Principle six calls for us to examine work processes organizationwide to make sure that all the mechanical process changes needed for full implementation have been identified.

In many cases, the next step is to identify the tools to support the reengineered processes and/or their enabling processes. The basic idea is to build or buy the tools, including information technology applications, that match the details of the reengineered work processes. Easier said than done, particularly with computer applications. Sometimes, however, companies take an alternative route. They only describe their reengineered processes at a general level, then select their tools or computer applications from the marketplace, and only then detail their process redesign, to fit exactly with the tools they purchased. Regardless of how the company proceeds, the bottom line is still the same: work processes and tools have to match to the letter for maximum performance and minimum confusion.

Reengineering calls for people to stop doing work the old way and to start doing it the new way. The change to the new way calls for new job descriptions, training in the new work process and its accompanying tools, and possibly alterations in employee compensation. To make this point more clearly, if 1,200 people are doing work a new way as a result of reengineering, that means 1,200 altered job descriptions, 1,200 folks to run through training, and 1,200 handshakes with employees as they and their managers consummate an agreement to do work the new way.

Red Zone Principle Seven: Use Program and Project Management to Build to Print

A big reengineering project calls for systematic program and project management to ensure that all the mechanical parts are worked carefully. We have found that the program manager, acting as the agent of the CEO or COO, is critical in managing the reengineering effort from its beginning to the very end. The program manager's job is tough enough during the early phases when the prime responsibility is to ensure readiness for the reengineering effort. The job really becomes difficult during the design and execution phases when multiple project teams need to form and focus first on targeted process redesign, then on implementation planning.

During the design phase of reengineering, the program manager works with senior executives to create project teams around the redesign, usually forming one team around each major process or subprocess to be redesigned. The program manager's job is to ensure that these redesign project teams have the needed resources, training, and tools to accomplish their tasks.

The program management task is frequently complicated by what are called the *quick wins,* the relatively small change opportunities that are discovered as the redesign process goes along. Quick wins can be very valuable for the company and improve performance in a relatively short time without the waiting for the total redesign. The program manager's job is to form project teams around as many of the quick wins as possible and put these teams to work to produce benefits. Quick wins sound good and frequently look easy, but when reengineering, absolutely nothing is easy. During the last weeks or months of the design phase, program managers often ride herd on two or three major redesign projects and up to a dozen quick win projects.

Keeping all those projects headed in the right direction, balanced in resources, and cooperative is one of the toughest Red Zone jobs. In addition, the program manager must have a take-no-prisoners approach to the quick wins. Failure on a quick win is not an option; failure here can jeopardize the entire reengineering maneuver.

The most critical challenge for program management comes, however, in the execution phase of reengineering when redesigns, and the mechanical changes that will give them life, must all be implemented. The challenge is to put the blueprint into effect without altering it so much that it loses value. Implementing the blueprint just the way it has been crafted will take a lot of energy, courage, and toughness. The program manager must work directly with the CEO and COO to ensure that the design gets implemented with integrity despite the obstacles that the organization will raise. Implementation of the design cannot be delegated to managers in the existing organization to work out for themselves. To do so will likely prove disastrous, as human rationalization processes take over: "We don't have to do it the new way, because we are essentially already doing it kinda' that way, aren't we?" Implementation of reengineered processes takes top-down leadership and control to ensure they produce the planned benefits.

To cap off the program management task, consider this. There has probably never been a major reengineering project in the history of the world that did not endure major interruptions by something else changing in the organization, be it key personnel moves, competitor attacks, or market upsets. The job of the program manager is to make the reengineering project a success anyway, working out the inevitable problems of balancing the project against the realities of today's company business.

Red Zone Principle Eight: Focus on Speed

Speed is important. The goal is to move briskly through the reengineering design and execution steps. If major reengineering is occuring with top management heavily involved, as they should be, critical executive attention will not be available for a fully effective strategic focus. The idea is to get through the reengineering maneuver as fast as possible to minimize that strategic distraction.

Speed is especially critical during the execution steps when the disruptive steps of starting to work in new ways begin. While elapsed times vary, most major reengineering projects seem to take 12 to 18 months from when serious consideration of the maneuver begins to the completion of implementation. The length of the project can vary a great deal, frequently depending on the amount of information systems work to be done. Even then the organization may not be finished because a number of continuing refinements will stay on management's agenda until the next major redesign. Yes, there will be another major redesign as technology continues to advance and know-how develops. If your company doesn't reengineer regularly, your competitors may leave you in the dust.

Red Zone Principle Nine:
Meet Special Needs of Workers

The most important need for workers during the reengineering maneuver is to know where they stand. Given the bad name that reengineering has on the street, continuing a robust communication program during the entire Red Zone maneuver is especially critical to ensure that people know what is going on with the project, why reengineering is necessary, and how the organization's—and therefore their—future will be unfolding.

Beyond understanding the changes in the organization, people will need direct help in responding. Because reengineering is about putting new know-how and tools to work, employees have an immediate need to improve their knowledge and skills. Effective, efficient, timely training ensures that people will be able to perform well in redesigned processes.

Workers who are part of reengineering project teams frequently need special attention. It is not unusual to have workers away from their regular jobs and organizations for weeks at a time to help design future processes. The usual camaraderie of the design teams will not overcome the job security issues that frequently arise among the very people who know the most about the redesigned processes. Top, and I mean *top,* management must be directly involved in reassuring these valued members of the reengineering project teams that they have a future in the organization.

A critical need of some employees, particularly those who have not experienced changes in their jobs before, is for direct encouragement to get on with the change. While some folks make needed job changes rather easily, resistance frequently runs high in others. Those who just refuse to go along with the change need special encouragement beyond the retention of a good job. That special encouragement might range from the message to get over it, to other verbal kicks in the pants. Finally, for those labeled in the reengineering literature as the *stragglers,* special encouragement might be direct communication that employees who fail to change will immediately lose their jobs. A recurring theme from interviews of reengineering project leaders is that if they had to do it all over again, they would not have waited as long to shoot the stragglers, putting them and the organization out of misery sooner.

Red Zone Principle Ten: Reward Management for Red Zone Performance

So you want big results from the reengineering maneuver? Then incent the key players in the organization to get those results. Put your money where your mouth is, and put major carrots out there for the managers who directly lead the reengineering maneuver to success. Direct and above-normal incentives should target both process goals and business results goals. Reengineering major processes in today's organization is a huge and difficult task. If you want it done right, you will need to pay for it. Positioning reengineering as just part of a top manager's regular job, while leaving big bucks in plain view behind today's short-term revenue and profit goals, will not get you a reengineered company.

As we have recommended before, incentives need to tie to multiple goals, including both process and business goals and be paid one to two years after maneuver completion. Avoid paying incentives for the accomplishment of process goals without corresponding achievement of business results. Also avoid paying incentives for either accomplishment if other parts of the organization have been trampled just to get to the reengineering targets. At this point, I say, "Just use common sense to dish out the rewards." For unknown reasons, however, many companies are reluctant to incent performance properly in the Red Zone. I'm not surprised that Red Zone performance continues to lag in these very companies.

APPLYING THE GAMEPLAN

Reengineering can easily be one of the most confusing and disruptive of the Red Zone maneuvers. Focusing strong leadership on getting results, including the company's best minds in the design process, and engaging strong, aggressive program management can turn this maneuver into a money maker.

CHAPTER 8

Red Zone Gameplan for Implementing Enterprise Solutions (ERPs)

In this Red Zone gameplan chapter we will discuss one of the most difficult to understand and messiest of the Red Zone maneuvers. Companies have been implementing big IT systems for a couple of decades, but little that they learned has prepared them for implementing an enterprisewide solution. While in the past, companies have been able to invest in information technology that could be custom fit to their business, many are unprepared to implement an enterprise system that cannot be customized, for which the organization must be redesigned. This chapter will begin with a high-level primer on the subject of implementing enterprise solutions and end with a discussion of the Red Zone principles as they apply to this messy and difficult situation.

THE PRIMER ON IMPLEMENTATION OF ERPS

It's a Jungle in Here

A discussion similar to this could be taking place at a location near you in Corporate America.

CFO to CIO: Okay, Bert, with R/3 as our ERP, what's our TCO over the next five years?

CIO to CFO: Well, Ernie, It depends. You gotta think beyond this first financial system module. We need to examine our whole supply chain.

Some new APS bolt-ons are a lot more user friendly than SAP. And Ernie, we're surely gonna want full-blown EC capabilities, for both B2B and B2C, but I'm not sure about running an e-biz on our current ISP's platform. You know, the guys who manage our Web site . . . If we brought it all in-house, we could run it off the new client-server platform we'll be buying anyway. Just need a little boost in processing power and more disk drives with redundant arrays. Let's see, we'd need a good DBMS, OLTP/OLAP architecture for mining, and some XML programmers, too.

On the other hand, some ASPs have really hot apps, like CRM, if we could get the right QoS and SLAs in place. They could totally change our support structure and learning curve. That answer your question, Ernie?

One of the most vexing challenges for company leaders is simply to understand what language the IT group is speaking. The rapid speed and sheer complexity of IT innovation has created a class of technology acronyms that become nouns within days of their first press release. Lured by seductive promises of linkages, integration, and functionalities that save time, save money, and increase competitive advantage, companies are investing millions of dollars to implement business automation tools called Enterprise Resource Planning (ERP) or, more accurate though less used, Enterprise Resource Management (ERM) or Enterprise Business Management (EBS) systems.

A Definition of ERP Implementation

The idea behind an ERP system is to integrate departments and functions across a company onto a single computer system that serves the particular needs of each department while offering direct connections between departments (connectivity). For instance, the finance department typically has its own software as does human resources, sales, manufacturing, and other functional areas, each optimized for the way work is processed in the department. They may also be running their software on their own computer network, which may or may not talk to another network. Producing monthly business reports might take days of accounting time to access, translate, and reconcile records stored in each database, and their accuracy would still be suspect.

ERP combines these disparate systems into a single, integrated software program that runs off a single database, enabling various departments to share information more easily and company leaders to see and react to the company's key business indicators more quickly. Just as Materials Requirement Planning systems had a revolutionary impact on manufacturing operations, ERP can have a tremendous payback if companies install the software correctly—technically and strategically.

The Promise

Let's take a customer order as an example. At its simplest level, fulfillment of the order involves taking the information from the customer, locating/making the product, shipping it, billing for it, receiving payment for it, and accounting for it on company books and commission checks. In the preintegration days, an order started as a conversation that got written up on a piece of paper. That sales order floated from in-basket to in-basket and was keyed, and likely rekeyed, into each computer system along the way. The end results of this process were often misplaced or lost orders, delays in order processing, and errors in quantity or price. Good luck to the poor customer with questions about order status without multiple call transfers retracing the paper's journey.

When an order is taken in an ERP system, the salesperson or customer service representative has all the information necessary to complete the order—customer credit rating and account/payment history, inventory levels at the warehouse, and shipping schedules. When one department finishes with its part of the order, the order information is automatically routed to the next in line. Information on order status can be accessed at any point by logging into and querying the ERP system.

The Reality

All this automation should help customers get their orders faster and more accurately. But all this automation also affects the people inside the company. Before, each group just did its part. If something went wrong with the order outside one department's walls, it was somebody else's problem. With ERP, customer service representatives are more than order entry clerks. The information on their PC screen—credit rating from the finance department, inventory levels from the warehouse, last payment information from accounts receivable—makes them businesspeople, responsible for making decisions regarding the customer and the order they did not have to make before. People in other departments face new responsibilities too. Inventories can no longer be kept in logbooks or clipboards on a nail. Information on inventory levels must be entered online and kept updated so the customer service reps can quote accurate information on items in stock.

Accountability, responsibility, and communication have never been tested quite like this before. In addition to requiring a technical installation, implementing an ERP system forces key business processes to change to match the system, and it requires training and changes to the job responsibilities of all those involved. They must perform new tasks, or the same tasks in different ways, to different levels of performance.

The Big But

The biggest caveat with an ERP system is that it is a generic representation of the ways a typical company does business, based on allegedly extensive best practices research. While most ERP packages are mind-numbingly comprehensive, they are for the most part designed for use by manufacturing companies that make product units. ERP vendors have labored to modify packages for process manufacturers (e.g., oil, chemical, and utility companies that measure products by flow rather than units). Due to the depth and complexity of the system, modifications at the code level for these and other industries have taken Herculean efforts.

The idea is for companies to adapt their internal business processes to those best practice processes that come embedded within the ERP package. As noted in the order fulfillment example, an installation means changing long-established business processes to accommodate ERP software, which in turn means changing many roles and responsibilities, including those of people at very senior levels. Not a relishable prospect for the undercommitted.

So the bottom line in plain English is simple but revolutionary to many. You don't buy an ERP package and customize it to fit your business processes. You in fact customize your business processes to fit the package. Rather like bringing the mountain to Mohammed. Amazingly, we still see corporate ERP buyers shocked by that realization, especially after an ERP purchase.

Reasons to Implement ERP

So, the decision to implement an ERP involves a project of breath-taking scope, gut-wrenching adjustments to people and processes, and price tags large enough to make even the most seasoned CEOs lose many nights's sleep. What possible benefits could be worth this much pain? In a December 22, 1999 article, "The ABCs of ERP," *CIO* magazine listed the three major reasons companies implement ERP.

1. *To integrate financial data.* With different systems using different sets of numbers for financial reports, CEOs and division heads get different versions of the truth. An ERP system produces a single version of the truth so everyone is operating from the same page in measuring performance.
2. *To standardize manufacturing processes.* Companies with international business units may be using different methods and computer systems to make many of the same products. By standardizing manufacturing processes and using a single, integrated computer system, companies can increase productivity and quality. Newly merged and acquired companies are common targets for ERP implementation (or reinstallation if the parent has already implemented a package).
3. *To standardize HR information.* In companies with multiple business units, tracking employee time and benefits is extremely labor intensive. ERP provides a simple method for tracking and communicating these and other company programs and news.

In the *CIO* article, authors cite a 1999 Meta Group study that looked at the benefits and total cost of ownership (TCO) of an ERP system. TCO included the cost of hardware, software, professional services, and internal staff for installation and the following two years of service, which is when the real costs of maintaining, upgrading, and optimizing the system are felt.

- Among the 63 companies surveyed, the average TCO was $15 million, with a range of $400,000 to $300 million. With such a wide range, it's hard to draw absolute conclusions; however, the one number worth noting is the TCO for a single user over that period—$53,320.
- The study found that it took 8 months after the new system was in place—31 months total from project initiation—to start seeing the benefits. The median annual savings from the new ERP system was $1.6 million/year.

The Corporate Root Canal: Why ERP Implementations Are a Red Zone Condition

A few oversights in the budgeting and planning stage can send ERP implementation costs spiraling out of control faster than almost any other IT project. The mere mention of enduring another ERP project sends managers in many organizations running for cover. Covering some infamous budget-busting, career-endangering implementations, *The Wall Street Journal, Business Week, Fortune,* and other publications have characterized ERP implementations as the "equivalent of a corporate root canal."

Not without some justification. According to a study on ERP implementations by Robert Austin and Richard Nolan of the Harvard Business School, a remarkable 65 percent of executives believe ERP systems have at least a moderate chance of hurting their businesses because of implementation problems. In a 1998 report called "Chaos," the Standish Group published some eye-opening results of 8,000 software projects (not all ERPs) that showed significant time and cost overruns and content deficiencies. Based on their sample:

- The average project exceeds its planned budget by 90 percent and its schedule by 120 percent.
- 31.1 percent of the projects are cancelled before they ever get completed.
- 33 percent of all projects are over budget and late.
- 52.7 percent of projects will cost 189 percent of their original estimates.

- Only 16.2 percent of projects will be completed on time, on budget.
- The average time overrun is 222 percent of the original estimates.

Implementing an ERP system is an exercise in strategic thinking, precision planning, and negotiations within and between multiple departments and functions. Executives and managers must be aware of the success factors involved before implementation begins. As reported in *Information Systems Management* by scholars researching critical implementation issues, "Once an ERP system is implemented, going back is extremely difficult; it is too expensive to undo the changes ERP brings into a company." ERP projects involve changing the way a company works, and the company (read *leaders* here) has to be responsible for doing just that. It's easy to blame the complexities of the technology for expensive snafus, but (and here's another big *but*) the technology itself is not the biggest problem to resolve. Poor planning and/or poor project management top the list of reasons for implementation snafus. The top ten list of bubble and budget busters includes difficulties with testing and integration, data conversion, training, project scope creep, consultant creep, and staff disillusionment and loss. Derek Slater's complete discussion of "The Hidden Costs of Enterprise Software" can be accessed online at <www.cio.com>.

As this book goes to press, a new wave called *extended ERP*, which connects a company and its suppliers and customers with a single system, is emerging. If implementing an ERP is a Red Zone, implementing an extended ERP is a dark Red Zone and requires even greater care and attention. Summing up, the most common reason for the performance drop is that everything works differently, and people take some time to adjust to the new way to do their job on a new system, be it an ERP or an extended ERP. The expectation is that work was going to be better with the flip of a switch. As mistakes and frustration levels rise, management panics and the business hiccups before settling into the new routine.

No primer on implementing enterprise systems would be finished without some real examples of companies that succeeded and failed in this Red Zone. These brief examples were selected to show how messy some real world implementations are. The examples hopefully make the point that a good deal of leadership is needed to keep this maneuver under control and to synchronize the technical implementation with modifications of work processes and performance systems.

Singing the Blues: W.L. Gore

There are too many examples of failed ERP attempts in which the companies lost not only the capital invested in the system and millions paid to consultants, but also a major portion of their business. In November 1999, W.L. Gore & Associates, Inc., a privately held manufacturer of electronic components, surgical appliances, adhesives and sealants, and outdoor accessories (e.g., Gore-Tex® brand fabrics), filed suit against PeopleSoft and Deloitte & Touche, alleging that they improperly installed PeopleSoft's human resources management system and damaged Gore's business.

The lawsuit alleges that Deloitte & Touche consultants were not the PeopleSoft experts they had represented themselves to be. Jay Eisenhofer, an attorney representing Gore, says that the Deloitte team was always on the phone to the PeopleSoft customer service hotline, asking for guidance.

Oddly enough, Donald Duck figures into the dispute. To test the system, the Deloitte team created fictional employee files using Disney characters such as Donald Duck. Eisenhofer told the *Wall Street Journal* that the team couldn't get the fictional names out of the system and disrupted business by printing out paychecks, benefits, and tax statements for Donald and his cartoon mates when the system went live in July 1997.

"Within a very short time of going live, Gore's human resources, benefits, and payroll administration functions were in chaos," said Eisenhofer in a November 1999 *InfoWorld* article, "Consultant, ERP Firm Face Lawsuit over HR App." He added, "Gore associates were not getting paid, and Gore could not track vacation time or benefits." Gore is said to have brought in another team of consultants from PeopleSoft to delete the cartoon names and reinstall the software.

According to the suit, Gore paid Deloitte approximately $2.8 million for the software implementation, not including the cost of the software itself, although the estimate provided by Deloitte was for less than half that amount. Gore alleged fraud, negligence, and the assignment of incompetent consultants to the project, claiming unspecified damages plus a refund of the $2.8 implementation fees and a further $650,000 in charges. In cases like this, courts have frequently awarded triple damages.

At the time of the filing, neither Deloitte nor PeopleSoft had commented on the lawsuit. However, a Deloitte spokesperson later said in a July 17, 2000 *Business Week* article, "First, Sue All the Consultants," that the assignment was completed "to the client's satisfaction" and that Deloitte suspected the problems had occurred when Gore tried to make changes on its own.

Culture plays an important part in the story as well. Gore has been recognized as one of *Fortune* magazine's 100 Best Companies to Work for in America. It has no traditional management structure. The family-run company is known for its consensus-driven, *boneless* structure. Associates, not employees, communicate directly with each other and are accountable to fellow members of multidisciplined teams. Sponsors, not bosses, guide associates toward projects that match their skills and interests, helping them chart a career path that maximizes their contributions to the enterprise. Leaders emerge naturally, defined by what is called *followership*. Apparently, some Gore employees have acknowledged that the company's unusual culture and structure could have been a factor in its implementation difficulties.

THE RED ZONE MORAL TO THE STORY:

The moral is simple. Don't try a Red Zone maneuver with a "consensus-driven, boneless structure." Red Zone calls for clear direction, lockstep coordination, and a fast close. This maneuver calls for business unusual rather than business as usual.

And Some Who Are Singing Praises: Chevron

As we've seen, the out-of-control costs of a massive ERP implementation can end executive careers and damage the reputations of major consulting firms. Implementing SAP R/3, Chevron's IT managers executed a project that was fraught with dangers, yet they avoided many of the big traps.

Three years into their implementation, work on the project was still on schedule, but the number of expected users had quadrupled to 10,000, and cost estimates were up by a third to about $130 million. Chevron CEO Ken Derr calmly gave the team the green light to continue what would be one of the world's largest R/3 implementations. According to "Slick Moves," a February 3, 1997 article in *PC Week,* Norman Osborn, manager of Chevron's Advanced Financial Information System project, reported that Derr said, "We seemed to be on the right track, and we seemed to have good reasons for our costs as well as our benefits increasing." Not the reaction you would have expected? Naturally, there's more to the story.

Initial support for the R/3 project came from Chevron's CFO, who wanted to revamp the company's collection of some 200 25-year-old financial systems and processes. After an evaluation of ERP packages, R/3 was selected for a pilot implementation at Chevron's Warren Petroleum subsidiary, an integrated oil patch company like its parent. By all accounts, the implementation and results within the subsidiary were very successful. As published in the *PC Week* article, one implementation team member said with pride, "We got this to be a top management driven project with heavy emphasis on change management right from the beginning. This wasn't just about implementing SAP but about getting an old, inflexible organization ready for the inevitable change. And it worked pretty damn slick!!"

Senior management had given the green light. However, Jim Zell, CIO at Chevron, reported in an August 17, 1998 *Industry Week* article, "Proof Positive," that, "As we developed a rollout strategy, we couldn't get the individual businesses to hold themselves accountable for the benefits." So rather than rushing headlong into implementations in all 15 operating companies, the IT project leads asked each company to develop its own business case, looking at implementation costs and bottom line benefits. Taking this approach, the team had key business data to defend the decision to go forward to the CEO. Plus, the top managers of the operating companies spent the time and effort necessary to understand the system, its benefits, and its limitations, as the team earned their buy-in for the implementation.

After nine months to assemble the business cases, the company projected a total implementation cost of $75 to $100 million. Current cost for financial processes was $124 million per year. The initial set of business cases indicated costs could be reduced by at least $25 million per year—a payoff in 3 to 4 years—with the system rolled out to 2,500 users.

So how did dangerous times come into play? As it turned out, most of the business cases underestimated current expenses, costs of implementation, and payback. After widespread implementation started in 1994, the scope started changing rapidly. Many operating companies wanted to broaden implementations to cover more functions and users. As SAP started introducing new releases of R/3 with new modules for purchasing and project management, the operating companies wanted this functionality, too.

The team controlled the appetite for more technology by continuing to demand ROI and business case justification for each new expansion of the project. To avoid unpleasant surprises, they continued to communicate their approach and their results to senior leaders. The biggest increase in cost and complexity came from building links to legacy systems and from "stress testing" to be sure that R/3 could handle the now massive workload. Plain and simple, the need for additional computing hardware and disk storage drives up costs in any project.

But the team did manage some innovations to keep costs under control. The user pool had expanded to 10,000. The cost of training these additional users could have blown the budget and ROI potential to bits. For the initial rollouts, Chevron had used standard classroom training covering R/3, new business processes associated with the system, and PC use. The training price tag per user was $4,000. Because a training cost of $40 million would have shredded the budget, the team decided to develop their own computer-based training (CBT). Their CBT—with animation, Windows help features, and online quick reference—replaced classrooms and reduced system instruction by half. Users had to take the 40-hour CBT training and pass a test to get certified.

The team became so good at implementation that they were rolling out R/3 in up to five operating companies simultaneously. In fact, said Osborn, that was the only way the project stayed on schedule in spite of the sizeable increase in the scope. Postdeployment, Chevron refers back to the original business cases to evaluate the returns. The team plans to use the same formula as units press for more R/3 modules, like Sales and Distribution, along the way. They stuck with careful documentation of the business case and ROI and managed executive expectations very carefully.

THE RED ZONE MORAL TO THE STORY:

Get the best players in the game, keep top management in the lead, conduct

thorough due diligence on the enterprise system before you start, and keep learning.

RED ZONE PRINCIPLES

Red Zone principles for the implementation of enterprise systems are critical for success. This chapter will build on the principles of Chapter 4 and will include several important variations and distinctions.

Red Zone Principle One: Declare the Company in a Red Zone

While just about anybody in an organization can figure out that a merger is a Red Zone maneuver, few realize that implementing an enterprise system is one. After all, companies have been implementing computer systems for years. What's so different about this one? The unexpected answer is just about everything.

Enterprise systems bring two key elements to the implementing organization: connectivity between parts of the organization that had not been connected before, and standard work processes that are baked into the system. Most companies have implemented software that affects one functional area at a time, like a new financial package that impacts the departments of finance or accounting. An implemented enterprise system may impact dozens of departments simultaneously, requiring the folks in those departments to agree to work together as never before.

Also, departments typically have been working with computer systems that they believe are the best in class or that are their own proprietary systems, which they believe give a competitive advantage. Moving to an enterprise system represents a change in organizational strategy, saying that the department will now use a standard solution exactly like that of many competitors. Department members must move from a mindset of "Our system is special and we need to keep improving it." to a mindset of "Our system is not special; it's standard off-the-shelf stuff, which the software vendor will improve by periodic new releases." Vastly increased connectivity and movement to a standard solution represent big change for the organization, in both information technology and user departments.

To add to the complications, the value from an enterprise system frequently is not gained by initial implementation but by subsequent use of the system and subsequent process improvements. That is, once the system has been implemented and users begin working together in a more connected way across departments, performance improvement opportunities frequently appear. However, further changes in the way users work together are usually necessary to achieve improvement, becoming what some have called a second wave of implementation. The second wave is problematic to many organizations because employees were bunged up and burned out over initial implementation. It seems awfully difficult for users even to think about a second wave while they are still licking their wounds from the first wave.

The biggest problem right off the bat is selling top management on the idea that implementing an enterprise system is a real Red Zone maneuver. Obviously, they would not be considering implementation if a business case had not already been made for the potential big gain. But frequently, the case for a potential big loss has not been made. Somehow, the subject does not come up in conversations with the enterprise software vendor: surprise! Top management's first step when contemplating an enterprise system should be intense due diligence research on several firms that have completed similar implementations. If due diligence is done thoroughly, the firm considering the implementation should find a number of firms that can tell them how difficult, upsetting, and tumultuous such an implementation can be.

If top management does its due diligence well, they will understand how tough other firms have found ERP implementations to be, and they will think Red Zone. The information technology professionals will also be thinking Red Zone because of their technical knowledge of enterprise systems. They will understand that they are about to undertake a big, difficult project. The final challenge in preparing the organization will be to convince system users that they will have more hard work and changing to do than just about anybody.

We believe that top management must declare a Red Zone when they decide to go forward with implementation. The declaration should include both the potential big wins or gain, and the nature of the big losses that are possible from a failed implementation. Top management must also make the case for extremely hard work for several months during at least two waves of implementation. Frankly, I can't think of a better way to make the point than the *Wall Street Journal* phrase "corporate root canal."

Red Zone Principle Two: Put the Best Players in the Game

Implementation of an enterprise system is a top-down management exercise. Firms that spend $15 million to $250 million on software alone—in addition to system integration, documentation, training, and change management—will want the organization to use that system to make money for the company. In company environments where users are accustomed to taking or leaving a new computer application, depending on their preferences, introduction of an enterprise system is a shocking change. Only the most senior executives on both the line and staff sides of the organization have the authority and power to make the enterprise system decision and then enforce it. While many CEOs have tried to duck responsibility, organizations with successful systems have stand-up CEOs who actively led the implementation.

Contrary to popular belief, the second most important executive to the implementation is the COO, who represents the user community that will work with the system to make money for the company. The COO is directly responsible for fully preparing the users to use the new enterprise system. Full preparation includes a lot more than training on the new bells and whistles of the technology. Preparation includes altering all work processes that touch the system to ensure alignment and changing the roles and responsibilities of users. In those cases where only selected modules of an enterprise system are implemented, like financial or human resources modules, the top organizational executive responsible for the target functional area (e.g., the CFO or the CHRO) most take on those duties just discussed for the COO.

The third key executive role is played by the CIO, the usual owner of the information technology resource for the firm, who must ensure a successful technical implementation of the enterprise system. The CIO is many times called on to be the day-to-day leader of the executive team during the implementation. The savvy CIO leads by pointing out when and where the CEO can throw his or her weight to support the system and by working with the COO to ensure that user preparation is proceeding as needed.

Every top executive will have a Red Zone role. That is, they should each have an important and visible piece of the Red Zone action in addition to their day job, their usual duties in the day-to-day running of the company.

Red Zone Duties of the Chief Executive Officer (CEO):

- *Chief advocate to the company.* The CEO ensures that the company fully understands the reason for moving to the new enterprise system, the organizational implications of that move, and the need to get on with it.
- *Chief customer advocate.* The CEO ensures that customer goals wind up at the top of the list for the implementation.
- *Chief advocate to the board and to investors.* The CEO's goal should be to keep the Board of Directors informed, involved, and supportive of the enterprise system implementation, especially when the inevitable obstacles show up.
- *Chief communications officer.* The CEO explains the new organizational strategy represented by the implementation of the new system to the firm. For many companies, moving to an enterprise system is a major shift in how the company will do business.
- *Owner of the program management office.* This office will work day to day to support both the COO in user preparation and the CIO in technical implementation. The CEO, working through the program manager, must ensure that the implementation moves forward around, under, and through the day-to-day business changes during the implementation.
- *Master program manager.* The CEO is the major provider of resources, internal obstacle remover, and ultimate budget and time clock keeper.

Red Zone Duties of the Chief Operating Officer (COO):

- *Chief user preparation officer.* The COO is responsible for getting users ready to use the new system just as technical implementation is complete.
- *Day-to-day change leader.* The COO works with the CEO and the program manager to understand what changes in work processes,

plant/equipment, and tools will be necessary to move to the new system and leads needed process changes and plant alterations.

- *Chief performance officer.* The COO and direct reports will be the folks on the spot for organizational performance during implementation and after the new system goes live.
- *Day-to-day owner of the customer scorecard.* The COO owns those parts of the organization that must be altered to produce the desired customer scorecard.
- *Chief performance improvement officer.* The COO's job is to ensure that long-term performance improvement comes from the enterprise system's new connectivity.
- *Leader of day-to-day executive teamwork.* The COO provides leadership as the executive team focuses on internal issues associated with the implementation (the CEO works external as well as internal issues).

Red Zone Duties of the Chief Information Officer (CIO):

- *Chief technology officer.* The CIO ensures proper completion of the technical implementation of the enterprise system and ensures that technical risks associated with the system implementation are managed and mitigated.
- *Chief information technology strategist.* The CIO ensures that the company's technology strategy accommodates the new enterprise system and, after implementation, works directly with the COO to ensure that performance gains from organizationwide use of the new system are realized, consolidated, and technically supported.
- *Information technology resource provider.* Works directly with program management and the COO to ensure that information technology resources are available for user preparation (e.g., providing user training on the enterprise system).
- *Leader in metrics.* The CIO works directly with the CEO and CFO to put in place the metrics and scorecards for measuring results of the system implementation.

Red Zone Duties of the Chief Sales Officer (CSO):

- *Customer advocate.* The CSO is responsible for key customer interaction and market impact, and focuses on customer relationships during implementation. Also, the CSO owns the customer scorecard that shows how system implementation will add value for customers.

- *Marketplace information resource.* The CSO keeps the CEO and the executive team in sync with the marketplace during and after the implementation.
- *Chief communicator to customers.* The CSO explains how the system will produce value for them.
- *Chief communicator to the firm.* The CSO keeps the organization informed about the system implementation's potential impacts on customers.

Red Zone Duties of the Chief Financial Officer (CFO):

- *Leader in metrics.* The CFO measures the results of the system implementation, making adjustments to the balanced scorecard as necessary.
- *Resource manager.* The CFO assists the CEO with the resourcing of funds to implement the system.
- *Challenger of assumptions.* Devil's advocate for investment in the system.
- *Compensation and incentive designer.* The CFO works with the CEO and the human resources officer to ensure that monetary incentives are in place to motivate key organization members to implement the system in the short run and raise performance levels in the long run.

Red Zone Duties of the Chief Human Resources Officer (CHRO):

- *Staffing leader.* The CHRO identifies and finds the personnel to run the business while the company's best players work on system implementation and user preparation.
- *Chief people advocate.* The CHRO monitors stress and strain on the organization and recommends support to people as needed.
- *Performance management leader.* The CHRO aligns employee performance management systems with the enterprise system work processes as well as with changes in incentive compensation criteria.
- *Compensation leader.* The CHRO works with the CEO and CFO to put in place monetary incentives to motivate organization members to implement the system in the short run and raise organizational performance levels in the long run.

- *Line management support provider.* The CHRO provides trained human resources generalists to assist line management in fully using the new enterprise system.

Not only is implementing an enterprise system the place for strong individual leaders with authority, it is the place for top-notch executive teamwork. While the tendency in many organizations has been to look at system implementation as solely the CIO's game, the executive team must be absolutely together on this one. Team building sessions with top management may be required, beginning with the sharing of due diligence information about the results of similar implementations in other companies and extending into the clear assignment of Red Zone roles.

This Red Zone maneuver is typically vendor intense. The implementing company will probably have extensive contacts with the system vendor; the systems integrator; and various training, documentation, and change management firms. The selection of the vendors and their ongoing management is therefore a critical part of implementation. My experience is that the best vendor management comes from giving that responsibility to the program manager, who in turn works directly for the CEO, thereby ensuring the single point of management responsibility needed to direct vendors and resolve the inevitable conflicts between them.

Red Zone Principle Three: Focus on the Customer

Never is the customer more likely to be forgotten than during the implementation of an enterprise system. While the ability to deal better with customer transactions is usually one of the strongest reasons to move to an enterprise system, the implementation battle in the trenches is sometimes so difficult and intense that it is easy to forget the customer.

We believe that the implementing company must complete a customer scorecard (like the one shown in Chapter 4) as a part of the design sequence. The customer scorecard should show those attributes of the company's products and services that the new enterprise system will impact positively. Attributes like time to place an order, availability of information about orders, and number of contacts needed to get order status information are likely to be impacted immediately if the implementation is successful.

Using a customer panel can ensure that the customer gets in two cents's worth. Additionally, the customer panel becomes a ceremonial feature that keeps customer value as the implementation's focus. After all, if the new system doesn't help the company serve the customer better, is it really worth all the implementation trouble?

Red Zone Principle Four: Set Clear Red Zone Goals

Three categories of goals are needed to effectively guide an enterprise system implementation: technical implementation goals, user preparation goals, and business results goals. Goals for the technical implementation are well understood by both information technology departments and the systems integrators who frequently are hired to assist. Those goals usually revolve around implementation timetables and budgets for the various modules of the enterprise systems. Budgetary goals are critical for enterprise systems because the price frequently runs into the tens or even hundreds of millions of dollars. These technical goals are key to the effectiveness of the detailed program and project management that will be discussed in principle seven.

Setting goals for the preparation of system users is also critically important. Frequently overlooked, the user community must be prepared to use the new system when it is technically ready. The easiest and most effective goals here are to set time schedules for each user community or department. Obviously, senior management must coordinate technical and user preparation goals to synchronize the implementation: technical systems should be released for use just as users are certified ready to use them. In addition, senior management should set budgetary goals for user preparation. Guidelines range from as little as 10 percent of the technical cost of the enterprise system to 30 percent, numbers that can easily run into millions of dollars.

Management must go beyond the typical enterprise implementation goal of being on time and on budget to goals that describe what the enterprise system will do for the company. I have seen two different kinds of results goals set for enterprise systems implementation. The first kind focuses on the amount of dollars to be saved. I have found that kind of goal to be hard to measure and easy to fudge. I prefer to add a second kind of result goal that focuses on some tangible measures of company performance with overall dollar impacts. For instance, in Chapter 4's third principle, I gave a customer scorecard example that contained three attributes that could become implementation goals: time to place an order, availability of information about orders, and number of contacts needed to get order and status information. An enterprise implementation that meets goals in these three categories will surely provide long-term value to the company.

The three kinds of goals—technical, user preparation, and results—must be coordinated to ensure good guidance for the implementation's management. Obviously, we do not want to meet one set of goals at the expense of the others, and we clearly do not want to forget that the real goal of the implementation of the enterprise system is to have a positive bottom line impact on the company.

Red Zone Principle Five: Blueprint for Success

The goal of the blueprint step in Red Zone system implementation is to build a compelling picture of the organization as it will use the new enterprise system to do the work of the company both differently and, hopefully, better than work is done now. The better and more complete the picture of how the organization will work after the Red Zone maneuver, the better the firm's chances of a successful implementation with full goal achievement.

The blueprint should clearly and precisely show the organization acting in several ways that are especially important for this Red Zone maneuver.

- *Using an industry standard enterprise system instead of the custom or proprietary system the organization may have been using before.* The organization must understand that the new software will not be customized to meet the company's every need. The point must be made clearly that the enterprise system may or may not be better than the company's current system for each particular situation. The move to the enterprise system is about getting connectivity between different parts of the organization and moving to a standard solution that will not call for in-house customization or applications development.

- *Using the enterprise system to serve customers.* The blueprint follows the customer scorecard and guides the setting of results goals.
- *Using the new system as an integral part of routine performance of work.*
- *Employees use the system to transact employee business.* This element applies if the enterprise solution has a human resources module.
- *Employees work together across the organization (connectivity).* Employees both handle transactions and solve problems together for overall performance improvement.
- *Handling changes to the enterprise system.* The system will be upgraded through new releases, rather than needing in-house customization.

Completion of the blueprint is the final step in Red Zone design that links customer-scorecard to Red Zone goals with the description of how the organization must look and operate after the implementation of an enterprise system.

Don't Move! Don't go to Red Zone execution principles until a clear picture exists of the improved business designs.

- Clear understanding of how the Red Zone system implementation will positively impact the customers.
- Clear goals for the maneuver in implementation targets and end results.
- Completed blueprint for the organization after the maneuver, describing how it will use the implemented system to do better business.

RED ZONE PRINCIPLES FOR EXECUTION OF AN ENTERPRISE SYSTEM

The Red Zone execution principles for enterprise system implementation are especially critical because the Red Zone goals and blueprint are likely to represent a comprehensive and challenging change to the organization. A lot of leadership horsepower will be needed in this execution phase.

Red Zone Principle Six: Focus on Mechanics

The goal of this step is to identify those mechanical parts of the organization that must be altered to bring the blueprint to life. Once again, those mechanicals are:

- Work processes
- The plant, equipment, and tools needed to support those work processes
- The performance systems that help focus employee behavior on those processes and tools

For an enterprise system implementation, identifying and altering the mechanicals can be a major and difficult operation. The difficulty will to a large degree depend on how similar the organization's current work processes are to those work processes incorporated into the ERP system. In all the cases that I have seen, however, a significant number of mechanical changes in work processes is necessary for any enterprise system implementation.

- *Work processes.* The detailed steps the organization takes to do what it is designed to do. For an enterprise system implementation, the primary process task is to alter existing work processes to align with those processes baked into the enterprise system. For example, an implementing company might have a purchasing process that requires staff workers to take specific data collection steps before initiating an automated purchase order within their existing system. Implementing a new enterprise system might require different data collection steps before purchase order initiation. Those different steps and the way the purchase order is generated in the new system constitute a change in work process that needs to be thought through, tested, written into procedures, and placed into the training program that will be used with the procurement staffers.
- *Plant/equipment/tools.* Those concrete items that the firm's employees use to support work processes. In this case, the primary item is the enterprise system itself. For an enterprise system implementation, other information systems are often implemented

in parallel, thereby complicating the overall environment. For example, customer relationship management systems are frequently implemented alongside the enterprise system.

- *Performance systems.* The organization's collection of roles, goals, training programs, and incentive structures will need to reflect altered work processes. Full implementation will require all workers who touch the new system to change some aspects of their roles and be trained in using the altered procedures and the new enterprise system.

Red Zone Principle Seven: Use Program and Project Management to Build to Print

The job of the program manager, the right-hand person to the CEO, should focus on getting two things done at once. Program management works to ensure that the enterprise system, and any other technical systems accompanying it, is technically implemented on target, on time, and on budget. Program management also must work to ensure that the users are thoroughly prepared, ready to put the new system into play just as it is ready. Accomplishing both tasks in parallel not only involves a great deal of planning and day-to-day supervision, but working across many organization lines with technical and user communities who have different missions and priorities.

The projects that make up the enterprise implementation program are best organized around the technical systems and user organizations to be impacted. (Figure 8.1). Some crossfunctional membership is useful in the project organizations. For example, the technical project team focused on configuring and implementing the enterprise system should include some users to ensure the presence of their perspective. The user preparation projects are designed to get work processes aligned with the technical system and to alter user roles and responsibilities and provide work process training. User preparation cannot go forward successfully without intense communication and coordination with the personnel who are at work on the technical projects.

Once the enterprise system has gone live, program management must shift its emphasis to exploiting the new system for company advantage. The projects that make up the enterprise exploitation program are best organized around organizationwide work processes that

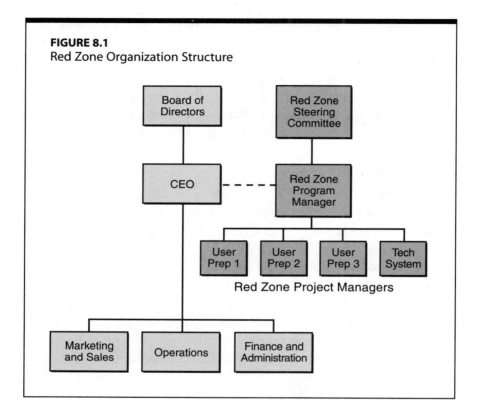

FIGURE 8.1
Red Zone Organization Structure

serve internal and external customers. Crossfunctional membership is a requirement for project teams to find better ways for the organization to work together by using the new system.

Program management should stay active until top management is satisfied the implementation has achieved the results goals. At this point, program management can be discontinued until the next hurdle for the enterprise system. That next hurdle will be implementing the subsequent releases of the enterprise software that company management decides will be of value. In other words, the software vendor who designed and built the enterprise system will always be improving the system to provide greater functionality and trying to sell those new releases to its current customers. In practical terms, some program management functions barely complete one cycle of system implementation and exploitation before top management decides to implement the next release. Implementing a new release may or may not be another Red Zone, depending on the amount of process change involved. Buyer beware.

Red Zone Principle Eight: Focus on Speed

Because the goal of enterprise system implementation is to allow the company to operate in a more connected way, the sooner the system is implemented and exploited the better. Time frames frequently run 12 to 24 months for the system selection and technical implementation. That means that at the end of that time, the company has a system that works technically. If the user community has been successfully readied in parallel, the company will have a new system up and running with "rookie" users. Depending on the enterprise system, some benefits should be available immediately. However, to gain long-term value will take another six months to two years of hard work as users cooperate to find ways to exploit the system for customer and company value.

The CEO has a big job as he or she holds the time clock on this Red Zone maneuver. Many organizations are so fatigued by the implementation itself, they tend to back away from exploiting the systems once the go-live point has been reached. The CEO's job is to keep the organization at work to figure out ways to exploit the system to get the second wave benefits.

Red Zone Principle Nine: Meet Special Needs of Workers

The special needs of workers who are a part of a Red Zone ERP implementation are rooted in the fact that they are frequently sprinting a marathon. Implementing an ERP system takes intensive effort for a long time and workers wear out. Important considerations for workers during this Red Zone include:

- Making sure that workers on Red Zone project teams have someone covering for them in their regular jobs.
- Ensuring that project personnel have job protection (i.e., employees will have acceptable choices about the kind of work they do. In many cases, personnel on the implementation project team become so familiar with the new enterprise system that they are kept on system duty, not given the chance to return to their regular jobs.)

- Taking special care of workers might go hand in hand with taking special care of the organization in this Red Zone. Turnover can be a problem with this Red Zone maneuver as workers leave to exploit their new enterprise skill sets and market value.

Red Zone Principle Ten:
Reward for Red Zone Performance

Incentives for this Red Zone maneuver must be based on the goals set for the maneuver. Care must be taken not only to incent the accomplishment of short-term technical and user preparation goals but to put important incentives behind long-term results goals.

Top management must use good judgement in sizing the incentives and in detailing the criteria that will be judged for reward. The incentives must be large enough to get the attention of Red Zone players, but not so large that those players will kill anything or anybody to get to the dollars. The criteria for awarding incentives must be several in number and to some degree conflicting. For example, the criteria for a reward to the technical project manager should include not only the implementation schedule and budget but the adequacy of the manager's cooperation with the user preparation project manager. Failure to add user preparation criteria could result in effort directed solely at the technical go-live at the expense of the rest of the enterprise program.

APPLYING THE GAMEPLAN

Getting an enterprise system running in an organization is a tough technical challenge. Getting the users prepared when it is ready is sometimes an even tougher challenge. The principles in this gameplan will save months and millions if properly applied.

CHAPTER 9

Red Zone Gameplan for Implementing e-Business Solutions

The newest of the Red Zone maneuvers is implementing e-business solutions in an existing company. Such implementations, adding the "clicks" of e-business to the "bricks and mortar" of the established company, seem to offer great potential, but they come with the potential for big losses. New e-business solutions can further a company's supply chain effectiveness, its way of dealing with customers, or its transactional relationships with employees, but they can also upset established business partnerships with customers, suppliers, and employees. This chapter will begin with a high-level primer on the subject of e-business solution implementation and will end with a discussion of the Red Zone principles as they apply to this situation.

THE PRIMER ON E-BUSINESS IMPLEMENTATION

A Definition of e-Business Implementation

For our purposes, we are limiting our discussion of e-business implementations to those companies adding clicks to their bricks or implementing an e-business solution to replace or supplement an existing business system. Rather than looking at Webcentric firms such as amazon.com, eBay, and E*Trade who opened for business on day one over the Internet, we're focusing our Red Zone coverage on firms that are or want to become *Web enhanced*. Web-enhanced firms are for the most part traditional companies, such as Federal Express, Office Depot, and Hewlett-Packard, that are making significant investments in the Internet to strengthen existing business. Target goals for Web-enhanced companies include:

- Improving distribution channels for products, services, and information
- Enhancing existing business processes
- Improving linkages with suppliers
- Enhancing customer relationship management (CRM) strategies

E-business may involve multiple interactions with multiple constituencies:

- *Business-to-customer (B2C).* B2C encompasses interactions between the customer and the business such as sharing product information, creating virtual display space, developing products, ordering products, and providing customer service. For instance, gateway.com and dell.com provide product specs and allow customers to configure their PCs online, while ford.com and gm.com provide information on their products and dealerships.
- *Business-to-business (B2B).* B2B includes a host of upstream and downstream transactions, which enhance channel coordination and customer/supplier/partner relationships and enable the design, buying and selling, and distribution of products and services. For instance, jcpenney.com shares packing, shipping, inventory, and product movement with suppliers, and phillips66.com shares product movement trends and forecasts with pipeline partners.

Companies in every industry are seeking new ways to interact with customers and suppliers, reach new markets, communicate, share knowledge, and ultimately create value. Thanks to the Internet, organizations have the capability and opportunity to fulfill these goals, and the challenge of doing so when speed and intensity of change and competition are increasing exponentially. Successful e-businesses are developing a deep, real-time understanding of both internal processes and the external dynamics of the marketplace on a monthly, weekly—even daily—basis. What a payoff! And what a price. As we'll discuss, transitioning to e-business can alter the very core of how companies manage growth and plan the future, and it calls for Red Zone principles.

How e-Business Enhances Traditional Business

For many old economy companies, e-business solutions offer striking opportunities for cutting costs and saving time in transaction processes. Many firms get started in e-business by focusing on customer self-service and e-procurement. Implemented and operated successfully, these two areas provide relatively fast payoffs and paybacks. Key resources become available quickly, and energy from initial success can fuel the next steps in the strategy.

Southwest Airlines is a great example of online pricing and transactions in the B2C space. Southwest uses its <www.iflyusa.com> Web site for online ticketing, as well as investor information, advertising, sales, promotions, and PR materials. The company's look-to-book ratio is twice that of rival American Airlines's Travelocity site, and higher than any other retailer on the Internet. Online sales accounted for 30 percent of sales in August 2000. By the end of third quarter 2000, its Web site had generated over $1 billion in passenger revenues, according to *Flight International*. Additionally, because customers are looking up scheduling and fare information as well as booking and purchasing tickets themselves, Southwest's call center, where per-transaction costs run higher, has less call load.

In the B2B space, W.W. Grainger is an example of an enterprise that was supposed to be Internet roadkill, according to *Fortune's* Big Business Online Report Card in the November 8, 1999 issue. To place orders for maintenance-repair-operations items, customers had to use a 7-pound, 4,000-page catalog listing 70,000 products. This $5 billion distributor of power tools, motors, light bulbs, and machine maintenance and repair supplies (and much, much more) could have been bypassed by manufacturers and suppliers of the equipment it sells. Instead, orders on the company's Web site were $140 million in 1999, more than any of its competitors or suppliers. The bad news is that most customers still haven't switched to the e-purchasing option. The good news is that those customers who do order online are pleased with their experience and are spending 20 percent more annually than they did before. They can search quickly through even more products than the print catalog

(220,000 items) and get up-to-date information on prices (discounted for certain customers) and availability. Also, to no one's surprise, the company reports a noticeable upsurge in orders after store closing times across time zones.

In addition to online transaction processing, firms might consider investing in e-business solutions that leverage an existing competitive asset.

- *Leverage a firm's product line.* Like cassette tapes and CDs did for audio, the Internet offers the opportunity to repackage existing products in a new format. This can enhance productivity and profitability. Bertelsmann AG, the $16 billion global media giant, has begun storing new books (and much of its 20,000 volume backlist) published by its Random House unit as digital files, which can be printed quickly and easily on demand or down-loaded to e-books, if the concept ever catches on. With digitized content, including artwork and promotional material, Bertels-mann can market books online in perpetuity, principally through barnesandnoble.com of which it owns a 40 percent stake. Because it also owns printers, warehouses, and the biggest book club in the United States and Europe, the firm can make money all along the publishing chain. "Our strategy is to integrate the Internet into all of our core businesses," says CEO Thomas Middelhoff in a January 27, 2000 article in *New Media Age,* "Don't Write Off Ber-telsmann Just Yet."
- *Leverage a firm's logistical system.* Direct catalog companies such as Lands' End, L.L. Bean, and Sharper Image have been early adopt-ers of Web-based commerce models, using the Internet as an ad-ditional sales channel. Lands' End sells more clothing online that any other retailer, $136 million in 1999, about 10 percent of total revenue and twice its online sales in 1998.
- *Enhance channel coordination and relationships.* J.C. Penney shares packing, shipping, inventory, and product movement with suppliers.
- *Strengthen the value chain.* Manufacturers can use the Web to pro-mote channel partners. Godiva provides an extensive locator ser-vice so visitors can download detailed maps of the retailer nearest them.
- *Strengthen partner and supplier communication.* The Internet extends partner/supplier linkages by enabling firms to provide detailed

information on products, services, and projects. Boeing maintains a site for suppliers and partners with a continuing stream of technical specs, which in turn enables suppliers to turn around orders/actions that meet Boeing's most current technical needs.

- *Optimize communication to key markets.* Pharmaceutical manufacturers like Johnson & Johnson provide online information to consumers and researchers about diseases, prescriptions, and treatments.

- *Fully integrate the marketing communication mix.* Megamall developer and operator Simon Properties uses its Web site to serve multiple constituencies. It provides specific information sections for investors, analysts, and journalists as well as general information about the company, its good works, and links to mall locations.

- *Extend service excellence.* Nordstrom's is famous for its above-and-beyond, employee-empowered customer service. The company has extended this strategy into the e-marketplace with an online version of its popular personal shopping program. Via e-mail, Nordstrom's Personal Touch America customers can communicate their personal preferences for style, fabrics, sizes, and colors as well as gift needs. Nordstrom's will recommend gift selections and have them wrapped and delivered on the designated day.

- *Technical support for products.* Software companies and electronic manufacturers have been quick to embrace the Internet's potential for online tech support. Consumers usually look to the product developer or manufacturer, rather than the retailer, to provide technical support. Microsoft and Sony Electronics are just two firms that have developed extensive online support resources. Apple's popular site gets over 1.5 million visitors a day. In addition to assisting customers with specific needs, these sites have the potential to enrich the relationship, providing valuable downstream feedback previously only received by manufacturers's resellers.

There's No Business Like e-Business

The speed, scope, and reach of the Internet is influencing business relationships in profound ways. The opportunities for firms are vast: to refine, or redefine, who they are, what value they offer, and to whom.

E-business challenges today's managers to develop a thorough under-standing of the multifaceted impact of the Internet and Internet-based technology. The issues go beyond technology and dive deeply into organizational structure and culture.

Many old economy businesses have come late to the e-party. When traditional businesses rushed to dip a toe into e-business waters, Silicon Valley pundits often scoffed at their early efforts, and well-published B-school profs claimed these folks just didn't get it. In truth, many didn't. But not for the reasons you might think. It wasn't the e-ness of it at all.

Many of these businesses had no business launching any e-aspect without first examining exactly how it would support their larger busi-ness goals and strategy, and how it would complement existing pro-cesses and channels. If the planning for these efforts was poor, the implementations were even worse. Knee-jerk reactions resulted in a va-riety of launched-too-early, launches-postponed, and if-you-launch-it-they-will come/care/spend missteps. Why else would savvy retailers like J.C. Penney, Target, and Wal-Mart proclaim Web store doors open with only a small percentage of merchandise available? Why else would a well-established brand like Levi's so irritate its retail channels by for-bidding them from selling Levi products on their online sites, only to later shut down its own e-business site and refer site visitors back to Levi outlets and still-steamed trading partners?

In a September 2000 article, "Get There from Here," Chris Newton, an analyst with AMR Research, told *Manufacturing Systems,* "The whole move [toward e-business] is still in its infancy. Nonetheless, whether a company is a Fortune 100 company, or a smaller company, its executives are under pressure to move into the e-business arena, and they also be-lieve their competitors are further along than they are. As a result, there is a growing hysteria about, and pressure for, e-business capabili-ties." He continues, "Many of these executives, however, have no idea how to transition their companies. They may know where they want to go, but they don't know how to get there."

Being slow to go *e* has turned out to many firms's advantage, saving them from having to repair damaged brands and reputations. Established firms are now getting it and going to the Web. On the surface, they have a significant advantage: recognized brand names, existing customer bases, strong links with suppliers, facilities to support fulfillment and distribution, and employees who know the products. But the fact remains that most traditional enterprises have some level of cultural inertia to overcome before they can take advantage of the e-opportunity.

E-business also poses other challenges. For instance, established firms may be able to spend less on marketing thanks to brand strength and customer base. But, for e-business purposes, their information about customers may well be inadequate. A major retailer may know to the nth degree what sells and in what quantities. But fine-tuned inventory doesn't equate to in-depth knowledge of individual customers or their preferences. The Web is ideal for collecting and exploiting such individual buying data. To derive any benefits from e-business implementation, most firms need some degree of organizational retuning before they open an e-door to suppliers, partners, and customers.

Why Implementing an e-Business Solution Is a Red Zone Condition

To start with, e-business is hard and risky. GartnerGroup analysts, discussing their ten-year roadmap for e-business, predict, "a bumpy ride for both traditional brick and mortar organizations and the newer dot-com enterprises." At the group's Symposium ITxpo '99 conference, covered in the November 30, 1999 issue of *Australian Banking & Finance*, analysts warned that, "While technologically aggressive businesses face failure from immature technology, an unready market, and poor e-business strategies, more conservative organizations that seek to avoid all risk by ignoring the 'Net-age' completely are also doomed to failure." That certainly drives the point home.

Alexander Drobik, GartnerGroup vice president of e-business transformation, emphasized that, "Such failures will not be because transformation to *e* is wrong, but because the business model, strategies, and implementation will have failed." Drobik shared his e-timeline:

- The early part of the 21st century will bring a high level of disillusionment.
- By 2004, we will see a steady "slope of enlightenment" as the true e-businesses begin to emerge.
- By 2006, many businesses will have made the transition, most likely to a brick-and-click mix, and the distinction of clicks from bricks will cease to exist.

"At this point [2004–2006]," Drobik said, "e-business will be completely embedded into an organization's business process." He pointed out the importance of sound business practices combined with a vision that cuts between the hype, the reality, and the practicality.

E-business is also expensive—and risky. The capital investment threshold can be daunting. Initial expenditure on hardware and software depends on existing infrastructure, but none is small. After that point, Forrester Research has found that average annual operating costs for a large transactional Web site exceed $2 million (hardware, software, people, and administrative costs associated with processing electronic payments). Access to the technical and design skills to implement the Web site is difficult in today's market, not to mention the crossfunctional project management expertise required to design, prepare, and launch the solution.

No primer on implementing e-business solutions would be complete without a couple of real examples of companies that succeeded or stubbed their toes in the Red Zone. These examples hopefully make the point that fooling around with e-business solutions can have a big impact on a company's marketplace and is serious Red Zone business.

Compaq Computer: When Even Giants Stumble

As we'll see, the issue of cannibalizing sales gets complicated when a company doesn't own the distribution channel its e-business might cannibalize. The Compaq-Dell rivalry is well documented. Former Compaq CEO Eckhard Pfeiffer seemed to have an extremely well-developed obsession with staying ahead of Dell—at any cost. Under Pfeiffer's leadership, Compaq successfully reinvented itself to get into the low-end PC market, competing with companies like Dell and Gateway. Within six years, its sales increased from $3 billion to $25 billion as the company emerged as the world's top-ranked desktop computer maker.

For years, Wall Street has gushed over Dell's direct-to-consumer business model for selling PCs. On the other hand, Compaq depended on a network of resellers for about 75 percent of its sales, a more complicated model to maneuver. In line with the times, in November 1998 Compaq announced it was aggressively expanding its own e-business direct sales program, Direct Plus. Probably looked like a great move on paper. To no one's surprise, its reseller network went into revolt. Customers could bypass them to buy from the Compaq Web site for 8 to 9 percent less than what resellers charged. *Fortune* published an excellent review of the events in the September 6, 1999 article, "Internet Defense Strategy: Cannibalize Yourself: Call It Survival by Suicide." Steven Harper, a small reseller and chairman of Compaq's Small and Medium Business Advisory Council, said "When they first showed it to us, we just hated it." Compaq's move "basically set our price," Harper said. "It forced us to play this little cat-and-mouse game: 'I wonder if my customer knows the price on the Web.'"

Compaq's new Prosignia line would be available online, and the product's ad campaign gave little mention that it could still be purchased from a reseller. Ted Warner, a $12 million per year reseller, was angry enough that he started steering customers toward Hewlett-Packard hardware. Others followed suit. Over the next few months, Compaq's sales in the crucial small and midsize business segment waned noticeably. While Compaq blamed the slippage on industry problems, analysts perceived another linkage: Compaq was losing the hearts and minds of its resellers.

Compaq vice president Michael Pocock held a series of meetings to listen to the resellers. In heated discussions, resellers expressed their concern that Compaq was obsessed with Dell, especially to the detriment of its relationships with the network that gave the company its leadership position in PC sales. Compaq faced an unmistakable dilemma: stay the course and risk collapse of a channel, or backslide through some unpleasant circumstances of its own making.

Compaq chose to compromise, improving the health of neither channel. It suspended the right of some third-party Web sites to sell Compaq products. It also introduced new programs to help resellers set up their own online storefronts and pocket an agent fee for steering business through Direct Plus. (Remember that some PC makers at this time were offering $500 to $800 computers, and margins on PCs were thinner than wiring on chips.) In his spin, Pfeiffer called the approach "customer choice," hoping to reaffirm the company's role as "the number one channel-friendly vendor in the industry."

In April 1999, Pfeiffer announced that first quarter profits would be less than half of what Wall Street had forecast. The announcement sent Compaq's stock downward by 22 percent, the biggest drop in eight years. After a week of tumbling stock prices, Compaq announced Pfeiffer's resignation, effectively immediately.

Analysts agreed that falling computer prices, increased pressure from Dell, and friction between Compaq and its resellers were to blame for the company's recent rash of poor financial news. "When Compaq needed its resellers to come through at the end of this quarter [first quarter, 1999], they weren't there, and Compaq suffered," said Aaron Goldstein, vice president and principal analyst at Ziff-Davis, in an April 19, 1999 *Dallas Morning News* article, "Top Two Officers at Compaq Computer Step Down." Goldstein continued, "They alienated their resellers and must now work hard to repair those connections. But the bottom line in this is that Compaq will continue to be a top player in the industry, and I think they will become a stronger company because of this."

There was no shortage of armchair quarterbacking. In a September 6, 1999 *Fortune* article on Internet defense strategies, Lester Thurow, professor of management and economics at MIT offered his take. "I think you've just got to bite the bullet and take six months of low sales. It is the valley of death. For at least one year, you report a disaster . . . But it's obviously clear that Dell's doing it right. I don't think there's any other choice." Harvard Business School's Clayton Christensen added, "It's easy for academics and journalists to trivialize how difficult this is," he says. Nonetheless, "the evidence is just overwhelming that companies that try to manage the health of their distribution channel won't end up on top. If the channel is going to be disrupted, that's a force more powerful than any company." Now that's a Red Zone message if we ever heard one.

For 1999, Compaq continued to be the number one PC vendor worldwide, with a near 14 percent market share, followed by Dell. However, in the United States, Dell outsold Compaq for the entire year, and many analysts said they expected Dell's dominance to continue.

RED ZONE MORAL TO THE STORY:

Adding an *e* to the business is a critically important move, which can have a major negative impact if not aligned and complementary to existing business strategy. E-capability is an important new weapon, but a weapon that can be used to shoot oneself in the foot if it's not strategically aimed.

The e-Business That Ate a Business: Its Own

Charles Schwab is America's biggest online retail brokerage. Until 1996, the company operated largely as a discount telephone broker with some branch offices. While still an upstart by old-line brokerage standards, Schwab launched an online trading operation, being among the first traditional brokerage firms to start an e-business. To promote the new business and attract customers, eSchwab charged lower commissions, $29.95 a trade, while Schwab's traditional customers were paying an average of $65 a trade. The two-tiered pricing system was awkward, irritating brokers and existing customers alike. Some customers were keeping a small account with Charles Schwab to maintain access to live brokers, then executing trades through eSchwab. The fear, uncertainty, and doubt factor reigned in branch offices.

David Pottruck, co-CEO (with Charles Schwab) and *force majeure* for the online business, had met his moment of truth as a leader. He made a radical leadership decision: online would be the line. To bolster its online trading system, Schwab added a research and guidance service under a new flat-fee payment plan. Under the plan, all Schwab customers would have access to all brokerage services—telephone, branch and online—for $29.95 a month for up to 1,000 shares and 3 cents per share thereafter. The move was designed to help Schwab tighten its hold in the online trading market and to lure more customers away from Merrill Lynch, Prudential Securities, and other full-service brokerages. The move also helped resolve customer service issues by eliminating two-tier pricing for trading services.

The organization went through many unpleasant moments while resolving problems of sales cannibalization and channel conflict. Branch employees were apprehensive about the decision. As covered in the September 6, 1999 *Fortune* article, "Internet Defense Strategy: Cannibalize Yourself: Call It Survival by Suicide," Pottruck says, "All of them thought they would have no more business and were going to lose their jobs. It attacked our old business."

Board members were apprehensive as well. At the same level of business, slashing commissions would take an estimated $125 million off revenues, and Schwab stock would surely take a major hit without an immediate and significant inflow of new, active customers. Folks, you can't get much more Red Zone than this. Reflecting back on that time and his decision, Pottruck now says, "I can't tell you honestly that I didn't lose a lot of sleep about it. I thought, 'Maybe all we're going to do is give away revenue, profit, and share price'."

To prepare employees for the transition, Pottruck staged a "crossing the chasm" ceremony in which he walked across the Golden Gate Bridge with 100 or so of Schwab's top managers in tow. Symbolically, this gesture represented leaving behind one business model and embracing a new, Internet-based model. The board was next. He said simply, "It's not going to get any easier, so we might as well move forward and take the pain." The board agreed to go, too.

In January 1998, the firm restructured itself into a single, mainly online business. So eSchwab ate Schwab. Company stock lost almost a third of its value. But, over a short time period, the strategy worked and gain triumphed over pain. In the first six months, total accounts jumped from 3 million to 6.2 million and $51 billion in new assets flowed in.

The company has become the leader among online trading companies. As reported in *Fortune's* November 8, 1999 Online Report Card for Big Business, eSchwab grabbed 42 percent of a new market. In the first quarter 2000, they led in trading volume with a 21 percent share of the average 1.4 million daily trades. eSchwab also has opened other opportunities as "a place not just to trade stocks but also to write checks, buy insurance, and pay bills electronically." The transition was painful and expensive, but Schwab has emerged with hundreds of billions in online customer assets and a capitalization that rivals Merrill Lynch's. "You can't steal second," says Pottruck, "with one foot on first."

RED ZONE MORAL TO THE STORY:

Putting together a clicks play that is closely aligned with the existing bricks play is what leverage is all about. But even with alignment and leverage, successful e-capability may bring new economics into play—new economics that will give new shape to the entire business at the price of disrupting the old order.

PRINCIPLES

Now for the Red Zone principles that apply to the management of e-business implementations. The goal in this chapter is not to duplicate the principles of Chapter 4; instead we want to show variations and distinctions on those principles for this particular Red Zone maneuver.

Red Zone Principle One:
Declare the Company in a Red Zone

Implementing e-business systems is a Red Zone for three reasons:

1. Implementation is very difficult from a technical point of view.
2. It can be very disruptive to the existing order.
3. Many business folks are still caught up in e-uphoria, the hype about *e* curing all.

Implementing e-business brings out conflicts like no other Red Zone: conflicts between brand new and tried and true, between young and old employees, and between notions of the new economy and the old. The bottom line is that top management should warn the organization that they are about to enter a Red Zone requiring their best ideas and greatest tolerance of each other. During this difficult time, strong business practices and principles, not untested assumptions about the magical qualities of e-business, must rule.

In the earlier chapter on reengineering, we mentioned that alarm bells go off for many employees when they hear the word *reengineering*. Top management's challenge with e-business is to ensure that alarm bells do go off for the organization, alarm bells that can be heard above the e-uphoric panting.

Red Zone Principle Two:
Put the Best Players in the Game

As with any Red Zone maneuver, e-business implementation requires massive amounts of direct leadership from the executives. Each and every executive has a distinctive role they must play well for the organization to enjoy the benefits of e-business solutions. We have seen several problems come up in e-business deployment that must be avoided. First, CEOs and COOs who do not have strong technosavvy cannot step aside from their leadership roles in this Red Zone maneuver. Handing over the leadership of e-business deployment to those with the technical skills may leave core business knowledge and experience out of the equation.

Second, top management should avoid the intuitive assumption that if a player has strong information technology skills, that player will also be a whiz at e-marketing, or e-customer relationship management, or e-supply chain, or e-anything that the company is implementing. Assuming that your CIO has marketing skills because he or she knows CRM applications is like assuming that your Chief Sales Officer knows information technology because he or she knows those same applications.

Red Zone Duties of the Chief Executive Officer (CEO):

- *Chief advocate to the organization.* The CEO must know in the gut that adding clicks to support the company's bricks is a good and defensible move with great promise.
- *Chief strategy officer.* The CEO ensures that both the competitive strategy and the e-strategy are clear. The CEO must be able to state clearly the strategy of the company and the role of e-business capability in furthering that strategy.
- *Chief process selector.* The CEO works with the COO to target the organization's work processes that e-business capability will enhance or complement.
- *Goal setting leader.* The CEO works with the COO to set business goals for e-deployment.
- *Chief customer advocate.* The CEO ensures that the firm's new e-capability adds value from the customers's point of view.
- *Supply and distribution designer.* The CEO works with the chief sales officer and the COO to ensure that supply chain/distribution channel architecture meets the company's strategy.
- *Chief communications officer.* Communicates the business reasons for e-deployment, the specific business goals and the continuing status of the change to the firm.
- *Master program manager.* The CEO is the major provider of resources, internal obstacle remover, and ultimate time clock keeper on the e-deployment and the business objectives associated with it.

Red Zone Duties of the Chief Operating Officer (COO):

- *Chief targeting officer.* The COO ensures that the right and best processes are targeted for e-business solutions.
- *Goal owner.* The COO owns the specific business goals of the e-business project.
- *Chief executor of the e-business blueprint.* The COO works directly with the CIO to ensure that e-business implementation and organizational preparation to use the new systems are in sync and properly done.
- *Day-to-day change leader.* The COO works with the program manager and the CIO to understand, identify, and schedule all the mechanical changes needed to meet the e-business project's objectives.

Red Zone Duties of the Chief Sales Officer (CSO):

- *Key distribution channel architect.* During planning and actual e-deployment, the CSO is responsible for ensuring that the firm's distribution channels will allow it to achieve its strategy.
- *Process selector.* The CSO works directly with the CEO and COO to target work processes for e-business.
- *Customer advocate.* The CSO's key focus is on customer and distribution channel relationships. Also, the CSO is responsible for key customer interaction, market impact, and prevention of customer loss and ensures that a customer scorecard has been completed to explicitly take into account improvement of customer value.
- *Marketplace information resource.* The CSO keeps the CEO and the executive team in sync with the marketplace (customers and distribution systems) during and after implementation.
- *Chief communicator to customers and the distribution system.* The CSO explains how e-deployment will work for them and bring them value.

Red Zone Duties of the Chief Information Officer (CIO):

- *Chief customer information officer.* The CIO comprehends the information opportunities of e-business and works with the chief sales officer to improve customer relationships and profitability.
- *Chief information technology strategist.* The CIO ensures that the company's technology strategy accommodates e-business systems and, after e-business implementation, works directly with the COO

to ensure that performance gains from organizationwide use of the e-business systems are realized, consolidated, and technically supported.

- *Chief e-business system architect.* The CIO works with the COO and CSO to ensure that the systems selected (or developed) will meet the requirements for reaching business goals.
- *Chief technology officer.* The CIO ensures proper completion of the technical implementation of the e-business systems and ensures that technical risks associated with implementation are properly managed and mitigated.
- *Information technology resource provider.* The CIO works directly with program management and the COO to make information technology resources available for user preparation (e.g., providing user training on the e-business systems).
- *Leader in metrics.* The CIO works directly with the CEO and CFO to put in place the metrics and scorecards for measuring results of the system implementation.

Red Zone Duties of the Chief Financial Officer (CFO):

- *Leader in financial due diligence.* The CFO works with the CEO to understand and document the economics of the e-business initiative, ensuring that the CEO and COO know at all times its anticipated costs and benefits. The CFO also requires that the business rationale for e-business be as tight and realistic as possible to protect against euphoria.
- *Leader in metrics.* The CFO puts in place measures of the results of the e-business initiative, making progress toward the specific business goals visible.
- *Resource manager.* The CFO assists the CEO with the resourcing needed to complete the e-business initiative.
- *Compensation and incentive designer.* The CFO works with the CEO and human resources officer to put in place monetary incentives to motivate organization members for e-business success.

Red Zone Duties of the Chief Human Resources Officer (CHRO):

- *Process selector.* The CHRO works with the COO and CIO to target processes and e-business systems that are related to employee transactions.

- *Performance management leader.* The CHRO works with the COO to align employee performance management systems with work processes impacted by e-business deployment as well as changes in incentive compensation criteria.
- *Organizational development leader.* The CHRO works directly with the COO to ensure that the deployment issues that impact employees are identified and worked through.
- *Training and development leader.* The CHRO identifies the competencies needed to use e-business systems and provides the training employees will need to develop those competencies.
- *Chief of outplacement.* The CHRO assists the COO in dealing with the performance issues of workers who are unwilling and/or unable to align with the e-business systems.

The entire executive team must supply leadership during this Red Zone maneuver, staying watchful of divided teamwork and being careful not to underbudget needed manpower. In short, the right horses must be in this race from a technical point of view, and care should be taken not to allow polarization between the techies and the nontechies.

Red Zone Principle Three: Focus on the Customer

Let's face it, the e-business play is more about CRM and supply chain than anything else, and for success we need clear scorecards, like the one shown in Chapter 4, for both customers and suppliers/distribution channels. Adding e-business capability will probably touch customers in a totally different way and the company will understand their specific needs and buying habits better than ever. But problems can arise if the company is not clear on its CRM strategy and exactly what it wants to gain from e-deployment. Customers are still kings, and any e-business deployment must explicitly take them into account. Failure to identify a CRM strategy up front in planning will result in a default CRM strategy you may not want.

We often overestimate what our competitors are doing in new technology, including e-business systems. In times of e-uphoria, we may tend to believe the hype and assume the worst about the competitive landscape. An organization must invest time and energy to determine where the competitors really are and where they are going.

Disruption of distribution channels and the cannibalism of sales is a continuing threat in e-business deployment. Treating resellers like customers and completing a customer scorecard for them will allow e-business architects to better understand the potential reaction and/or disruption of channels.

Red Zone Principle Four: Set Clear Red Zone Goals

New economy goals are not substitutes for old economy ones. Goals for managing an e-deployment must be the familiar ones of speed, cost, value to customer, and satisfaction—not number of mouse clicks. The purpose of an e-deployment is to solve a real-world business problem, to add clicks to bricks, strengthening the company's existing work processes and assets. The initiative must have clear business goals. E-applications are not new business processes; they are parallel, redundant processes or substitutes for existing ones.

The goals for e-deployment are akin to those for reengineering: work process goals and business result goals. Work process goals guide the implementation toward faster, better, and cheaper work, while business result goals anchor the implementation to market share, profitability, and return. Goals for customer value and efficiency in distribution channels are also critical. Just remember that every time an organization changes the way it talks to a customer, it impacts and potentially disrupts distribution channels, because those channels carry relationship dimensions as well as products/services.

Work process goals can be set aggressively: reduce the time it takes to place an order with a supplier by 90 percent, or increase the speed by which the customer can contact the company about a problem by 100 percent. Result goals, on the other hand, should be set like other business goals, at feasible but challenging levels. In a mature industry filled with established companies, major changes in business results are unlikely, even with highly touted e-solutions.

Red Zone Principle Five: Blueprint for Success

This blueprint step generates a picture of the organization as it will operate with e-enabled processes in place. The first and most important step is to develop the e-business strategy. Methodologies for this vital step are beginning to emerge. While the words vary a great deal across methodologies, the ideas are essentially the same and include steps like those below, taken from our firm's approach for e-Maturity Assessment and e+Strategy selection.

- Assessment of the company's overall business strategy as the foundation for e-strategy development
- Assessment of the company's business products/services/processes to identify leverage points for exploitation with e-business solutions
- Assessment of the company's current capability for hosting e-business solutions (including IT technology strategy)
- Assessment of the business environment with special emphasis on e-business: competitors's direction, trends, and capabilities, and customers/suppliers's direction, trends, and capabilities
- Exploration of what is possible today and tomorrow with e-business solutions
- Development of e-strategy options/scenarios that could add value to the client company in both the short and long term (including quantified business plans)
- Presentation and discussion of options with key business and technical personnel to identify the desired e-strategy.

After developing an e-strategy, management must aggressively lead the process to select the e-applications to fulfill the strategy. Blueprinting goes further to picture the whole organization, not just the new systems. The finished blueprint must show a complete picture or people will get the impression that their work world will turn totally to clicks. Employees must be able to see and understand the completed organization with its e-business systems up and running, in parallel or substituted for existing systems processes. The blueprint must also show how people will be working, including changes in culture, attitudes, mindset, etc. Standard ingredients of the blueprint should be the same as listed in Chapter 4: organization chart, goals/measures, process flows, system architecture, and vignettes of how people will need to perform.

Don't Move! Don't stop the Red Zone design engine, the sequence of design steps, and go to the execution principles until a clear picture exists of the organization as it will operate after the clicks have been added to the bricks. Before execution begins, top management must be clear on:

- How e-business solutions will enhance both customer value and supply chain value/integrity.
- How the organization's major work processes and e-business systems will work together to meet performance improvement goals.

RED ZONE PRINCIPLES FOR IMPLEMENTATION OF E-BUSINESS

The Red Zone execution principles for implementing e-business solutions are critical. Coming up with the systems design and finding the vendors with the right technology pales in comparison to the job of implementing the needed organizational changes. Strong leadership will be needed to resist the urge to slam in the e-business solution without thoroughly integrating that solution into the day-to-day operations of the company.

Red Zone Principle Six: Focus on Mechanics and Plan for Complete Operations Integration

Successful execution of the Red Zone maneuver properly begins with the identification of the necessary mechanical moves. Execution will succeed only after the new e-solutions have been fully integrated into the day-to-day operations of the company. The mechanicals we work on for any Red Zone stay the same. Once again, those mechanicals are:

- Work processes
- The plant, equipment, and tools needed to support those work processes
- The performance systems that focus employee behavior on the new, redesigned work processes

Once again, the bottom line is the same: work processes and information technology tools have to match to the letter for maximum performance and minimum confusion.

We have found the term *operations integration* to be particularly helpful in communicating about both enterprise and e-business solutions. The term seems to be meaningful to technical personnel, who are involved in the technical implementation and the systems integration that goes along with it. We use Figure 9.1 to show the importance of operations integration in bringing value to the organization.

The following actions must be taken to complete operations integration of the e-business solution:

- Clearly communicated vision of the e-solution at work
- Direct communication of expectation/requirement for use of the e-solution
- Work processes altered and aligned to match the e-business solution
- Work processes documented and worker instructions placed in company policies and work procedures

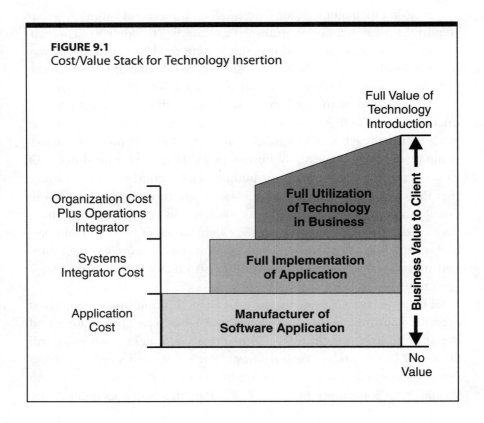

FIGURE 9.1
Cost/Value Stack for Technology Insertion

- Roles of workers modified to align with work processes and e-solutions
- Users/workers trained on work processes incorporating the e-solution
- Performance management system in place to reward desired performance and to penalize failure to use the e-solution

In most companies, operations integration is a significant effort that takes careful management and attention to detail. When coupled with the complexities of e-solution technical implementation and systems integration, disciplined program and project management clearly are required.

Red Zone Principle Seven: Use Program and Project Management to Build to Print

Program management for e-business solutions is very similar to that required for implementing enterprise solutions (Chapter 8). The program manager's primary duty is to implement the blueprint just the way it has been drawn, or at least as close as humanly possible, despite the inevitable conflicts on the technical and user sides of the equation.

The program manager should focus on getting two things done at once: technical integration and operations integration. The first task ensures that the e-business solution, and any other technical systems accompanying it, is successfully implemented from a technical point of view on target, on time, and on budget. The second task is to ensure that the users of the new e-business system are thoroughly prepared to put the new system into full use as soon as it is ready. Accomplishing both tasks in parallel not only involves a great deal of planning and day-to-day supervision but working across organization lines with technical and user communities, who have different missions, priorities, and— sometimes—different levels of e-uphoria.

The projects that make up the e-business solution program are best organized around technical systems (the e-business application) and the affected user organizations. Some crossfunctional membership will be useful in the project organizations. For example, technical project teams focused on configuring and implementing the e-business system should have some user personnel assisting their work to include the user perspective. User preparation projects, key parts of operations integration, are designed to alter and align user work processes with the technical system and to alter user roles and responsibilities and to provide work process training. User preparation cannot go forward successfully without intense communication and coordination with the technical personnel.

The primary goal of the program manager is to ensure that the e-business solution is fully implemented and fully utilized for the good of the company. Full implementation is tough; full utilization will call on a great deal of skill and hard work as the program manager works directly with the CEO and COO to ensure complete operations integration.

Once the e-business system has gone live, program management must shift its emphasis to exploiting it for company advantage. The projects that make up the exploitation program are best organized around organizationwide work processes that serve internal and external customers. Crossfunctional membership is a necessity for project teams designed to find better ways for the organization to work together.

Program management should stay active until top management is satisfied the e-business implementation has achieved the results goals. At this point, program management can be discontinued, until the next hurdle for the e-business system is encountered, such as implementing the next software release from the e-business vendor. In practical terms, some program management functions barely complete one cycle of system implementation and exploitation before top management decides to implement the next purchased release or module. Implementing a new release may or may not be another Red Zone, depending on the amount of process change required to align with the system.

Red Zone Principle Eight: Focus on Speed

Just as with the other Red Zone maneuvers, the idea is to move into fully utilized e-business solutions as fast as possible. However, I have watched several firms with a different kind of speed issue in this Red Zone maneuver. While most Red Zone maneuvers tend to go on too long, with e-business the tendency seems to be to go too fast. The excess speed clearly comes from top management who wants results quickly, sometimes too quickly. Pushing too hard has resulted in two kinds of problems: moving into e-business implementation before the strategy is clear, and slamming technical solutions into the organization. The word *slamming* means to implement a technical solution with little or no effort given to operations integration.

Moving before the strategy is clear usually results in bad business results or, if the company is lucky, a canceled project. Slamming usually results in intense organizational confusion, worker frustration, and a far longer delay in utilization of the system than would have been required to do operations integration up front, in parallel with technical implementation. As with any other Red Zone maneuver, think 12 to 18 months from start to full utilization of an e-business solution.

Red Zone Principle Nine: Meet Special Needs of Workers

While most of the special needs that we have described for other Red Zone maneuvers apply to implementing e-business solutions, two stand out. First, workers will have a very high need for information about the impact that moving to e-business solutions will have on them and their jobs. Unless the workforce is already heavily experienced in the information technology world, confusion will reign, and rumors about job impacts will run rampant. Given the hype that e-business solutions have on the street, conducting a robust communication effort during the entire Red Zone maneuver will be especially critical. The goals should be to ensure that people know what is going on with the project, why e-business solutions will be useful, and how the organization's, and therefore their, future will unfold in the e-world.

The second special concern with the e-business Red Zone has to do with worker skills. While skill level is a critical factor in any Red Zone maneuver, it is especially critical in this one. If the workforce is low on technical skills, the move to e-business solutions will be a tough one. We heard of one manager who got a real sense for how tough an implementation was going to be when she saw workers looking at a mouse for the first time and then rolling it on the computer screen.

Effective, efficient, timely training ensures that people will perform as needed in their e-business job. Top management must face the fact that some workers just may not be able to make the needed transition to the e-world. Those workers must be dealt with fairly and honestly, finding them a place in the company where they can be valuable employees.

Red Zone Principle Ten:
Reward for Red Zone Performance

Rewards and incentives work for this maneuver just like they do for all the others. Putting those incentives in the right place is critical here, however. Focusing reward dollars on nebulous and short-sighted goals like "getting our company into the e-world quickly" will result in quick, sexy Web sites and slammed-in solutions. Rewards must tie closely to the process and result goals discussed earlier in this chapter under Red Zone principle four. Strange as it may seem, best results during an e-business implementation come from rewarding achieved business results, not implemented e-technology.

Yes, we do want to provide incentives for completion of the technical e-business solution on target, on time, and on budget, but not at the expense of the organization's preparation and integration. Incentives need to be tied to multiple goals, including both process and business goals, and paid over one to two years after the e-business maneuver is essentially complete. Avoid paying incentives for the accomplishment of process goals without corresponding achievement of business results. And avoid paying incentives for either accomplishment if other parts of the organization have been trampled just to get to the e-business targets.

APPLYING THE GAMEPLAN

Implementing e-business solutions is the rage, technology sellers are going great guns, and the hype is in sixth gear. Top management's job is to plot a safe and sane journey through this newest of the Red Zone maneuvers. Strong leadership focused on getting results, good heads in the blueprinting process, and aggressive program management can put an organization on the leading edge, without going overboard to the bleeding edge.

CHAPTER 10

Red Zone Gameplan for Changing Culture

In this chapter, we will discuss one of the most difficult and least understood of the Red Zone maneuvers. While people talk a great deal about changing an organization's culture, few agree on how to do it. Suffice it to say that many managers talk about the desirability of changing culture but few are willing to bite the bullet and go after a full-fledged culture change. One manager even said that changing a culture is like moving a graveyard; you can't count on much help from the residents. This chapter will begin with a high-level primer on the subject of culture change and will end with a discussion of the Red Zone principles as they apply to this fuzzy situation.

THE PRIMER ON CULTURE CHANGE

A Definition of Culture Change

Everybody has at least one loved one who's historically hard to buy gifts for. My wife is one of those people. When birthdays and anniversaries roll around, I'm often roaming the aisles at local department and jewelry stores. The salesperson inevitably asks, "What are you looking for today?" At that moment, it's just not something I can easily put into words. So I respond, "I can't explain it exactly, but I'll know it when I see it." Organizational culture is not unlike that, hard to describe but important none the less.

In a 1998 article on "The Integration Challenge" in *Management Review,* Tom Davenport defines culture as, "the DNA of an organization, invisible to the naked eye, but critical in shaping the character of the workplace. It controls the form and function of what the organization ends up being." In an observation that appeared in "Irreconcilable Differences" in the April 1999 issue of *HR Magazine,* Mitchell Lee Marks, author of *Joining Forces: Making One Plus One Equal Three in Mergers, Acquisitions, and Alliances,* suggests that on a very practical level culture is, "a lot like breathing. You don't think about it, you just do it. But, if I covered your mouth with my hand, you'd be thinking about breathing."

"Official" cultures in most organizations evolve from a set of principles developed and promulgated by the founders and passed on by subsequent leaders. These principles acquire shades of meaning over time as the firm meets challenges and launches major projects, a sort of corporate genealogy replete with personalities and folklore. Organizations have unwritten rules for how employees, without any direction, should act under varying conditions. These unwritten rules are based on and reinforced by acts, thoughts, and perceptions and passed among rank-and-file workers over time. When employees behave in conformance with the rules and customs, they are accepted by the organization. When they don't, they receive some form of social sanction ranging from direct feedback to a lower (or no) raise or bonus, lack of promotion, or termination.

Our firm's very simple working definition of culture over the years has been "how we do things around here." Culture is the day-to-day way employees approach the work of the company and deal with each other. Culture is the result of how the organization has reinforced behavior in the past and the predictable path of action for the foreseeable future.

How Does Culture Impact Organizational Performance?

As we've discussed, dozens of different and equally valid definitions of culture exist. Let's simply say that culture is an organizing concept encompassing how work is done and how people are selected, developed, managed, led, and rewarded. To support the organization's goals and strategies, culture too must align with structure, work processes, and human resource systems.

Culture does indeed directly impact the bottom line, according to some scholars. In their book *Corporate Culture and Performance,* John Kotter and James Heskett suggest that companies whose cultures align with organization direction and work processes have a significantly better chance of growing their revenues and even their stock prices. That sounds like enough promise to put many managers into the mood to try the Red Zone culture change maneuver.

David Pottruck, co-CEO of Charles Schwab & Co., credits Schwab's corporate culture as the single most important factor in the firm's transition to an e-brokerage powerhouse. According to a review of *Clicks and Mortar: Passion Driven Growth in an Internet Driven World* that appeared in the July-August 2000 issue of *Financial Services Marketing,* Pottruck and coauthor Terry Pearce describe Schwab as "a company built around a fine, ethical chairman whose main mission is helping people reach their financial goals." Supporting the leader is a cadre of committed executives who truly believe and act with the same fundamental sense of mission and zeal. Further, to ensure those values aren't diluted as they're transmitted down the line, a mechanism makes sure every message is on target with the company's fundamental values. The executives and their messages must be 100 percent in sync 100 percent of the time.

Six Sigma, Culture Change, and Organizational Performance

Six Sigma, the zero-defect or near-perfection concept developed by Motorola, produces a corporate cultural shift toward highest quality expectation and total customer focus that permeates the organization. The concept grew out of various quality initiatives at Motorola, sparked by competition from abroad. A consultant for Motorola University explains its significance in a November 2000 article, "It's Not Difficult to Change Company Culture," in *Supervision.* "If a company were to have the attitude 'Why bother?', I would ask them what they would do if they woke up tomorrow morning and their number one competitor announced they had improved efficiency ten times, improved quality ten times, and are committed to delivering a better product with better service in half the time—all at the same price? Sound familiar? It happened to Motorola, General Motors, and others in the 1970s, courtesy of Japan."

A decision to introduce Six Sigma is a decision to alter an organization's culture and requires more than an investment of dollars. Craig Erwin, quality engineering manager at Motorola Semiconductor Products, notes in the *Supervision* article that, "Achieving Six Sigma takes some vision. You have to have a plan, necessary resources, the commitment of everyone, and uncompromising matrices [to identify improvement rates]. Then you set aggressive goals along the path and hold people accountable." That's Red Zone talk.

Some companies have tried to use Six Sigma as a cultural change tool, with mixed success. Noel Tichy, author of *The Leadership Engine: How Winning Companies Build Leaders at Every Level,* explains in a June 8, 1998 *Computerworld* article on "GE's Quality Gamble" that at GE, legendary CEO Jack Welch changed the culture first. "He cleaned up his portfolio, got the business focused, got good players in place, did Work Out [a companywide initiative to eliminate bureaucratic obstacles and encourage best practices], changed all the management processes, then came along with Six Sigma on top of that."

Much has been written about GE's Six Sigma success. Welch and his team launched their initiative in late 1995. The results for GE companywide have been stunning—a gross annual savings of up to $6.6 billion or 5.5 percent of sales. One of the first companies to adopt Six Sigma was GE Plastics. CEO Gary Rogers highlighted their journey in his October 2000 article," GE Plastics Adopts a New Profit Center," in *Modern Plastics,* pointing out the depth of change it brings. "When you live Six Sigma as we have since 1996, it's hard to remember when it wasn't part of our company DNA. Back then, we didn't know where the initiative would lead, but it was clear that this was going to be the most challenging and important initiative in the history of our company."

Rogers credits Six Sigma for his company's industry-leading success in e-business. "We used Six Sigma to revamp customers systems at [distributor] GE Polymerland, and the drive for on-time delivery has given us the fulfillment capability needed in a transparent e-world. Six Sigma has truly become the way we work. It has also opened a wealth of new opportunities. We are now well over $20 million per week in Internet orders—and none of our new services such as Vendor Managed Inventory, Colorxpress, and Visualfx would have been possible without it."

M&As, Culture Change, and Organizational Performance

Nowhere is culture more evident than during and after mergers and acquisitions (M&As). According to a Hewitt Associates survey of major U.S. organizations, integrating culture was the top challenge for 69 percent of the 218 surveyed companies. In a 1992 then Coopers & Lybrand study of 100 companies with failed or troubled mergers, 85 percent of executives indicated that differences in management style and practices were the major problem. Tom Davenport explains in the April 1999 issue of *HR Magazine,* "There are two ways to screw up a merger. One is to pay too much; the other is to integrate so slowly or badly that you destroy value, rather than creating it. And misapprehending culture is the number one culprit in screwing up integration."

When organizations start to mesh workplace cultures, productivity in the acquired company can drop as much as 50 percent. Even if the merger or acquisition ends up being a success, the new joint organization can take from three months to three years to recover from the culture shock. In the meantime, the clock is ticking—the marketplace still demands products and services to certain standards, and the market is measuring the new entity's potential for success.

- Price Club, whose employees have been described as having a "real estate, strip mall mentality," merged with Costco Wholesale, whose employees have been described as "committed lifers" because so many had risen through the ranks. Although both firms were discount retailers, they couldn't work together, and the merger was dissolved in less than a year.
- The 1993 merger between Mellon Bank and money management wizard Boston Co. looked great on paper. Offended by Mellon's cost-centered management style, a key executive of Boston Co. left and over the next three months took 30 of his coworkers along with $3.5 billion in assets and many of the firm's clients.

Drivers for Changing Corporate Culture

In his latest book, *The Corporate Culture Survival Guide,* Edgar Schein points out that, "As companies age, if they do not evolve, adapt, and change elements of their culture, they grow increasingly maladapted and the culture becomes a serious constraint on learning and change. The organization clings to whatever made it a success. The very culture that created the success makes it difficult for members of the organization to perceive changes in the environment that require new responses. Culture becomes a constraint on strategy."

One example of this paralysis is Digital Equipment Corp. (DEC). From an early point in its history, DEC had a demonstrable cultural bias against marketing and a noted arrogance toward end users of its products. During the glory days of mainframe computing, these attitudes may not have had great impact on its competitiveness. But they surely hurt the company when businesses began switching to PCs and client-server systems, and DEC failed to read the market, adapt, and respond.

The key areas to address to bring about effective culture change follow the Red Zone litany from our other chapters:

- Mobilization of leadership to take ownership of the change
- Creation of roles and work processes that align with the strategic and structural changes
- Development of human resources strategies to support the culture change, including performance management processes as well as training and development support. A sound set of reward plans (tangible and intangible) must support the business goals and strategy, roles and responsibilities in business processes, and the culture change.

Schein says, "There is no right or wrong culture, no better or worse culture, except in relationship to what the organization is trying to do and what the environment in which it is operating allows." It is better to build on existing strengths than to focus only on weak elements. Schein concludes, "Never start with the idea of changing culture. Always start with the issues the organization faces. Only when those business issues are clear should you ask yourself whether the culture aids or hinders resolving those issues."

I can't emphasize enough the importance of using an organizationally significant business problem or opportunity as the driver for culture change. Organizational significance means that:

- Leadership is in complete agreement about the dire consequences of not fixing the problem or the immense value of seizing the opportunity
- The problem or opportunity can be translated clearly and made viscerally relevant to employees
- Multiple business processes are involved
- Multiple layers of people are directly impacted

How Organizations Approach Culture Change

As both Lenin and Mao are credited with saying about the challenges in implementing their respective "cultural revolutions," one often takes two steps forward and one step backward—or even worse, one step forward and two back. Implementing initiatives to change organizational culture are often no different, as we'll see in the following examples. For the most part, the organizations and culture changes covered are massive in scope, like works in progress. We've selected these cases to illustrate different points along a relative success continuum.

CSX: Getting Back on Track

Business culture in rail transport is more than a century old and, as in other industries from that era, is based on a command and control management structure. Concerned, and rightfully so, about safety, senior management at CSX imposed rules and regulations they thought would improve performance. They did so without a great deal of input from front line employees. Line employees who reported unsafe conditions said they were either ignored or harassed. To no one's surprise, fewer and fewer reports were made. Over time, the disconnect between labor and management increased, both in communication and in results. Accidents and injuries rose. Pressure from labor unions and federal regulators grew. In 1997, a scathing audit from the Federal Railroad Administration (FRA) found numerous track and signal defects, overworked employees, and a management culture that emphasized on-time performance over safety.

Clearly, major change was in order. At the beginning of 1997, CSX officials took the extraordinary step of entrusting their safety and employee-discipline programs to their 28,000 rank-and-file workers. Given the rail industry's sometimes violent labor history, this approach represented an extraordinary switch. Management would partner with two of its biggest adversaries, the Brotherhood of Locomotive Engineers and the United Transportation Union, which represented about half of CSX's workforce. To incorporate the regulatory perspective, CSX hired Jim Schultz, a former senior official with the Federal Railroad Administration (FRA), as chief safety officer and charged him with implementing the changes.

The program contained two fundamental changes in approach to safety and decision making, which were designed to eliminate intimidation and to encourage more frequent and accurate reporting of unsafe conditions and incidents so that root cause analyses could be done.

- Employees would now select their own safety committee at each terminal hub, rather than having it selected by management.
- The new disciplinary process would be the responsibility of employees. With the empowerment program, employees with safety infractions sit down in neutral territory and discuss the events with peer groups. If no serious injuries have occurred, they most likely return to work unpunished. Only the most serious violations warrant a formal hearing. When the new program was kicked off, previous discipline was forgiven, and employees started with a clean slate.

An article in the April 7, 1999 edition of *The Wall Street Journal*, "CSX Unit Breaks Tradition to Overhaul Safety Rules," describes the highs and lows of the implementation. To sell the program to employees, CSX enlisted Curtis Wall, a train conductor and local leader for the United Transportation Union, to be a full-time labor liaison, probably the first job of its kind in the firm's history. CSX introduced its culture change initiative at company headquarters and at its Montgomery, Alabama, terminal. "I've never seen anything like this in my 20 years," said Robert Cobb, a train conductor and union leader for 250 employees at the Montgomery facility. The empowerment program was then applied throughout Florida and the Southeast. During 1999, it was piloted in the Midwest and Northeast service lanes. CSX was proceeding full speed ahead in employee empowerment, while other rail carriers moved more cautiously. "The language being used by CSX and other railroads is similar, but the difference is CSX is applying it," said James Brunkenhoe-fer, national legislative director for the United Transportation Union.

When the program went into effect in 1998, reported accidents and injuries increased for several months. These results were likely related to employees's willingness to test the program by reporting incidents. What was actually good news about initial program participation unset-tled executives who were eager to demonstrate progress on safety to both regulators and shareholders. Despite these somewhat discourag-ing results, CSX executives stood firm and resisted the temptation to drop the new program.

Perseverance paid off. After the initial increase, results started to look more encouraging. Despite continued skepticism based on decades of mistrust, local union leaders seemed to warm to their broader respon-sibilities. (A large portion of line employees started in the 1960s and harbored institutional memories of poor management and labor rela-tions.) Wall commented, "This hasn't been an easy sell, but we have to make people believers. Our credibility is on the line." There were some early victories. The March 1999 employee injury rate was the lowest for any March in the decade, and train accidents were down 20 percent compared to 1998. Also, suspensions and dismissals were down com-pared to 1998.

Executives were now challenged with balancing an increasing num-ber of requests for safety improvements with bottom line profits. Indus-try watchers reserved judgment on the change effort, citing lack of substance and failure of other short-lived joint labor-management ini-tiatives. Still, regulators were encouraging. FRA administrator Jolene Molitoris credits CSX leaders for their commitment to change, even though accident and injury rates climbed initially and internal resist-ance was high. "I don't think there is any railroad that has done more than CSX at tackling this culture change," she said.

To facilitate continuous improvement in labor-management rela-tions, Carpenter's executive team and chief labor negotiator Ken Peifer constructed a "social compact" with employees including biweekly con-ference calls between national and state labor leaders and CSXT offi-cers. As related in "Hear Their Rising Voices," in the January 2000 issue of *Railway Age,* "We talk of the state of our railroad and the railroad in-dustry in open terms," said Peifer, crediting regular and open dialogue as the reason for frequent unanimous agreement on matters of fatigue and quality of life issues—matters of fierce contention at other carriers.

"The objective is flexibility in new business opportunities," said Peifer, which translates to increased profits, more secure union jobs, and more dues-paying union members. "By solving each other's problems, we're moving in the direction we all want to go."

With the groundbreaking labor-management agreement in 1998, Carpenter had laid a good foundation for culture change. In July 1999, Carpenter became vice chairman of CSX Corp., and Ronald Conway replaced him as CEO of CSXT. One of several Conrail senior managers who joined CSXT following the Conrail acquisition, Conway had earned high marks from customers and Wall Street as Conrail's operations chief. Upon his appointment, Wall Street hailed Conway's new role as an answer to improving CSX's performance record. As part of his performance improvement program, Conway initiated LAM (Local Area Management), a decentralized, regional structure he had developed at Conrail, placing accountability for asset utilization and customer service at the regional level. Pushing management decisions down the chain of command had improved Conrail's car cycle times by 20 percent and saved Conrail around $100 million over two years in increased productivity and reduced rolling-stock expenditure. What Conway promised *not* to upset was the emerging culture of trust handcrafted by Carpenter and Schultz. Substituting compassionate coaching and peer leadership for punishment "paid big benefits in the Conrail integration," said Conway in a September 1999 *Railway Age* article, "Can Ron Conway Rebuild CSXT to Customer Specs?" He added, "It's the right thing to do. It has differentiated us from other railroads."

We could have a happy ending if we stopped the story here. But time and troubles marched on. In March 2000, the FRA released a safety audit of CSX's track conditions (like the one in 1997 that sparked the new safety initiatives). The new audit found deteriorating track conditions, especially track widening, which had contributed to recent minor derailments. According to an April 28, 2000 *Business Journal* article, "CEO Vows Turnaround for Troubled CSX," John Snow, CEO of CSX Corp., responded that the company "has repaired or is in the process of repairing all of the defects identified in the report" and that he will personally head an internal company review of all track maintenance and improvement programs to make sure these efforts are fully effective.

In April 2000, Snow removed Ronald Conway as president of CSX and said that he was taking personal control of the company's rail unit—a unit Snow had headed from 1985 to 1989 before becoming president and CEO of the parent company. Continued service and safety problems arising from the Conrail breakup and integration, coupled with falling stock prices, proved a deadly career combination for Conway.

Snow commented in an April 11, 2000 article, "CSX President Fired over Service, Safety, Money Problems," in the *Philadelphia Inquirer* that "An awful lot of what he [Conway] brought to CSX will continue." Snow added that he would visit all major points on the 23,400-mile, 23-state rail network, launching a period of hands-on management, that would have CSX well on the road to recovery by July 1. "For the time being," Snow said, "the CSX headquarters will be on an airplane. Three months from now, you are going to see a fundamentally different railroad. You're going to see increased velocity and the number of cars on line go down. You're going to see a bias in favor of action on our problems. We're going to get back to the fundamentals, back to Railroading 101."

A few updates, in chronological order, at press time:

- Share price was gradually increasing, with third quarter results improved if not spectacular.
- James Schultz, the CSX chief of safety and culture change, announced his resignation, ending a three-year term with the railroad. He left to take a similar, yet "lucrative" position with Houston-based Waste Management, Inc. Citing his value to the carrier in a November 9, 2000 article in the *Florida Times-Union,* "Chief of Safety Leaves CSX Transportation," Michael Ward, CSXT executive vice president for operations, said, "The course that Jim Schultz has set for us over the last three years to change the culture of our company has had a profound effect on our labor management relationships and has become a model for other companies to follow."
- Within days of making that comment, Snow, in a November 29, 2000 company press release, named Ward president of CSXT, crediting Ward with the company's recent improvement, "Since moving to operations in April, Michael and his team have turned things around dramatically. Today we are delivering a much higher, much more consistent level of service to our customers. The railroad is now running fluidly and reliably, and our 35,000 employees are pulling together to increase efficiency in all areas to grow our business."

THE RED ZONE MORAL TO THE STORY:

Two steps forward, one step backward. You may not be able to change a century of culture in a year or two, but you can make dents that begin to genuinely reshape it. If you believe in the program, stay the course.

OSRAM Sylvania: A Light at the End of the Culture Change Tunnel

OSRAM Sylvania, based in Massachusetts, is a $1.8 billion manufacturer and marketer of general lighting products, automotive light sources and assemblies, and specialty materials, chemicals, and electronic components. The firm employs about 13,000 people and operates 22 factories in North America. For more than 30 years, Sylvania had adopted work practices and cultural norms from its telecommunications parent, GTE. In 1993, Sylvania was purchased by OSRAM, a Siemens company. Most of the company was reorganized along functional lines, reflecting the structure of its new German parent—with a traditional management-by-objective performance management program; job-based hierarchies from function to function; and a compensation process based on narrow grades, salary ranges, and control points. These practices targeted annual business plans and ensured equity throughout the workforce but placed little emphasis on defining, identifying, and rewarding individual performance excellence.

Siemens AG, as well known in Europe as GE is in the United States, is daunting in the size and diversity of companies within the organization, from medical engineering to design of public communication networks and high-speed microprocessors. According to an October 14, 1997 article, "Time for an Image Change," published in *Computing Canada,* almost 70 percent of the company's products are based on technologies that are less than five years old. Dr. Heinrich von Pierer, president and CEO, recognized that Siemens itself would need to boost earnings and reshape the organization's corporate culture. In the 1996 annual report, he discussed profound changes and challenges to Siemens's business, including technology changes, changes in purchasing processes as a result of deregulation, and the demand for customized solutions. He wrote, "We, too, must change to meet these challenges." But sheer size and diversity of the organization make the size of the challenges proportionately bigger. Still, positive changes can happen at local levels.

Within the OSRAM organization, a variety of subcultures developed, shaped in large part by the management styles of several strong leaders and the relationship between business units and their biggest customers. For instance, the culture at the automotive lighting division had been influenced by Ford and Chrysler, where the emphasis was on systematic quality assurance and fast response to problems. On the other hand, the precision materials group had been strongly influenced by the operations orientation of prior leaders, who had emphasized business unit latitude combined with strict accountability for results.

During this transition to implement Siemens management practices, a new vice president of human resources was named. Geoff Hunt had been a successful general manager of the company's 1,200-employee glass manufacturing division. Hunt thought that work culture was a potential tool to help drive or at least track changes in the attitudes and behaviors of the workforce.

He approached the culture change project from his operations perspective. Recognizing the varying and potentially conflicting cultural crosscurrents, Hunt started the project by looking for ways to define the company's current and desired work cultures within the framework of a changing environment.

- Globalization of automotive lighting
- Consolidation in the retail customer base for consumer lighting products
- Continuing development of new light sources. Hunt and his fellow executive management team members understood that the highly proceduralized work culture, which had worked well in stable times, would not compete effectively in times of rapid, significant change.

The Executive Committee and senior management, using The Hay Group's Targeted Cultural Modeling™ process, agreed in general on cultural priorities. They identified seven key behaviors that would be more rewarded, encouraged, and supported to move toward the desired work culture, and six behaviors that should not be rewarded or encouraged.

Key Behaviors to Be Encouraged and Rewarded

1. Increasing decision-making speed
2. Delivering reliably on commitments to customers
3. Providing employees with resources to satisfy customers
4. Being flexible and adaptive in thinking and approach
5. Continuously improving operations
6. Significantly decreasing cycle times
7. Encouraging teamwork

Key Behaviors to Be Discouraged and Disincented

1. Respecting the chain of command
2. Promoting one's point of view strongly
3. Limiting the downside risk strongly
4. Being highly organized
5. Using proven methods to serve existing markets
6. Supporting the decisions of one's boss

Several key initiatives were launched to support the firm's business goals and culture change objectives. The projects had good synergy and payoffs. Hunt redesigned the firm's Performance Management Process (PMP). The major objective was to move from an entitlement-based culture to a performance-based culture. Performance would be redefined as a combination of critical elements: results achieved on job objectives, behaviors shown in specific competency areas, and demonstrated technical and other skills. The competency areas were defined on both a companywide and a role-specific basis to correlate closely with process-based and time-based work cultures.

The new PMP drove the commitment of more managerial and employee time toward performance management training, midyear performance reviews, employee development planning, and action planning for poor performers. It also required salaried employees to be evaluated on the four core competencies of:

1. Commitment to continuous improvement
2. Customer service orientation
3. Change management
4. Collaboration in addition to their role-specific competencies

The general lighting business unit launched a 30-month initiative to reduce cycle times using a methodology developed by the Thomas Group, a consulting firm. The reengineering program involved process improvement projects in manufacturing, customer support, logistics, distribution, and product development.

Results from a 1997 progress measurement check-up indicated that OSRAM Sylvania had made progress in its journey toward a process culture. However, the firm had not made much progress toward a time-based culture. In response, the company put into place a number of practices based on the principle that customer problems and opportunities should be handled at the most efficient level of the company.

THE RED ZONE MORAL TO THE STORY:

The overarching Red Zone moral is a testament to the ongoing nature of culture change. Organizations do not have to be perfect every time as long as they make overall progress toward goals and directionally correct decisions in response to challenges. The change programs were developed with the intent to change work culture and address business challenges. The programs were supported by and worked by top management, and progress was measured.

PRINCIPLES

Now for the Red Zone principles that should apply to the culture change maneuver. The goal in this chapter is not to duplicate the Principles of Chapter 4; instead we want to show variations and distinctions on those principles for this particular Red Zone maneuver.

Red Zone Principle One:
Declare the Company in a Red Zone

The culture change maneuver is all about changing selected organizationwide work behaviors to better meet long-term objectives. While we want to let the company know that the culture change will be tough and time consuming with a lot of confusion, trials, and errors, the Red Zone announcement should feature the conditions that the company is trying to impact. For example, if the organization has a culture of slow delivery times with low concern for customer feelings, it might best characterize its Red Zone maneuver as a customer satisfaction or customer retention move. Top executives can describe the potential gains that can come to both the organization and the customer as well as the potential loss if the change is done poorly. Rather than focusing the declaration on the phrase *culture change,* we recommend focusing on the business condition to be corrected.

Red Zone Principle Two: Put the Best Players in the Game

"Do as I say and not as I do" clearly does not apply in culture change. If any Red Zone maneuver depends on top management modeling, it is this one. The organization looks to both top management and all well-known, respected employees for instruction and reinforcement of any targeted culture change.

Leadership for culture change starts at the top and flows down to managers throughout the organization. The entire executive team must share the same vision and commitment to change. They must agree on the desired culture change as well as on the business focal points for making that change happen. While consensus on vision is a critical first step, this alone will not drive change. Leaders's roles and behaviors must also change. Entrenched culture, and in many cases the long tenure of leaders, makes such a leadership transformation a tall order. But the organization cannot change its culture until and unless its leadership changes and models the desired behaviors.

Red Zone Duties of the Chief Executive Officer (CEO):

- *Chief advocate to the organization.* The CEO has the message, the fire in the gut, and the actions that match. The CEO who does not personify the culture change kills it.
- *Chief advocate to the board and to investors.* The CEO's goal should be to keep the Board of Directors informed, involved, and supportive, instructing them on the purpose and methods of the culture change.

- *Chief customer advocate.* The CEO ensures that the culture change adds value from the customers's point of view.
- *Chief communications officer.* The CEO communicates the business reasons for the culture change, the specific business goals that are to be reached, and the continuing status of the change to the firm.
- *Master architect.* The CEO ensures that the blueprint of the new organization will include the new, desired ways of doing business. The CEO, working directly with the COO, must select the specific business situation that will be used to define, work through, and reinforce the desired changes in how the organization works.
- *Master program manager.* The CEO must be relentless in ensuring that all of the detailed mechanical changes necessary for the culture change get identified and handled, getting made on target, on time, and on budget. In addition, the CEO is a major provider of resources, internal obstacle remover, and the ultimate time clock keeper on the culture change and the business objectives associated with it.

Red Zone Duties of the Chief Operating Officer (COO):

- *Designer.* The COO is intimately involved in the design of the culture change blueprint, owning the business operations affected by the change.
- *Chief executor of the culture change blueprint.* The COO and direct reports will be responsible for meeting business objectives and ensuring that the desired organizational behaviors are used to meet those goals.
- *Day-to-day owner of the customer scorecard.* The COO owns those parts of the new organization that touch the customer.
- *Day-to-day change leader.* The COO works with the CEO and the program manager to understand, identify, and schedule the mechanical changes needed to meet the culture change's business objectives.
- *Role model.* The COO personally models the desired behaviors of the culture change initiative.

Red Zone Duties of the Chief Sales Officer (CSO):

- *Customer advocate.* The CSO focuses on customer relationships during the culture change, being responsible for customer interaction, market impact, and prevention of customer loss. Also, the CSO works directly with the CEO and the CHRO to identify desired behavioral changes and their direct impacts on the customer scorecard.

- *Marketplace information resource.* The CSO keeps the CEO and the executive team in sync with the marketplace during and after the culture change, continuing to place market impact high on their priority list.
- *Chief communicator to customers.* The CSO explains how the culture change will serve the customer better.
- *Chief communicator to the firm.* The CSO keeps the organization informed about how the culture change is impacting customers and the marketplace and personally models desired behaviors.

Red Zone Duties of the Chief Financial Officer (CFO):

- *Leader in metrics.* The CFO measures the results of the culture change initiative, making progress on the business goals associated with the culture change visible.
- *Resource manager.* The CFO assists the CEO with the resourcing to complete the culture change initiative.
- *Compensation and incentive design.* The CFO works with the CEO and human resources officer to ensure that monetary incentives are in place to motivate organization members for culture change success.
- *Role model.* The CFO personally models the desired behaviors of the culture change initiative.

Red Zone Duties of the Chief Information Officer (CIO):

- *Leader in metrics.* The CIO works directly with the CEO and CFO to put in place the metrics and scorecards for measuring culture change results. Also, works directly with top management and IT resources to ensure real-time information is available for progress reporting.
- *Role model.* The CIO personally models the desired behaviors of the culture change initiative.

Red Zone Duties of the Chief Human Resources Officer (CHRO):

- *Organizational development leader.* The CHRO works directly with the CEO, COO, and CSO to identify both desired behaviors and current behaviors that need to be changed or eliminated to make way for the desired behaviors. Also, works directly with the COO to identify and work through all people impacts of the culture change.
- *Chief communicator to the firm.* The CHRO works with the CEO to communicate the culture change, including desired and undesired behaviors, to the organization.
- *Performance management leader.* The CHRO alters the performance management system to reward desired behaviors and disincent undesirable behaviors.
- *Training and development leader.* The CHRO identifies the competencies needed for the culture change and provides the training employees need to develop them.
- *Chief of outplacement.* The CHRO assists the COO in dealing with the performance issues of workers who are unwilling and/or unable to align with the culture change. In a culture change, one commonly finds individual workers who, for whatever reason, absolutely refuse to change behaviors. In these cases, the CHRO works to support the transfer or termination of such workers.
- *Role model.* The CHRO personally models the desired behaviors of the culture change initiative.

The executive team must be absolutely together for a successful change of culture. Not only must each individual on the executive team personally model the desired new behaviors, he or she must work to reinforce and encourage other team members in the new behaviors. An executive team with chinks in its armor makes a powerful visual case that culture change is not really the new law of the land.

Red Zone Principle Three: Focus on the Customer

The key to launching an effective culture change maneuver is to link the change to the customer. In fact, a good test of the soundness of a desired culture change is to look at the direct value it would add to the customer. The way the organization would work with the customer is a good test of the usefulness of the culture change. In short, if top management cannot look at the customer scorecard, like the one shown in Chapter 4, and see direct impacts of the culture change, then why do it?

We believe it is critical for the CSO to be in the thick of things, working with the executive team to translate any desired culture change into value dimensions for the customer. Such a move would be radically different from many culture changes in which the entire sales organization is either left out or stays above it all as the rest of the organization attempts to change behavior.

Frequent culture change targets of responsiveness, information sharing, speed, attention to detail, and Six Sigma excellence can all be directly linked to the customer scorecard. Tying desired changes to concrete customer measures goes a long way toward making the culture change and its rationale understandable and concrete enough to work on.

Red Zone Principle Four: Set Clear Red Zone Goals

This principle calls for top management to translate their culture change ideas into concrete business goals. Crisp goals that reflect the culture change in terms of the customer are preferred.

Using the sample culture change dimensions mentioned previously, Red Zone goals might be as follows:

- *Customer responsiveness.* All customers with complaints are contacted personally within 24 hours.
- *Information sharing.* Customer records have all the required information about completed customer transactions within one hour.
- *Speed.* Suggestions from customers are routed to new product development within 24 hours of receipt.

Business goals can also be set by customer segment, including market share and customer satisfaction goals that anticipate increased responsiveness, information sharing, and speed. I cannot overemphasize the need to set good, clear, customer-oriented goals as a part of any culture change maneuver. Culture change is too difficult to pull off without some translation into goals that workers can understand and relate to.

Red Zone Principle Five:
Blueprint for Success

The goal of this blueprint step is to generate a word picture of the organization with the culture change in place. The blueprint must communicate to the company around several critical dimensions:

- *Business with the customer using the desired behaviors to meet the goals set in the earlier step.* The description here should be of using desired behaviors to interact with customers, adding value to the customers and improving results for the organization. In other words, the blueprint must show desired behavior in new work processes.
- *Behavior within the company between workers using the desired behaviors.* The description here should show how day-to-day work embodies the targeted behaviors.
- *Actions of the managers of the company as they reinforce the desired behaviors.* This description shows managers rewarding and reinforcing workers for using desired behaviors to meet organizational goals and disincenting workers for using undesirable behaviors.
- *Behavior of the managers as they act out the new culture.* The description here shows top managers modeling the desired behaviors.

While all of the maneuver blueprints that I have described so far show the company as it should operate after the Red Zone, in this case developing an anti-blueprint is useful. This anti-blueprint describes how the organization should *not* operate after the Red Zone maneuver, showing all the undesirable behaviors working together to produce an undesired effect on the customer and on the organization.

Don't Move! Don't stop the Red Zone design engine and go to execution principles until a clear picture exists of the organization as it will operate after the culture change.

- How the new, organizationwide behaviors will enhance customer value.
- How the organization will reward desired behaviors and disincent undesired behaviors.

RED ZONE PRINCIPLES FOR EXECUTION OF A CULTURE CHANGE

The Red Zone execution principles for culture change are especially critical because the change will be both time consuming and frustrating to many workers. Strong leadership is required to focus on the tangible parts of the culture change to ensure that desired results are slam dunked and that the organization cannot escape the onerous task of making changes in the way they may have been doing things for years.

Red Zone Principle Six: Focus on Mechanics

Successful execution of this Red Zone maneuver properly begins with the identification of the necessary mechanical moves. The mechanical moves for culture change fall into two categories: those associated with business objectives and those focused on the company's performance management system.

The first challenge is to identify the mechanical moves needed to meet the goals set for the culture change. Carrying on with the improved customer service example I have been using, if business goals have been set for responsiveness and speed of service, work processes that impact those goals must be identified and targeted for alteration. For example, for responsiveness, the organization might target its work processes for taking and validating customer orders to allow more accuracy and reliability. Once target processes are identified, then specific mechanical adjustments can be named. Once again, those mechanicals are:

- Work processes
- The plant, equipment, and tools needed to support those work processes
- The performance systems that help focus employee behavior on achieving the business goals

The second challenge is to identify mechanical changes in the performance management system to communicate, enable, and reinforce desired behaviors with rewards. While the performance system is important for all Red Zone maneuvers, it is especially critical for culture change.

The performance management system is top management's tool for steering the organization toward desired behaviors.

Specific subprocesses in the firm's performance management system must be examined to ensure that they can support changes of work processes and behavior. The subprocesses are focused on the following:

- Identifying the specific behaviors and competencies needed in each organizational position to support altered work processes
- Recruiting and hiring workers with the needed skills and competencies for each position
- Communicating the performance expectations of the company to job incumbents (including communicating the desired and undesired work behaviors targeted in the culture change)
- Training job incumbents to develop competencies underlying desired behavior in work processes
- Providing real-time and periodic performance feedback to enable employees to focus their job behavior on expectations
- Compensating job performance, including desired behaviors, and disincenting behavior that does not match job requirements
- Coaching employees whose job performance does not meet expectations

While these changes are simple and logical, they become difficult because the performance management system is one of the most difficult processes to influence. Altering this basic organizational process means that managers will need to deal differently with employees around the subject of performance, a subject that many managers find highly difficult to deal with at all. While many managers find giving positive feedback relatively easy, they find addressing performance that does not meet job expectations difficult.

Red Zone Principle Seven: Use Program and Project Management to Build to Print

The culture change maneuver belongs to the CEO. Nobody else has the credibility, power, and authority to make a culture change happen. We have found, however, that a program manager reporting directly to the CEO can assist greatly in ensuring that all needed work for culture change gets done.

The job of program management should be focused on the mixed bag of projects that get at the business results specified in the culture change goals as well as strengthening the firm's performance management system. Our firm's experience indicates that representatives of the organizations that participate in the processes should staff each of the business projects. For example, if a business goal is to increase customer responsiveness through smoother order entry with fewer errors, the assigned project team might have folks on it from customer service, sales, and accounting.

Program management must adopt a slam dunk attitude for Red Zone culture change success. The program manager can ensure that proper time and attention is devoted to the projects that go right after the business goals. These projects must not be allowed to fail because they are the vanguard for the overall culture change.

However, the program manager cannot take the most critical step in program management. That step is up to the CEO, who must ensure that every reward cycle validly evaluates and reinforces the desired behaviors at the heart of the culture change. Only the CEO has the horsepower to ensure and insist that top management religiously reward desired behavior and disincent undesired behavior.

Red Zone Principle Eight: Focus on Speed

The frequency of reward cycles determines the speed of culture change. That is, behavior changes come about when the organization hears that some behaviors are now desirable and that others are not, followed by a reward cycle that reinforces the behavior change message. While some organization members will respond directly and quickly to the requested behavior change, other organization members will not, waiting instead to see and sometimes feel the results of a performance appraisal/salary review event. Some organization members even wait for a second cycle to be sure. I will leave the explanation of this phenomenon to behavioral scientists, settling instead for this practical rule of thumb for top managers: count on having to get two reward cycles under your belt before you see the entire organization pick up the desired culture change.

Because most companies reward performance on an annual basis, they can assume a two-year period for an organizationwide culture change. I have seen some organizations speed up the reward cycle and provide midyear incentive compensation for behavior in the desired direction, but that has been rare.

When I use the term reward cycles, I mean high-integrity reward cycles in which top management is ruthless in the way it handles the rewards, making no exceptions to rewarding desired behaviors and withholding rewards for failure to use the desired behaviors. A reward cycle that has low integrity, with employees getting positive rewards when their behavior did not meet expectations, will actually slow down the culture change. The long and short of it is that workers need to hear the desired direction and see as well as feel the consequences of their behavior.

Red Zone Principle Nine: Meet Special Needs of Workers

Clarify the culture change behaviors for all employees. Too often, culture change is talked about generally, without adequate explanation of just what it is all about. While some employees will get the message of the culture change quickly, others will just plain have difficulty understanding exactly what is expected of them. Modeling by management seems to be the single best way to get the culture change message across.

Help workers make the change to the new culture. The kind of help workers need will vary from instruction and training in new competencies to stronger measures like an occasional kick in the pants to help them come to grips with required behaviors. While most culture changes our firm has worked in did not require new competencies that were beyond the reach of workers, some companies do require changes that are. In those cases, workers who are unable to make the shift must be treated fairly but with integrity to the culture change. Keeping workers in place whose competencies do not match the culture change sends yet another signal that change is desirable but not required. Top management might stick with the guideline of being patient, firm, and flexible, but not to the point of weakening the desired behaviors that are at the heart of the culture change maneuver.

Red Zone Principle Ten: Reward Management for Red Zone Performance

Provide substantial incentives to top management for bottom line culture results over at least three years. The idea of this Red Zone maneuver is to bring about a sea change of behavior that will better meet long-term goals. Top executives must both be held accountable for and profit from such a successful change.

Additional incentives should be provided to meet the specific business goals associated with the culture change. For example, if a goal is to reduce the time to resolve customer complaints by half, managers should be rewarded when that goal is reached. These incentives should be over and above the incentives for meeting year-to-year bottom line results. Changing the organization's culture to better meet business challenges builds the long-term franchise value of the company, and top management should be rewarded for doing just that.

APPLYING THE GAMEPLAN

Culture change is not easy, but if top management focuses on business reasons for the change, sticks with their promotion of desired behaviors, and uses high-integrity reward cycles, this maneuver can work successfully.

PART THREE

MASTERING RED ZONE MANAGEMENT

A harsh reality of business life is that companies will need to go through many Red Zone maneuvers as they journey toward success. Red Zone maneuvers will not be the exception but the rule. Given that reality, today's companies will need to master Red Zone maneuvers to complete them quickly and successfully. Mastery requires the development and integration of new organizational capabilities. Part Three identifies those needed capabilities and provides leadership role models in the Red Zone hall of fame.

CHAPTER 11

Mastering Red Zone Management

Time flies in the Red Zone as time has flown while writing this book. The early chapters of this book were written during the Olympics, providing the easy metaphor of Olympic-level commitment needed for Red Zone success. I am writing the last chapter of the book while waiting for the Super Bowl to begin on a rainy January day, a day that promises some real Red Zone challenges for the two teams, in a new year that promises some big Red Zone challenges for business. As the economy tightens, as dot.coms sort themselves out, as big companies enter yet again a time of cost trimming, as industry consolidations continue . . . the new year will doubtless contain Red Zone challenges and lessons. Fortunately, you don't have to wait to learn the lessons; you've been learning them as you have gone through this book. This chapter is designed to summarize six of the most important lessons to truly master Red Zone management.

LESSON ONE: USE RED ZONE MANEUVERS TO GROW YOUR BUSINESS

The seeds of Red Zones are alive and growing in the global business economy. Ambition and expectations have never been higher. Disruptive forces continue to offer both opportunities and threats. Industrial progress is happening. Strong, visionary management continues to look for chances to take their organizations to the next level of performance. They will use Red Zone maneuvers to make the trip to that next performance level. Remember, Red Zones by definition are good things;

leaders try to make them happen to move the organization forward. Unfortunately, one cannot avoid the possibility of big losses if Red Zones aren't done right. Figure 11.1 shows Red Zones in regular play in the life of today's growing company.

Red Zones are here to stay. That fact has a very important implication that cannot be ignored. Given the constant of Red Zones, we'd better do everything we can to master them. Mastery will be a requirement for all organizations that want to keep up with competitors and offer growing returns for owners.

Mastery requires the development and refinement of some new capabilities and resources, from championship-level mindsets and expectations, to specific Red Zone tools and plays, to winning people who have what it takes for Red Zone excellence. Today's organizations will truly need to muscle up to handle Red Zone challenges. Olympic-level motivation to win along with do-or-die commitment not to lose will be required in the foreseeable business future.

LESSON TWO: DEVELOP A RED ZONE MINDSET, INCLUDING SETTING OF RED ZONE EXPECTATIONS

Developing a Red Zone excellence set of expectations is critical. We cannot continue to look at Red Zone maneuvers as scary, problematic

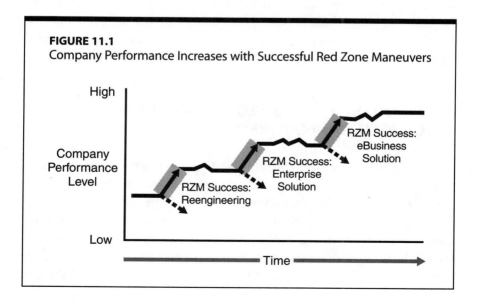

FIGURE 11.1
Company Performance Increases with Successful Red Zone Maneuvers

adventures, practically impossible to do well. We must stop being unnerved by the difficulty of Red Zone maneuvers and start focusing on their positive potential for improving performance. We must set the expectation of excellence.

I know of no better way to get the Red Zone excellence virus than to spend some time looking at the Red Zone Hall of Fame, populated by CEOs who are masters of the Red Zone. In the four vignettes that follow, you will read about courageous leaders who do not shy away from Red Zone maneuvers, but who use them to make great things happen for their companies. The names will be familiar, but read about them this time in the context of Red Zone management.

Jack Welch, General Electric, 1981–Present. General Electric (GE) is the fifth largest corporation in the United States with annual revenues exceeding $100 billion. GE's conglomeration of businesses includes the NBC television network, GE Capital Services, and numerous manufacturing operations that produce products for the medical, aerospace, consumer electronics, and energy generation industries. Jack Welch has guided GE through many Red Zone maneuvers since he became CEO of GE in 1981.

Welch has demonstrated an uncanny ability to move his company forward with Red Zone maneuvers. Shortly after being assigned his new position, he determined that a change in strategy was critical. To compete more effectively in the global marketplace, the company had to restructure and downsize its workforce. His decision to restructure the organization was scoffed at both inside and outside the company. "Peter Drucker asks a great question," Welch explained *In Lessons from the Top.* "If you weren't already in this business, would you enter it now?" Welch applied this question to all his business units and decided to keep only those that were either number 1 or 2 in their markets. Welch cut the number of employees by 45 percent and transformed the company from a producer of products to a provider of services. Ultimately, Welch's actions resulted in revenue growth from $25 billion in 1980 to $99.8 billion in 1998.

Welch also realized the need to change the company's culture, another Red Zone maneuver. He was determined to eliminate bureaucracy, improve communications, and encourage the exchange of ideas. Welch knew that a company of GE's size could operate more efficiently with an informal environment. "The winners of the '90s will be those who can develop a culture that allows them to move faster, communicate more clearly, and involve everyone in a focused effort to serve ever more demanding customers. To move toward that winning culture, we've got to create what we call a *boundaryless company*."

Welch accomplished this culture change by initiating a company-wide program to open communications. The new program, termed *Work-Out,* involved meetings where ideas and best practices were shared among departments. One of the benefits of these new communication forums was the ability to cross boundaries. Most companies of GE's size were known to operate in silos without sharing information. In reality, GE's success during the early 1990's can be attributed to Welch's successful changing of the corporate culture and the adoption of the Work-Out Program, a true Red Zone maneuver.

More recently, Welch yet again launched a culture change maneuver, his Six-Sigma initiative to improve quality. The new program called for a large investment in training tens of thousands of employees in a disciplined methodology to drive quality improvement. As covered in Business Week's June 8, 1998 article, "JACK: A Close-Up Look at How America's #1 Manager Runs GE," "Welch launched the effort in late 1995 with 200 projects and intensive training programs, moved to 3,000 projects and more training in 1996, and undertook 6,000 projects and still more training in 1997. So far, the initiative has been a stunning success, delivering far more benefits than first envisioned by Welch. In 1997, Six Sigma delivered $320 million in productivity gains and profits, more than double Welch's original goal of $150 million."

Percy Barnevik, ABB Group, 1987–1996. ABB Group is a large, multinational conglomerate that serves customers across various industrial markets. ABB operations include power transmission and distribution; automation; oil, gas, and petrochemicals; building technologies; and financial services. ABB was formed in 1987 from the merger of two European engineering companies: ASEA of Sweden and Brown, Boveri & Company of Switzerland. Percy Barnevik led the effort to combine the two companies into one global powerhouse. However, for the merger to succeed, Barnevik had to prove that he could succeed in the Red Zone by combining two diverse companies into one.

Barnevik was recognized for his ability to transform large companies into lean and efficient global competitors. Early in his career, Barnevik was appointed CEO of the U.S. subsidiary Sandvik Steel. He quickly learned the importance of being proactive and encouraging rapid change. In the March-April 1991 edition of *Harvard Business Review,* he related, "I tell my people that if we make 100 decisions and 70 turn out to be right, that's good enough. Why emphasize speed at the expense of precision? Because the costs of delay are vastly greater than the occasional mistake."

Eventually Barnevik moved on to an even greater challenge. He accepted the CEO position of ASEA, a large engineering group in Sweden, with a mandate to improve the company's performance significantly. To successfully change ASEA, Barnevik realized that the company needed a radical shake-up. In a single Red Zone maneuver, he decided to make two fundamental changes:

1. Restructure the organization to facilitate international expansion.
2. Eliminate bureaucracy and downsize the company's corporate headquarters.

Initially, Barnevik knew that speed was imperative to successful change. He also despised bureaucracy and developed his own method for downsizing corporate headquarters: the "30-percent rule." His approach is covered in Manfred Kets de Vries book, *The New Global Leaders: Richard Branson, Percy Barnevik and David Simon.* Barnevik stated that, "He broke it down by assuming that 30 percent of corporate staff could be spun off into separate and independent profit centers, another 30 percent could be transferred to the operational companies as part of their overhead, 30 percent could be eliminated. The remaining 10 percent could be kept on at headquarters as the minimum required." Ultimately, Barnevik reduced the corporate headquarters workforce from 2,000 employees to 200.

Barnevik did not stop there. He strongly believed that the electrical industry was going to experience a shakeout and that ASEA had to become more internationally diversified. Initially, he started acquiring small companies in neighboring countries. However, Barnevik was not satisfied until he decided to approach Brown, Boveri and Company in Switzerland. Both companies together represented a significant global presence. On August 10, 1987, the merger was announced; ABB was the official name of the new company. Similar to his experience with ASEA, Barnevik decided to start by downsizing the corporate headquarters. He applied the same 30-percent rule to the new company. Likewise, his next task was to streamline ABB quickly and convert its organizational structure into a matrix organization. As covered in the *Harvard Business Review* article, Barnevik supported "decentralization under central conditions." Ultimately, he created a new corporate culture that thrived on innovation and change. "ABB is an organization with three internal contradictions. We want to be global and local, big and small, and radically decentralized with centralized reporting and control." In time, Barnevik developed a truly transnational company with 210,000 employees in 140 countries, working in 1,200 companies divided into more than 5,000 profit centers.

Lou Gerstner, IBM, 1993–Present. International Business Machines (IBM) is the $87.5 billion computer manufacturing and technology services firm best known for developing the IBM personal computer. Big Blue is recognized as one of the technological leaders of the new economy. However, IBM has not always been successful. In the late 1980s and early 1990s, IBM's market share and profitability were in rapid decline. The CEO at the time, John Akers, was slow to adapt to the dramatically changing technological landscape. As a result, Big Blue's board of directors decided to replace Akers. In 1993, Lou Gerstner was hired as CEO, the first outsider to fill the position. IBM's board members selected Gerstner primarily for his ability to turnaround companies and make them profitable. In *Lessons from the Top,* authors Thomas J. Neff and James M. Citrin state that IBM presented Gerstner with two major challenges:

1. Turning around IBM and making it profitable
2. Returning IBM to its previous position as "one of the world's preeminent corporations"

In 1993, IBM suffered a loss of $8 billion. Gerstner realized that the company had to change its culture and focus more on the customer. As reported in *Saving Big Blue: Leadership Lessons and Turnaround Tactics of IBM's Lou Gerstner,* Gerstner stated, "If the CEO isn't living and preaching the culture and isn't doing it consistently, then it just doesn't happen." Gerstner traveled throughout the company, encouraging employees to adopt the perspective of the customer. His efforts had a profound effect on profits, and in 1998, IBM reported profits of $6.3 billion.

In addition to successfully changing the corporate culture, a tough Red Zone maneuver, Gerstner guided the company through the acquisition of Lotus Corporation. Initially, the Lotus group was apprehensive at becoming a part of Big Blue. However, Gerstner quelled their fears during a speech shortly after the acquisition. During the question and answer session, an employee asked Gerstner if he would dress up in drag, which was something Lotus' current CEO had done to boost morale. According to *IBM Redux: Lou Gerstner and the Business Turnaround of the Decade*, Gerstner said, "I'll make a deal. The day that we have 40 to 50 percent of the [groupware] market, and the day the guys on the West Coast throw in the towel, you'll see me any way you want to see me." Ultimately, the acquisition of Lotus was successful and in 1998, the company's groupware package, Lotus Notes, had more than 20 million users.

Gerstner also successfully changed the company's competitive strategy. When Gerstner took it over, most analysts thought that he would break up the company. However, according to Robert Slater's book, *Saving Big Blue*, Gerstner had other plans. "We believed the decision to hold IBM together was right at the time." He was more interested in transitioning the company from a producer of products to a company that offered total solutions. "Solutions require more than raw technology. They are combinations of software, hardware, and services that we integrate." Over the past five years, IBM has become known for its solutions. Gerstner proved himself successful by transitioning the company away from low margin products such as personal computers. Currently, Big Blue focuses more than ever before on providing integrated software and networking solutions to its clients. Gerstner truly has demonstrated the ability to lead his organization through Red Zone situations.

Larry Bossidy, Allied Signal (Honeywell), 1991–2000. Prior to its merger with Honeywell in 1999, Allied Signal was a $15.1 billion aerospace, automotive, and engineered materials manufacturer. Larry Bossidy became CEO of the New Jersey-based conglomerate in 1991. Prior to joining Allied Signal, Bossidy served under Jack Welch as Vice Chairman at General Electric. Upon joining Allied, Bossidy quickly demonstrated his ability to manage in the Red Zone by turning the company around.

When Bossidy was hired in 1991, he found disappointed and disillusioned employees. Allied's stock price had been stagnant for several years, and two major acquisitions with Bendix and Signal had failed to produce positive financial results. Unifying the company's diverse departments, each of which had its own unique culture, presented an immense challenge for Bossidy.

Bossidy realized that the company had to unify its efforts to successfully navigate the future. As a starting point, he reduced the workforce by 20 percent and immediately began to realign the organization. As reported in *Lessons from the Top*, Bossidy also composed a new vision statement that said, "We want to become a premier company, distinctive and successful in everything we do." Although his vision statement was clear, the company needed something more to stimulate change. The solution: Six Sigma, the quality improvement program. By implementing the program throughout the company, he facilitated a common goal across the company. Bottom line, Six Sigma worked.

In addition to establishing corporatewide quality initiatives, Bossidy also identified leadership principles that were imperative to successful change. He stated, "CEOs today have to be more hands-on than in previous eras." Likewise, Bossidy asserted that CEOs must reduce their time horizons for strategic planning. "With the pace of the world changing as it does, you've got to look at where you are ever more frequently, or the bus goes by."

Through a host of sweeping initiatives, Bossidy transformed the company into an industrial powerhouse that employed more than 87,000 people in 40 countries. Under Bossidy's leadership, the company leveraged a successful buyout of Honeywell, Inc. in 1999 and achieved annual sales upwards of $24 billion, ranking it among Fortune 500's top 75 companies.

These guys have it; they see Red Zone Management as a critical tool to move their organizations to today's levels of excellence. No wonder they are in the Hall of Fame.

LESSON THREE: DEVELOP A RED ZONE PLAN

I happened to be visiting one of our teams of consultants that was helping with a Red Zone maneuver at Florida Power & Light, when the inevitable happened: Hurricane Alert! It was pretty amazing to watch as the company seemed to effortlessly shift into hurricane mode with its preplanned organization structure, work processes, and schedule. In a flash, the organization was ready to respond to power shortages if the hurricane struck anywhere in their field of service.

Today's business organizations need a Red Zone mode that they can shift to when they tackle a Red Zone maneuver. Companies need a checklist they can follow when a Red Zone maneuver is initiated. That Red Zone checklist needs to be based on the company's Red Zone experience as well as benchmarks from Red Zone principles. The checklist must direct the company to official duties that will be the formal way of operating during the Red Zone. Today's organizations can ill afford to start from scratch every time they initiate a Red Zone maneuver. All the details need to be worked out, down to and including a Red Zone Duties page in the company's employee handbook.

Just as electric utilities on a coast train for hurricanes, companies need to train for Red Zones. Having the checklist is imperative, but all managers need to be trained in that checklist as well as in Red Zone pathologies and principles. Any or all of the company's executives should be able to train managers and employees on how the company will play in the Red Zone.

LESSON FOUR: PUT RED ZONE PROCESSES IN PLACE

This idea is simple enough. As the Red Zone gameplans in this book illustrate, certain organizational processes or capabilities are required to be successful in the Red Zone. The idea is to add those processes and capabilities before they are needed, not in real time during a Red Zone maneuver. For example, adding program and project management as an organizational capability is tough enough to do during stable times; it's really difficult to do during a Red Zone.

Additional capabilities that might need to be added are as follows:

- Planning and budgeting competence that enables the company to allocate resources properly for Red Zone success
- Customer scorecard competence that allows the organization to understand fully the dimensions of their products and services that are valued by the customer
- Appraisal systems that give feedback on and credit for Red Zone as well as normal run-the-business performance

- Flexible incentive policies with the impact needed for effective motivation during a Red Zone

Organizations that want to prepare thoughtfully for the opportunities of Red Zones must make concerted efforts to add capabilities in advance of the battle.

LESSON FIVE: SECURE RED ZONE RESOURCES

Skilled, experienced, been-there and done-that people are required for success in the Red Zone. They either have to be inside the organization, or the firm must access them on the outside. We need to start recruiting executives and managers based on their Red Zone qualifications, their combat history, not just their business success during normal times. Look for folks who have been in leadership positions in the Red Zone maneuver itself, not resident managers whose organizations successfully went through the Red Zones. Recruiting such folks starts with adding the Red Zone requirement to all management job descriptions. A manager must not only run a tight ship during times of smooth sailing, but must also be able to both navigate and captain the organizational ship through Red Zones. Actual Red Zone leadership experience has no substitute; plan to pay for it, because it carries a premium.

During a Red Zone, if the organization lacks an experienced leader on the inside, it may need to look on the outside. Red Zone resources are available as individuals and firms who can help coach you on your Red Zone journey or even provide some of the needed leadership for the trip. Our firm has been working with companies for over 20 years, providing explicit leadership, coaching, and program and project management to firms going through every kind of Red Zone covered in our gameplan chapters.

If you go outside to look for help, be careful. Not all consulting firms have the skill and experience for Red Zone; this is not the time or the place for "we've got all the answers" consultants to tell you everything to do or for the hordes of smart, young MBAs ready for their first Red Zone transit (on your nickel). Look for folks who know how to guide you on a journey that must be yours, not theirs, and who have the gray hair along with the flexibility and creativity to help you innovate your way through. You might also want to pick those folks who have great references for performing in the Red Zone on target, on time, and on budget.

LESSON SIX: KNOW YOUR RED ZONE CAPABILITY, AND USE IT TO COMPETE

Do you know how good your company is in the Red Zone? Is your Red Zone capability a competitive strength or a weakness? I think finding out is important so you can either count on your Red Zone capability or get busy fixing it. If you have not been assessing your company's Red Zone performance during maneuvers, you may not have an evaluation of your capability at your fingertips. Had you been formally using program management for Red Zone maneuvers, you probably would have some sort of assessment available for use.

To get a handle on your firm's Red Zone capability, convene a handful of perceptive organization members who have better than average insight and the courage to tell it like it is, and ask them to give your firm an assessment. A good starting point for the group might be to plot Red Zones in the history of your company and then talk through the effectiveness of your company in each Red Zone. Just for fun, you might ask the team to locate your firm on the following, very crude Red Zone capability scale that ranges from high capability (Red Zone Marauder) to extremely low capability (potential Red Zone victim).

High Capability: Red Zone Marauder

- Able to move easily into and out of Red Zones
- Gifted, flexible leadership with a track record of Red Zone success
- Above industry average use of Red Zone maneuvers
- Powerful, potent use of Red Zone maneuvers
- Able to use Red Zone as a tool of competition
- Able to balance achieving gain with mitigating the risk of loss

Red Zone Capable

- Sees Red Zone maneuvers as one of the ways to make things happen

- Industry average use of Red Zone maneuver
- Able to use a Red Zone maneuver competently
- Primarily motivated by the potential gain
- Able to balance achieving gain with mitigating the risk of loss

Low Capability: Potential Victim of a Competitor's Red Zone Capability

- Little or no proactive Red Zone capability
- Limited ability to react with a Red Zone maneuver
- Enters Red Zones more as a defensive maneuver
- Red Zone leadership is usually delegated
- Focuses on risk avoidance more than on gain
- Enters a Red Zone maneuver with a woe-is-us attitude

After identifying where your firm might be on the Red Zone capability scale, repeat the exercise for your most capable competitors. If you find yourself with more capability than your competitors, consider initiating more Red Zone maneuvers when they make sense to increase your organization's relative performance.

Companies with an edge in Red Zone capability have some real business advantages in this time of relentless change. Envision what your firm could do if it was good in the Red Zone:

- Pick up the business pace
- Be more proactive about opportunities
- Have more choices
- React faster to competitive surprises
- Use more competitive ambushes

If your assessment of your firm's Red Zone capability shows you behind your competitors, your choices are limited. Improving your firm's capability in the Red Zone may need to become your highest strategic priority, because without Red Zone maneuverability, your firm is for all intents and purposes dead in the water.

RED ZONE MANAGEMENT: CONCLUSION

The purpose of this book was to talk about the greatest challenges in business. The Red Zone is that special place where leaders can take their organizations to the front of the pack with maneuvers designed to move to the next level of performance.

I wanted to pose new rules or principles for Red Zones that show that something different is needed from managers and workers alike during these special times. I didn't want to frighten people away from Red Zones, but I did want to scare people deeply about using the normal management rules during a Red Zone maneuver. I wanted to show that a store of knowledge has accumulated on Red Zones. All companies may not be able to make it to the Red Zone Hall of Fame, but they can master the principles needed for basic competence.

One last use of the Red Zone metaphor. In football, winners want to get their hands on the ball. They want the ball because they have the confidence and the skill to get the job done, and they want the ball because they believe, they plan, they fully intend to score. I hope this book challenges management to take the ball and score in the Red Zone!

BIBLIOGRAPHY

Bingi, Prasad, Sharma, Maneesh K. and Godla, Jayanth K., "Critical Issues Affecting ERP Implementation," *Information Systems Management,* Summer 1999.

Chopra, Sunil and Van Mieghem, Jan A., "Which e-Business Is Right for Your Supply Chain," *Supply Chain Management Review,* July 2000.

Cliffe, Sarah, "ERP Implementation," *Harvard Business Review,* January-February 1999.

Crainer, Stuart, "The 50 Best Management Saves," *Management Review,* November 1999.

Davenport, Thomas O., "The Integration Challenge," *Management Review,* January 1998.

de Figueiredo, John M., "Finding Sustainable Profitability in Electronic Commerce," *Sloan Management Review,* Summer 2000.

Epstein, Marc J., "Organizing Your Business for the Internet Evolution," *Strategic Finance,* July 2000.

Garr, Doug, *IBM Redux: Lou Gerstner and the Business Turnaround of the Decade,* 1st ed., New York: HarperCollins, 1999.

Griffith, David A. and Palmer, Jonathan W., "Leveraging the Web for Corporate Success," *Business Horizons,* Jaunary 1999.

Hammer, Michael and Champy, James, *Reengineering the Corporation: A Manifesto for Business Revolution,* 1st ed., New York: HarperBusiness, HarperCollins Publishers, Inc., 1994.

Hammer, Michael and Stanton, Steven A., *The Reengineering Revolution: A Handbook,* New York: HarperBusiness, HarperCollins Publishers, Inc., 1995.

Holland, Dutch, *Change Is the Rule: Practical Actions for Change: On Target, On Time, On Budget,* Chicago: Dearborn Trade, 2000.

Holland, Dutch and Kumar, Sanjiv, "Getting Past the Obstacles to Successful Reengineering," *Business Horizons,* May-June 1995.

Jarrar, Yassar F. and Aspinwall, Elaine M., "Business Process Reengineering: Learning from Organizational Experience," *Total Quality Management,* March 1999.

Kets de Vries, Manfred F.R., *The New Global Leaders: Richard Branson, Percy Barnevik and David Simon,* 1st ed., San Francisco: Jossey-Bass, 1999.

Kim, W. Chan and Mauborgne, Renee, "Strategy, Value Innovation, and the Knowledge Economy," *Sloan Management Review,* Spring 1999.

Kotter, John P. and Heskett, Jamees L., *Corporate Culture and Performance,* 1st ed., New York: Free Press, 1992.

Neff, Thomas J. and Citrin, James M., *Lessons from the Top,* 1st ed., New York: Doubleday, 1999.

Neufield, Derrick and Parent, Michael, "From Bricks to Clicks," *Ivey Business Journal,* March 2000.

Picken, Joseph C. and Dess, Gregory G., "Right Strategy—Wrong Problem," *Organizational Dynamics,* Summer 1998.

Porter, Michael E., *Competitive Strategy: Techniques for Analyzing Industries and Competitors,* New York: The Free Press, 1980.

Schein, Edgar H., *The Corporate Culture Survival Guide,* 1st ed., San Francisco: Jossey-Bass Inc., 1999.

Slater, Robert, *The GE Way Fieldbook: Jack Welch's Battle Plan for Corporate Revolution,* 1st ed., New York: McGraw-Hill, 1999.

Slater, Robert, *The New GE: How Jack Welch Revived an American Institution,* 1st ed., Homewood, IL: Irwin, 1993.

Taylor, William, "The Logic of Global Business: An Interview with ABB's Percy Barnevik," *Harvard Business Review,* March-April 1991.

Vitiello, Jill and Manganelli, Raymond, "It's Totally Radical," *Journal of Business Strategy,* November-December 1993.

INDEX

Help Your Team Score Points in the Red Zone!

For special discounts on 20 or more copies of *Red Zone Management: Changing the Rules for Pivotal Times,* please call Dearborn Trade Special Sales at 800-621-9621, extension 4410.

Dearborn™
Trade Publishing
A **Kaplan Professional** Company